ENTROPY
aaron costain

FIRST EDITION. DESIGNED BY AARON COSTAIN.

PRINTED IN CHINA ON FSC® CERTIFIED PAPER.

FSC
www.fsc.org
MIX
Paper from responsible sources
FSC® C013314

SECRET ACRES
SA037

ISBN-13: 978-0-9962739-8-5
ISBN-10: 0-9962739-8-0

LIBRARY OF CONGRESS CONTROL NUMBER: 2017958123

PUBLISHED BY SECRET ACRES
200 PARK AVENUE SOUTH, 8TH FL.
NEW YORK, NY 10003

FOR RACHEL

one

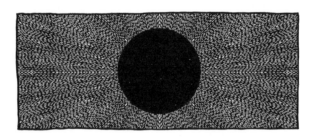

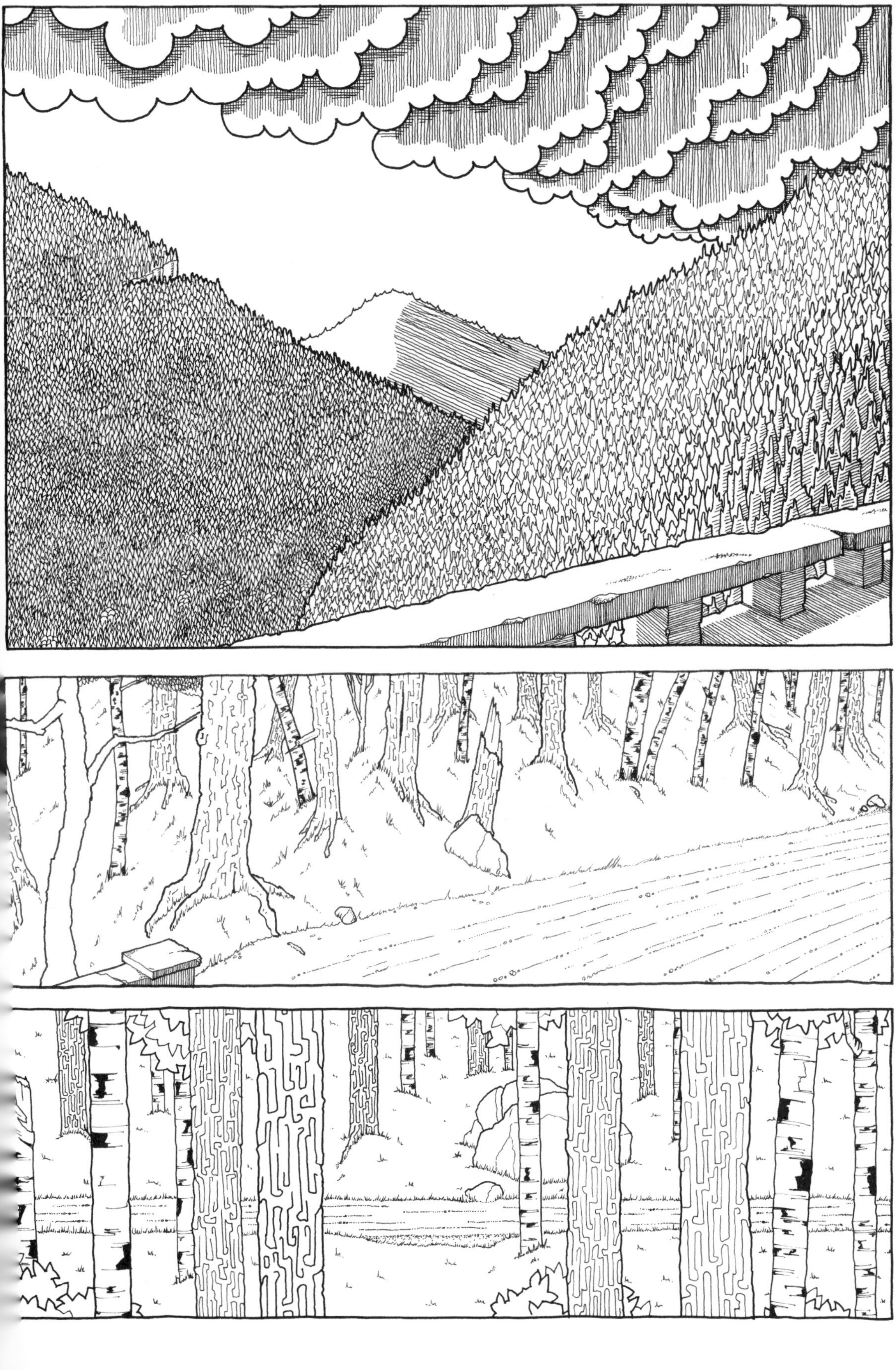

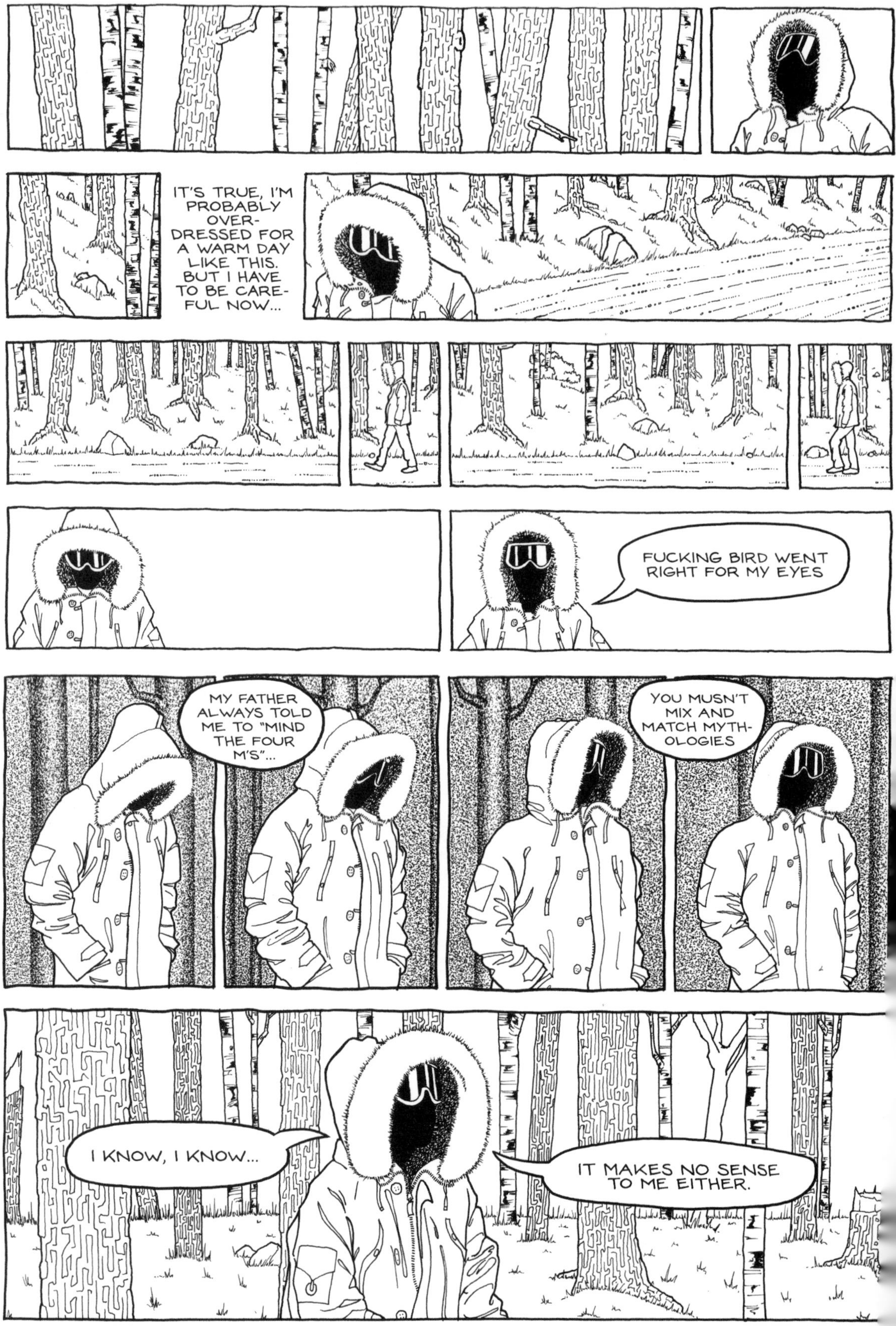
IT'S TRUE, I'M PROBABLY OVER-DRESSED FOR A WARM DAY LIKE THIS. BUT I HAVE TO BE CARE-FUL NOW...
FUCKING BIRD WENT RIGHT FOR MY EYES
MY FATHER ALWAYS TOLD ME TO "MIND THE FOUR M'S"...
YOU MUSN'T MIX AND MATCH MYTH-OLOGIES
I KNOW, I KNOW...
IT MAKES NO SENSE TO ME EITHER.

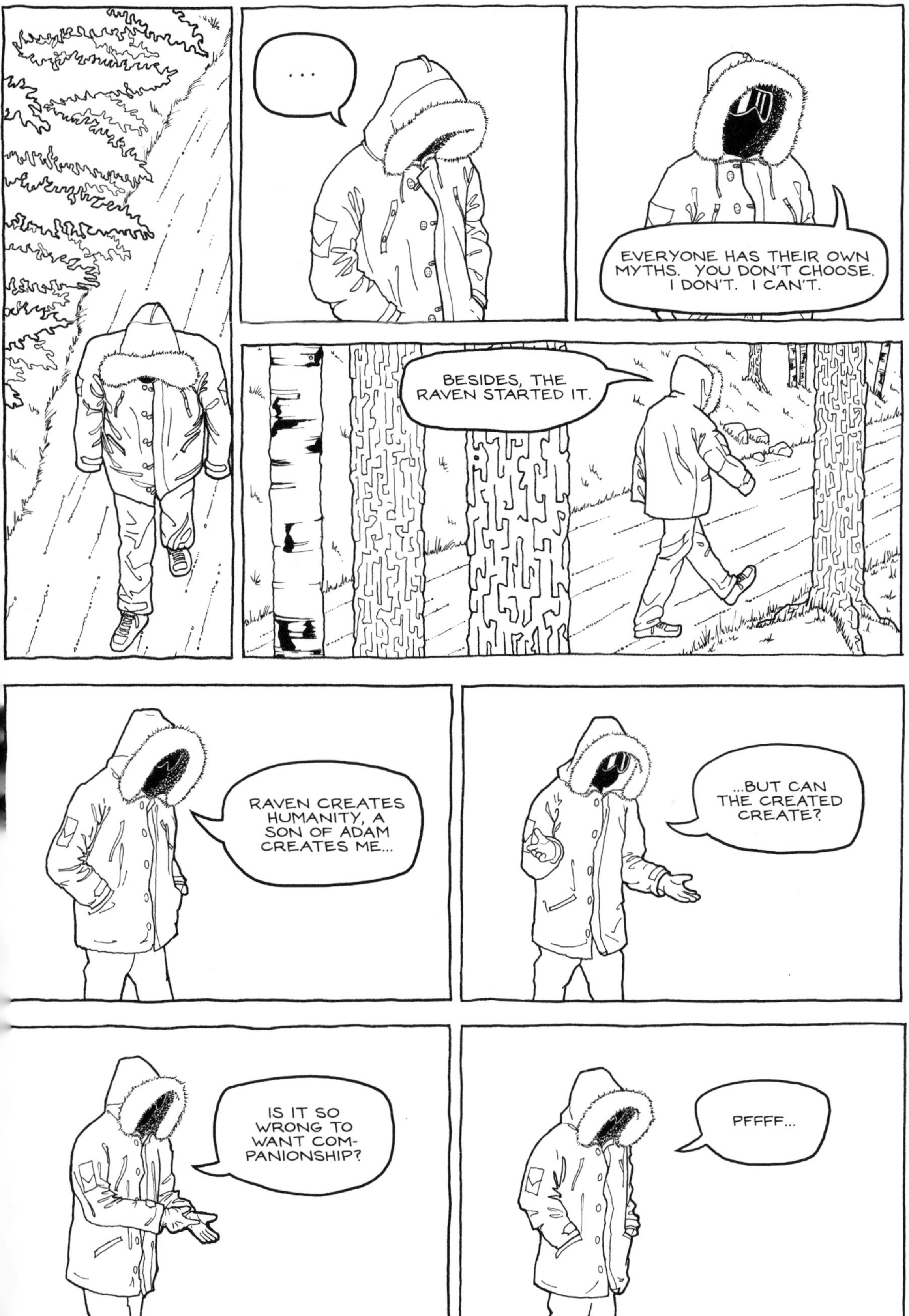
. . .
EVERYONE HAS THEIR OWN MYTHS. YOU DON'T CHOOSE. I DON'T. I CAN'T.
BESIDES, THE RAVEN STARTED IT.
RAVEN CREATES HUMANITY, A SON OF ADAM CREATES ME...
...BUT CAN THE CREATED CREATE?
IS IT SO WRONG TO WANT COM-PANIONSHIP?
PFFFF...

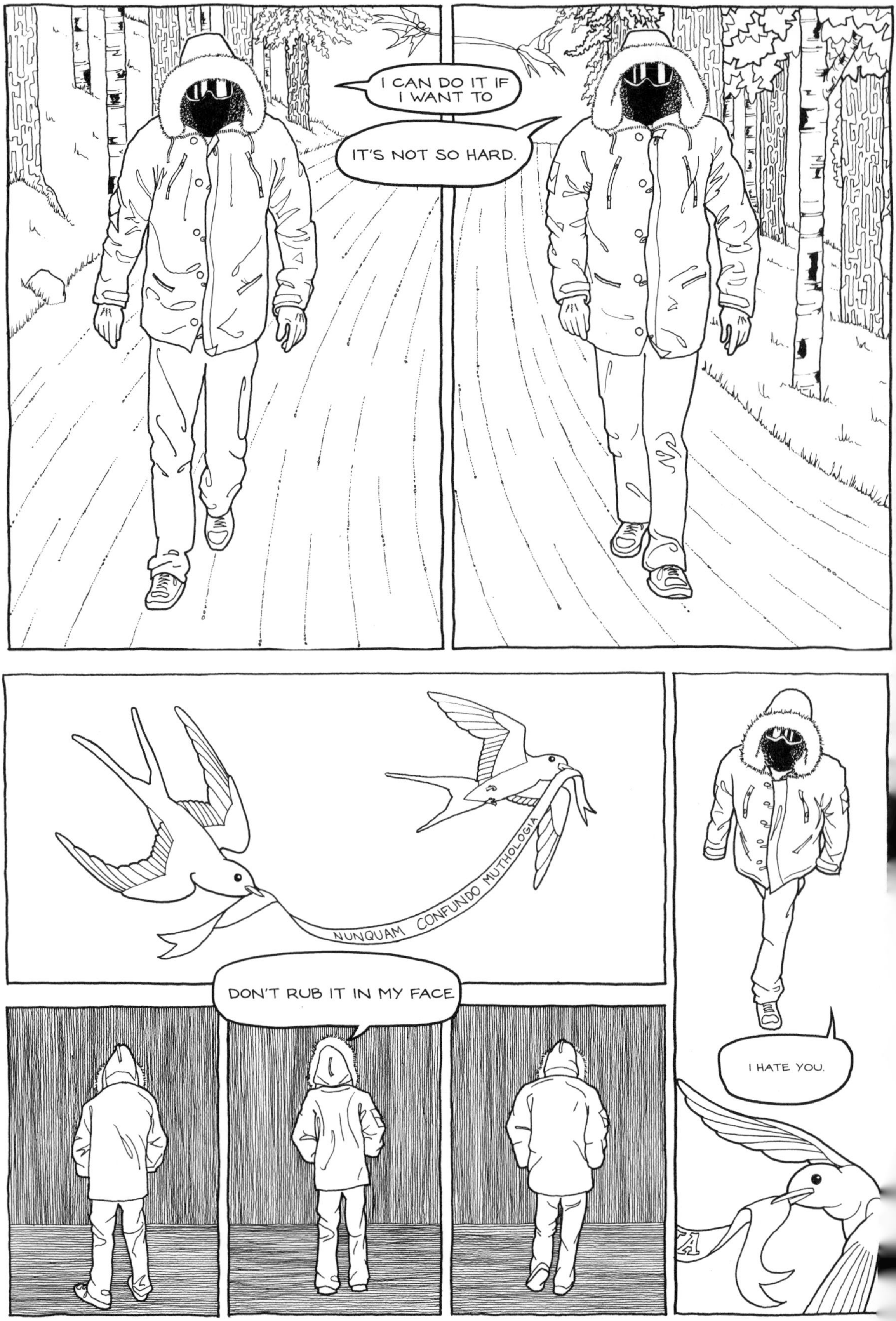
I CAN DO IT IF I WANT TO
IT'S NOT SO HARD.
NUNQUAM CONFUNDO MUTHOLOGIA
DON'T RUB IT IN MY FACE
I HATE YOU.

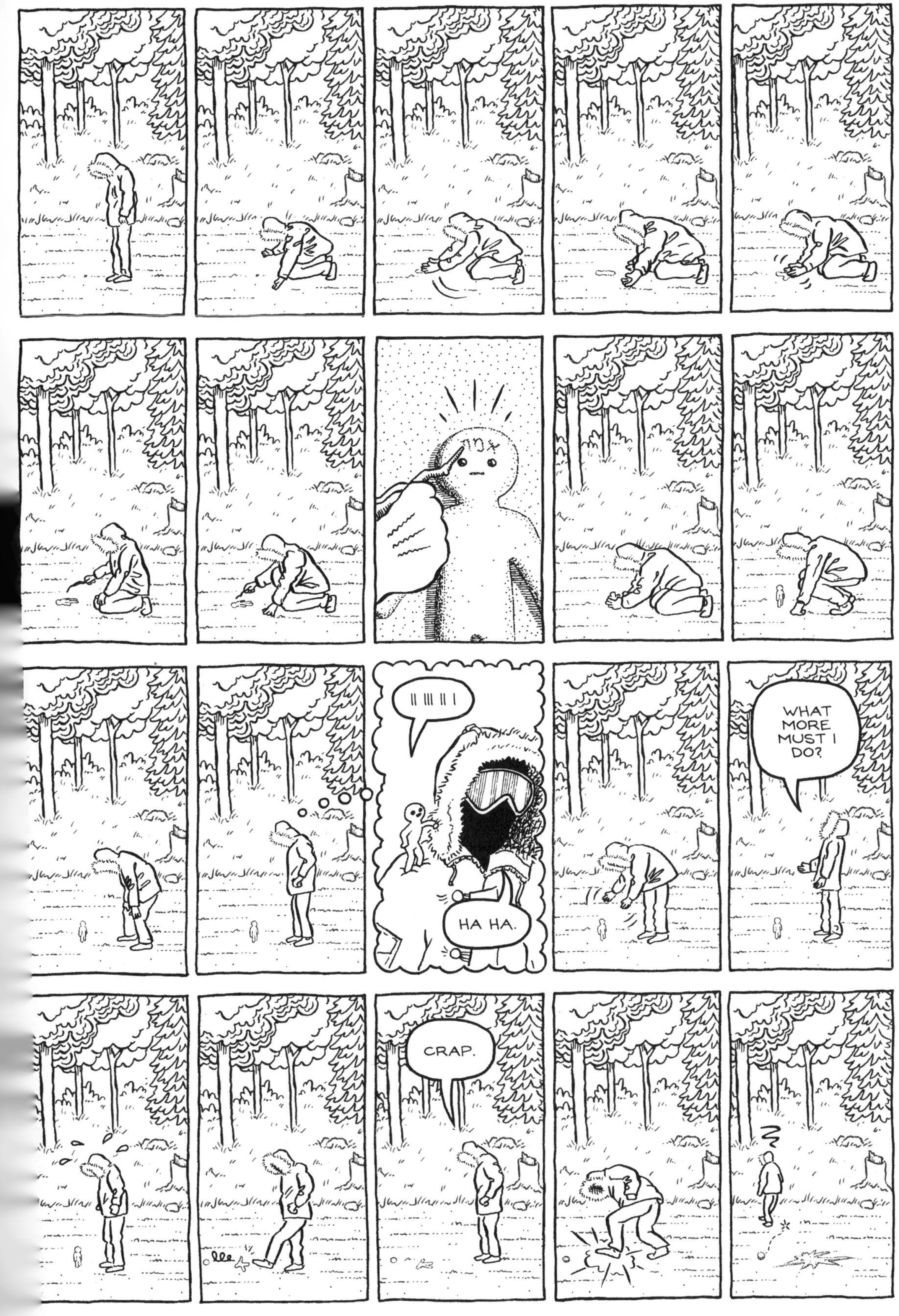
אמת
HA HA.
WHAT MORE MUST I DO?
CRAP.

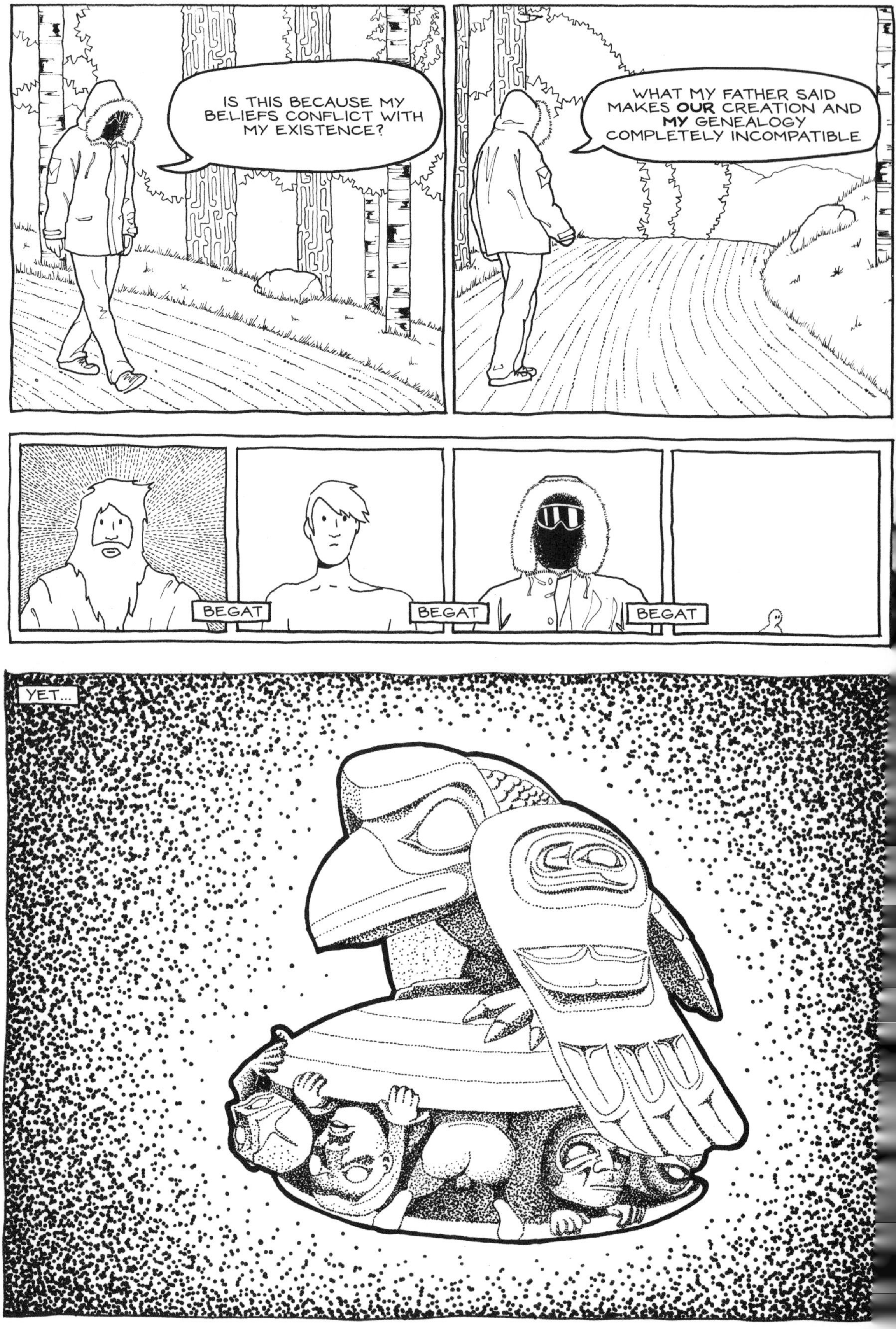
IS THIS BECAUSE MY BELIEFS CONFLICT WITH MY EXISTENCE?
WHAT MY FATHER SAID MAKES **OUR** CREATION AND **MY** GENEALOGY COMPLETELY INCOMPATIBLE
BEGAT
BEGAT
BEGAT
YET...

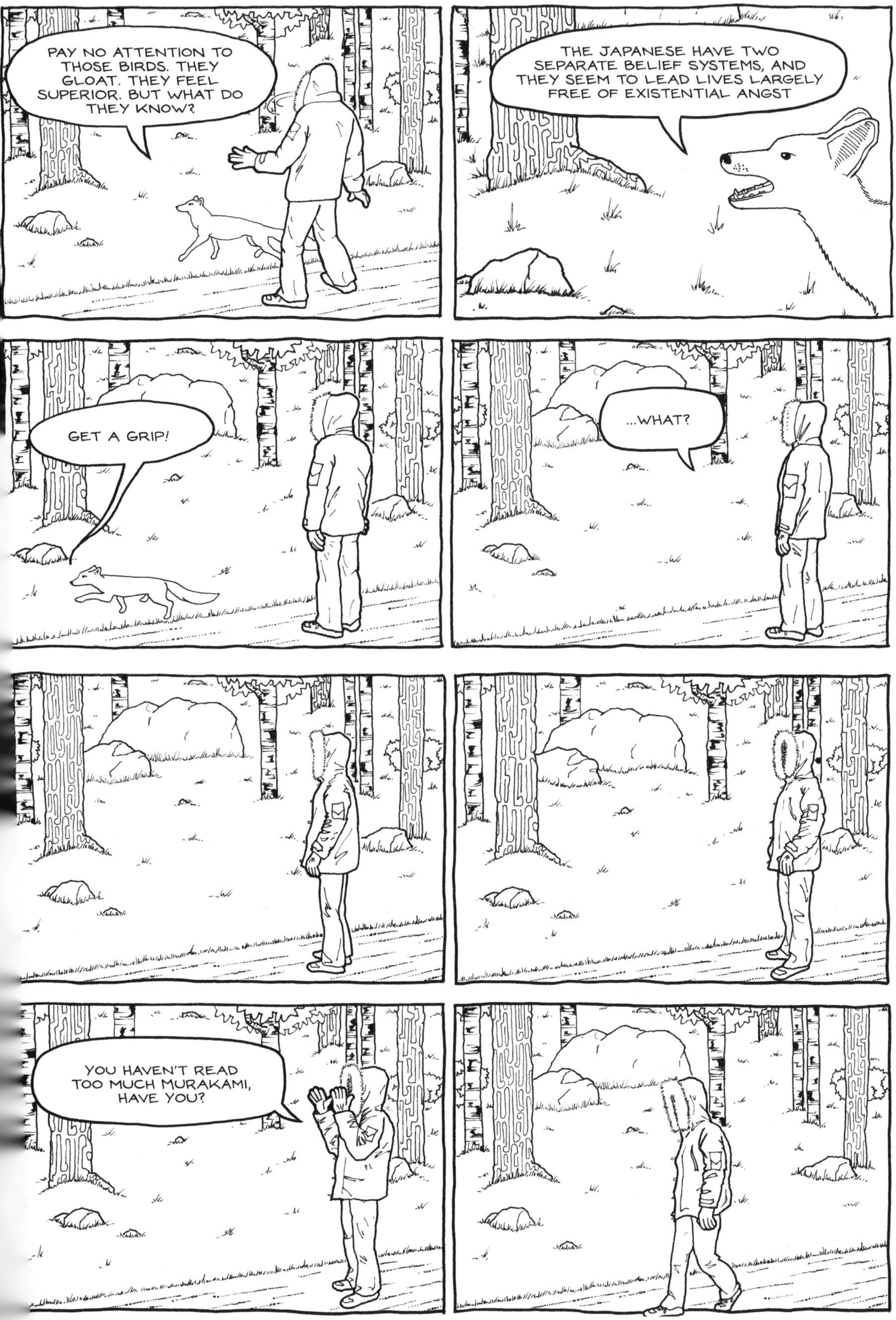
PAY NO ATTENTION TO THOSE BIRDS. THEY GLOAT. THEY FEEL SUPERIOR. BUT WHAT DO THEY KNOW?
THE JAPANESE HAVE TWO SEPARATE BELIEF SYSTEMS, AND THEY SEEM TO LEAD LIVES LARGELY FREE OF EXISTENTIAL ANGST
GET A GRIP!
...WHAT?
YOU HAVEN'T READ TOO MUCH MURAKAMI, HAVE YOU?

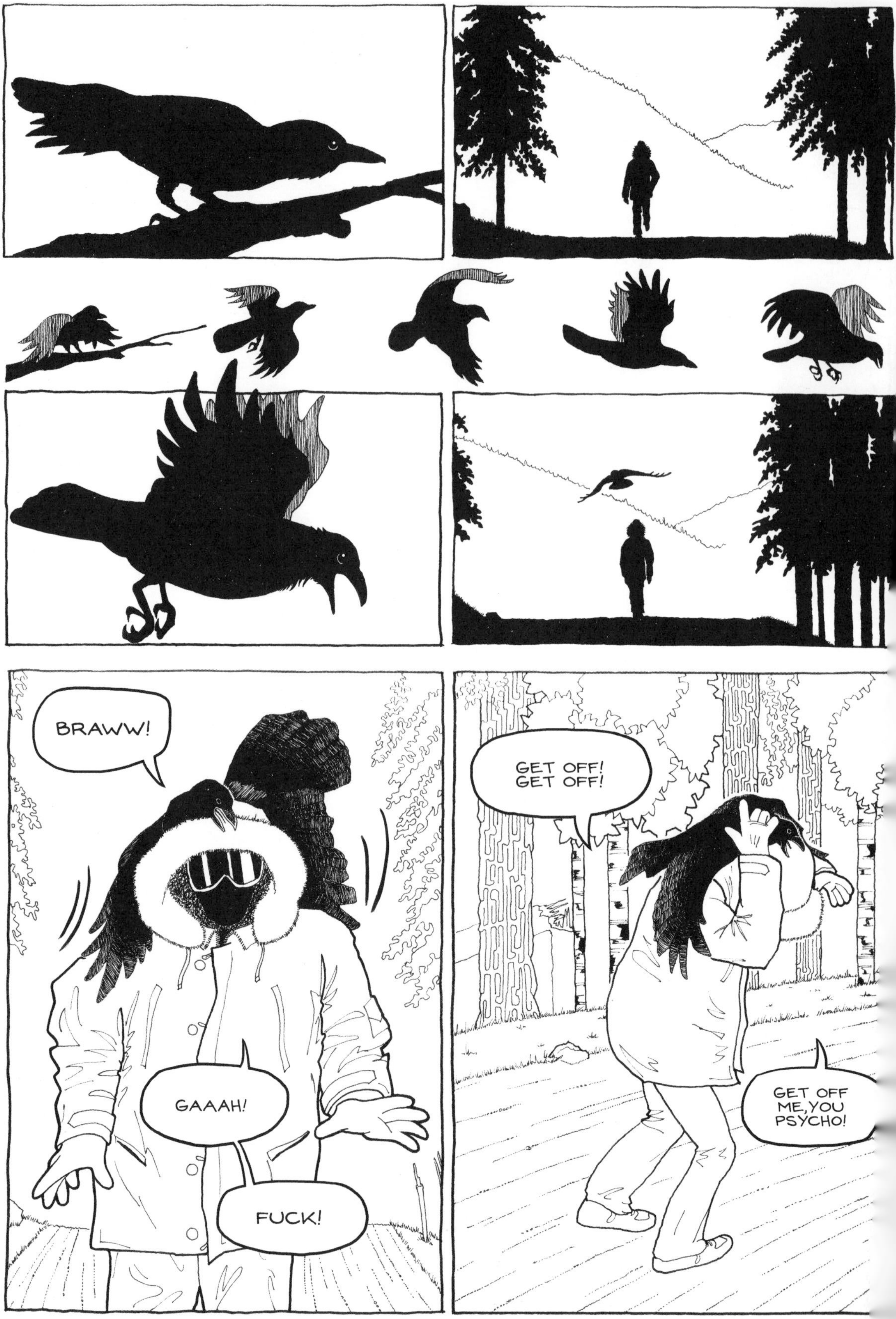

BRAWW!
GAAAH!
FUCK!
GET OFF! GET OFF!
GET OFF ME, YOU PSYCHO!

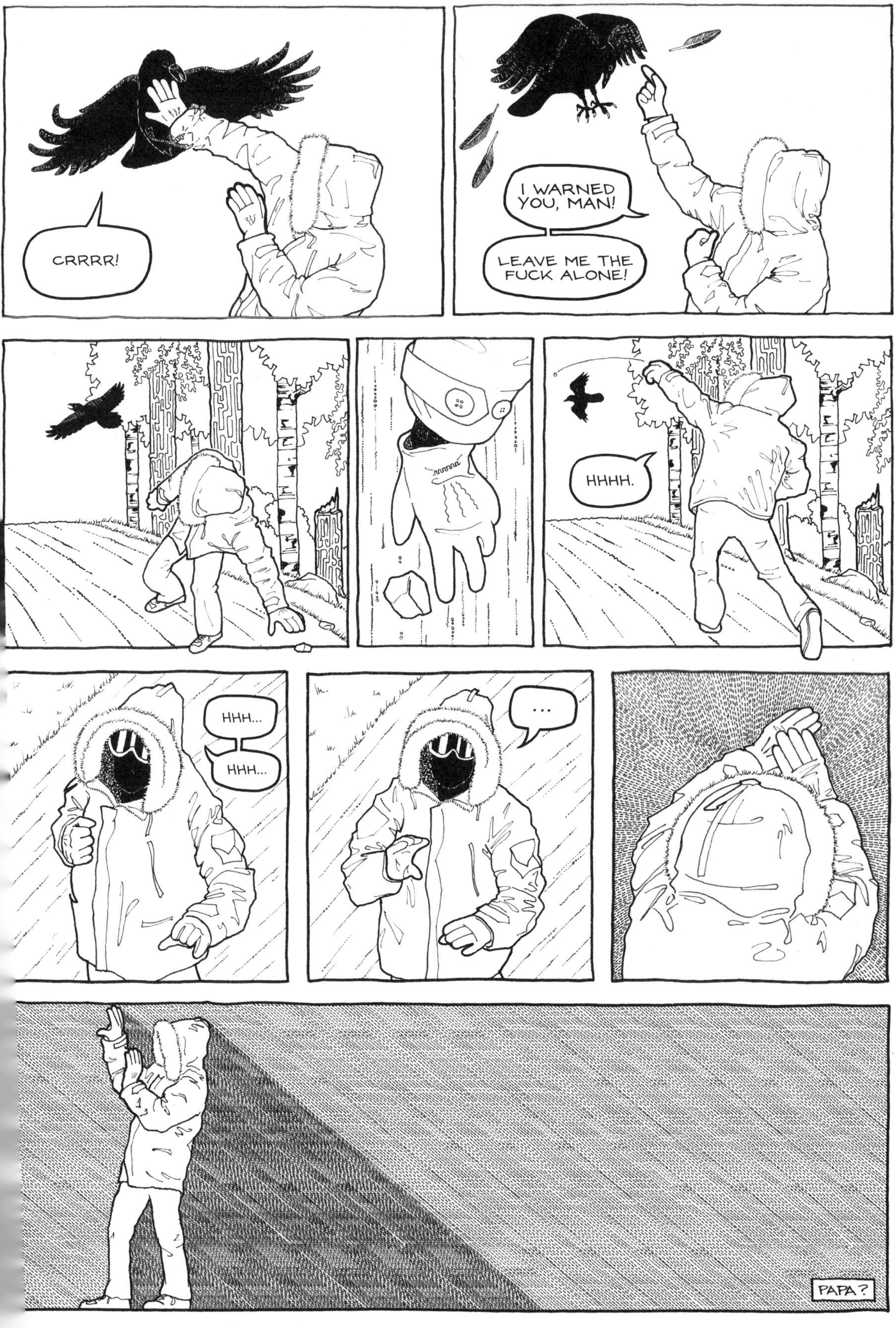
CRRRR!
I WARNED YOU, MAN!
LEAVE ME THE FUCK ALONE!
HHHH.
HHH...
HHH...
...
PAPA?

two

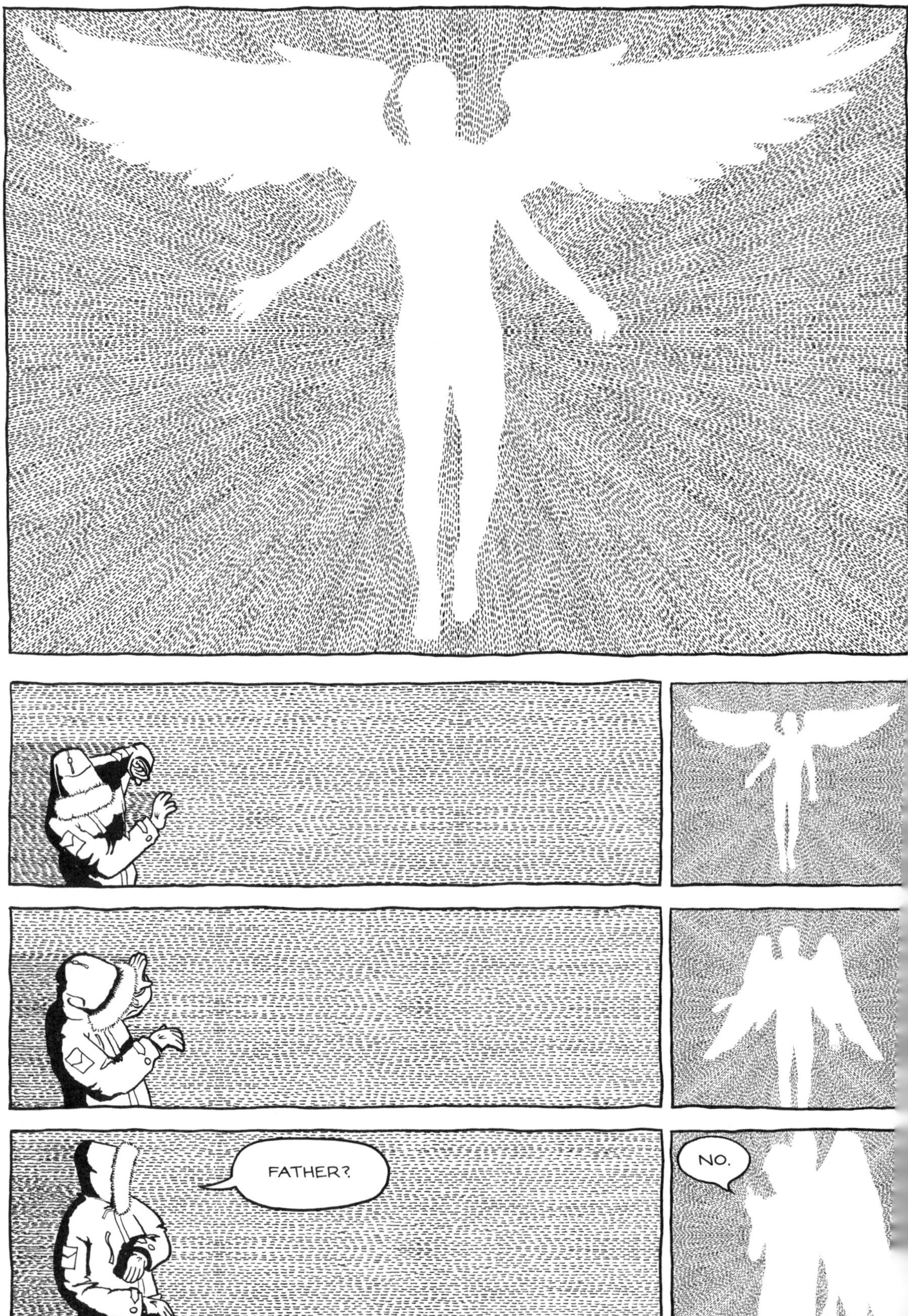
FATHER?
NO.

I AM A REPRESENTATIVE OF THE CREATOR.
GOD?
A CREATOR.
MINE?
NOT YOURS.
OH.
SO, UH... COULD YOU TURN IT DOWN A BIT?
YOU'RE KIND OF BRIGHT.
MY APOLOGIES.
SNAP!
AH.
THANKS.

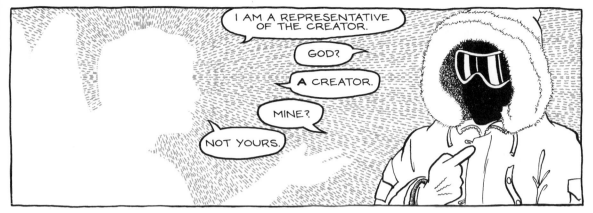

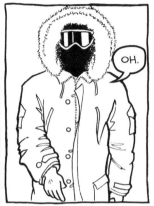

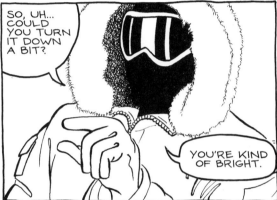

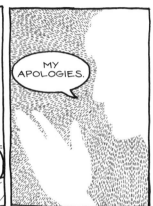

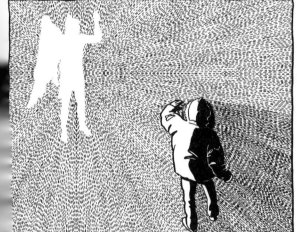

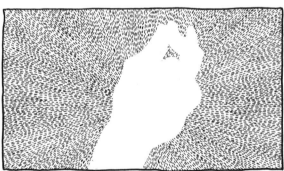

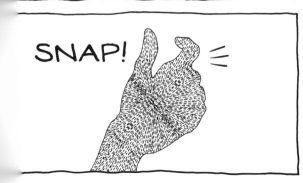

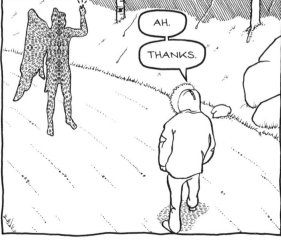

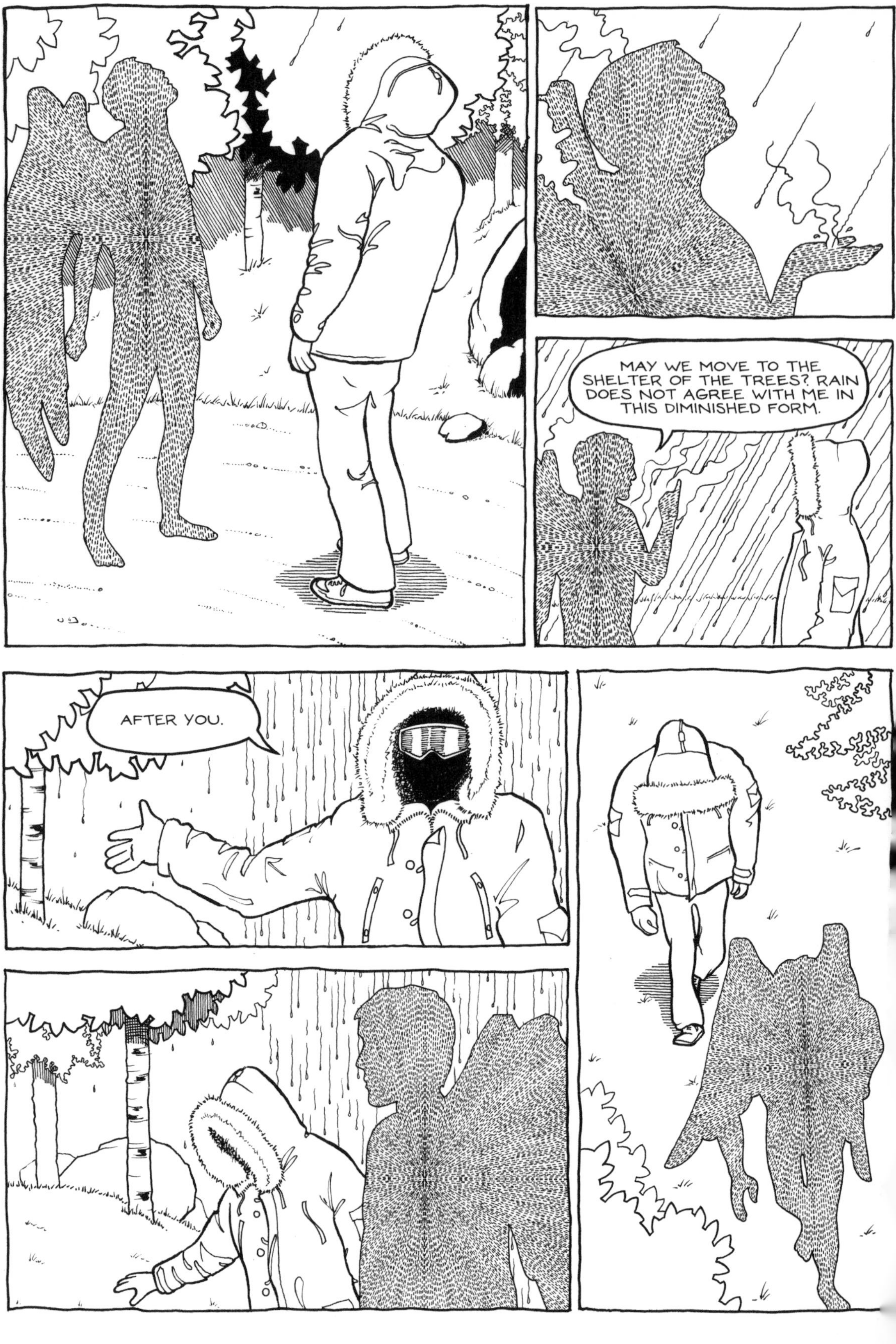
MAY WE MOVE TO THE SHELTER OF THE TREES? RAIN DOES NOT AGREE WITH ME IN THIS DIMINISHED FORM.
AFTER YOU.

SHALL WE PAUSE HERE?

THE GROUND IS FLAT AND STILL SOMEWHAT DRY.

HHH... HHH...

YEAH, HHH... I'M JUST GONNA SIT DOWN FOR A MINUTE...

...CATCH MY BREATH...

MMMM...

THERE'S SO MUCH I WANT TO ASK YOU.

THANK YOU, BUT I WOULD RATHER STAND.

C'MON.

SIT!

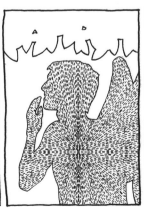

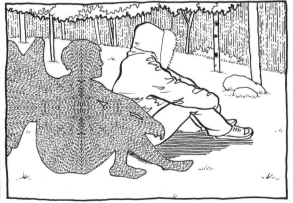

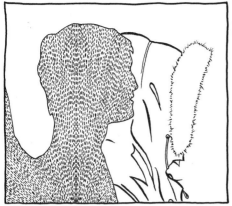

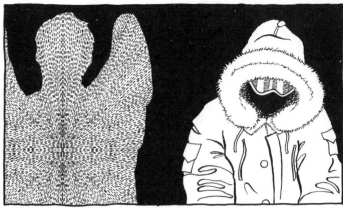

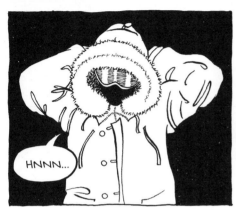

HNNN...

I DON'T EVEN KNOW WHERE TO BEGIN!

...I'VE BEEN TALKING TO MYSELF.

THE ANIMALS HERE CAN TALK...

AND THOSE THAT AREN'T LYING ARE SO INANE THAT THEIR CONVERSATION IS WORTHLESS.

I BARFED UP SOME MEAT I ATE YESTERDAY.

THEN I ATE THAT.

I'M GLAD THAT MOST OF THEM CAN'T SPEAK.

AHHHH! COME ON!

BLOP!

BUT THAT RAVEN IS THE WORST OF THEM.

HE'S GIVEN UP DIALOGUE ENTIRELY, AND FLIES INTO A RAGE AT THE SIGHT OF ME.

I USED TO THINK WE HAD SOMETHING OF A RAPPORT; HE WAS THE ONLY ONE WHO WOULD TALK STRAIGHT WITH ME.
... BUT YOU SEE, MY SPEAR MISSED SKATE BECAUSE HE EXISTS ONLY IN TWO DIMENSIONS - SO HE DE FACTO VANISHES WHEN SEEN FROM CERTAIN ANGLES.
WE WOULD DISCUSS THEOLOGY: MY ORIGINS, AND THE CREATION OF THIS WORLD.
YET I SENSED THAT HE WAS DELIBERATELY LEADING ME ASTRAY, AND HE BECAME UNREASONABLE WHEN I QUESTIONED HIM ABOUT IT.
CRAW!
FUCKING FUCK!
THAT WAS A COUPLE WEEKS BACK, AND SINCE THEN I'VE HAD TIME TO THINK THINGS THROUGH MORE THOROUGHLY.
I MEAN, WAS I REALLY MADE BY A SON OF ADAM, LIKE THE RAVEN SAID?
LOOK...
...IT WOULD EXPLAIN WHY I SEEM TO BE MADE OF DIRT!
AND LOOK HERE!
THIS IS WHAT THE RAVEN WAS GOING FOR!
אמת
ALL HE HAS TO DO IS REMOVE THIS ONE LETTER AND I DIE... I WOULD BECOME A LIFELESS PILE OF MUD!
I'M NOT WEARING THIS GETUP FOR MY COMFORT, YOU KNOW... I'M PROTECTING MY FOREHEAD!

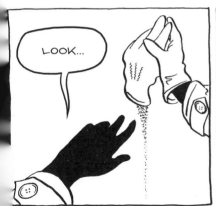

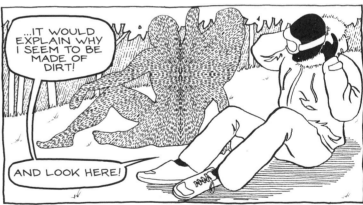

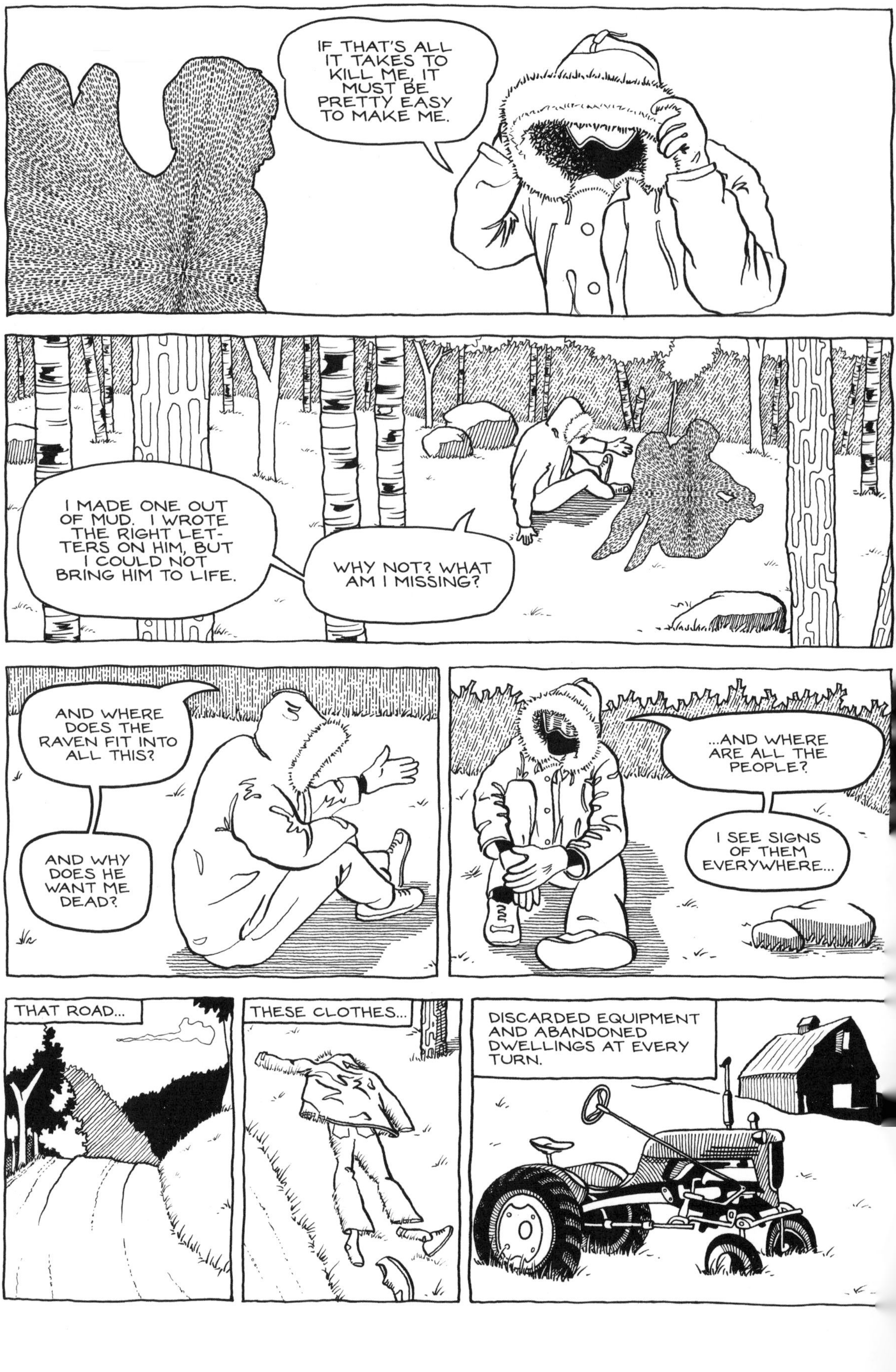
IF THAT'S ALL IT TAKES TO KILL ME, IT MUST BE PRETTY EASY TO MAKE ME.
I MADE ONE OUT OF MUD. I WROTE THE RIGHT LETTERS ON HIM, BUT I COULD NOT BRING HIM TO LIFE.
WHY NOT? WHAT AM I MISSING?
AND WHERE DOES THE RAVEN FIT INTO ALL THIS?
AND WHY DOES HE WANT ME DEAD?
...AND WHERE ARE ALL THE PEOPLE?
I SEE SIGNS OF THEM EVERYWHERE...
THAT ROAD...
THESE CLOTHES...
DISCARDED EQUIPMENT AND ABANDONED DWELLINGS AT EVERY TURN.

SO, WHERE DID THEY ALL GO? AND WHO THE HELL ARE YOU?

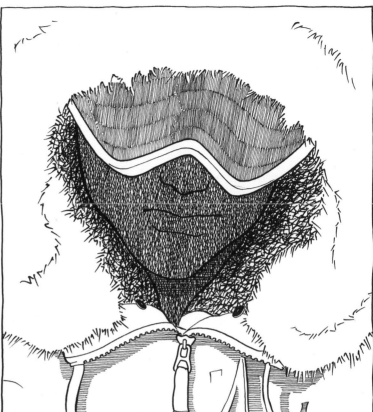

I TOLD YOU, I AM AN EMISSARY OF THE DIVINE.

I WAS SENT TO AID IN THE UNDERSTANDING OF YOUR SITUATION.

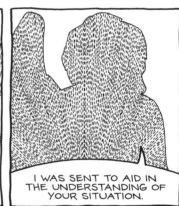

WHAT?

YOU ARE STILL HERE, AND WE DON'T KNOW WHY.

BUT FIRST LET ME TELL YOU ABOUT THE RAVEN.

I CAN ALSO AID IN **YOUR** UNDERSTANDING OF **HIM.**

AFTER THE DELUGE, THE WORLD WAS STILL; ALL WAS ENVELOPED IN A LIQUID SHROUD.

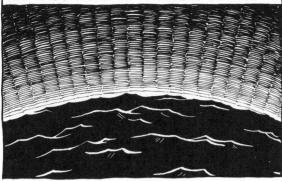

STILL, THAT IS, BUT FOR THE RAVEN.

AS HE FLEW OVER THE ENDLESS OCEAN, HE SAW THE FLOODWATERS HAD BEGUN TO RECEDE.

A SLIVER OF SAND HAD ARCHED ITS BACK THROUGH THE WATERS AND INVITED HIM TO REST HIS TIRED WINGS ON ITS SHORES.

RAVEN SAW MOVEMENT ON THE BEACH AS HE GLIDED TOWARDS THE SPIT; A GREAT CLAM SHELL ROCKED BACK AND FORTH ATOP THE NARROW STRIP OF SAND.

HE ALIGHTED ON THE SWAYING SHELL AND, HEARING MUFFLED SOUNDS WITHIN, PRIED OPEN THE EDGE WITH HIS BEAK.

SMALL HANDS GRABBED THE RIM AND FORCED IT FARTHER OPEN;

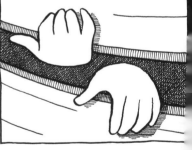

COARSE FACES STRAINED WITH EFFORT AS A DOZEN TINY MEN SPILLED FROM THE SHELL.

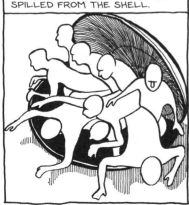

THESE PEOPLE WERE CRUDELY MADE, AS IF MOULDED FROM THE EARTH BY A NAÏVE HAND.

THEIR ACTIONS WERE AS VULGAR AS THEIR FEATURES; THE MEN SHOUTED NONSENSE AND MOVED WITHOUT PURPOSE.

NOT ONLY DID THEY NOT HAVE THE CAPACITY TO COMPREHEND THEIR NAKEDNESS, IT WAS IRRELEVANT; THEY HAD NO GENITALIA ON THEIR ILL-FORMED BODIES.

RAVEN GATHERED SOME DISCARDED LIMPET SHELLS, AND FORCEFULLY PLACED THEM OVER THE MENS' LOINS.

THIS CAUSED CONSTERNATION AMONG THEM, AND THEY FLED THEIR PERSECUTOR. AS THEY RAN, THE LIMPET SHELLS DROPPED FROM THEIR BODIES, FALLING TO THE SAND BEFORE THE MEN WERE SWALLOWED BY THE RECEDING TIDE.

RAVEN WAS ALONE ON THE BEACH NOW, BUT FOR THE GREAT CLAM SHELL AND A FEW OF THE LIMPETS LEFT BEHIND BY THE MEN.

THE LIMPETS BEGAN TO MOVE OF THEIR OWN ACCORD;

ONE BY ONE, PEOPLE BEGAN TO EMERGE FROM THE SHELLS: FULLY FORMED, MALE AND FEMALE BOTH.

THUS CAME THE FIRST OF HUMANITY, BORN OF THE ENDEAVOURS OF RAVEN.

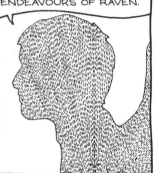

SO WHAT HAPPENED TO THE GUYS WHO RAN OFF?

THAT IS THE QUESTION!

THAT IS WHY I CAME TO TALK TO YOU.

YOU SEE, IT WAS THOUGHT THAT EVERYONE HAD PERISHED IN THE FLOOD...

YET **YOU** WALK ALONE THROUGH THESE MOUNTAIN ROADS. HOW IS THAT POSSIBLE?

SO I THOUGHT THAT I SHOULD SPEAK WITH YOU TO GAUGE YOUR INTELLECT, YOUR PHYSICALITY.

COULD IT BE THAT...

YOU ARE THOSE MEN?

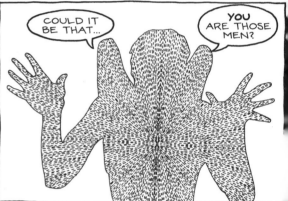

PERHAPS THEY SPLIT BETWEEN THEM THE INTELLECT OF ONE MAN; COMBINED, THEIR MINDS ARE THE EQUAL OF ANY SINGLE HUMAN FROM BEFORE THE FLOOD.

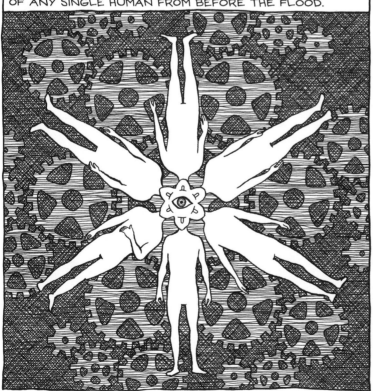

YOU YOURSELF HAVE SHOWN ME THAT YOU DO NOT POSSESS THE FLESH OF A MAN; RATHER, YOU ARE SOME AMALGAM OF TWIGS AND OTHER NATURAL MATERIALS, MUCH LIKE THE MEN FROM THE SHELL.

THIS IS EVIDENCE ENOUGH TO ME THAT MY ASSUMPTION IS CORRECT...

IT DID NOT HAPPEN ACCIDENTALLY, THOUGH. SOMEBODY PURPOSELY COMBINED THOSE MEN TO MAKE YOU. BUT HOW WERE THEY FOUND AFTER THEY WERE LOST AT SEA?

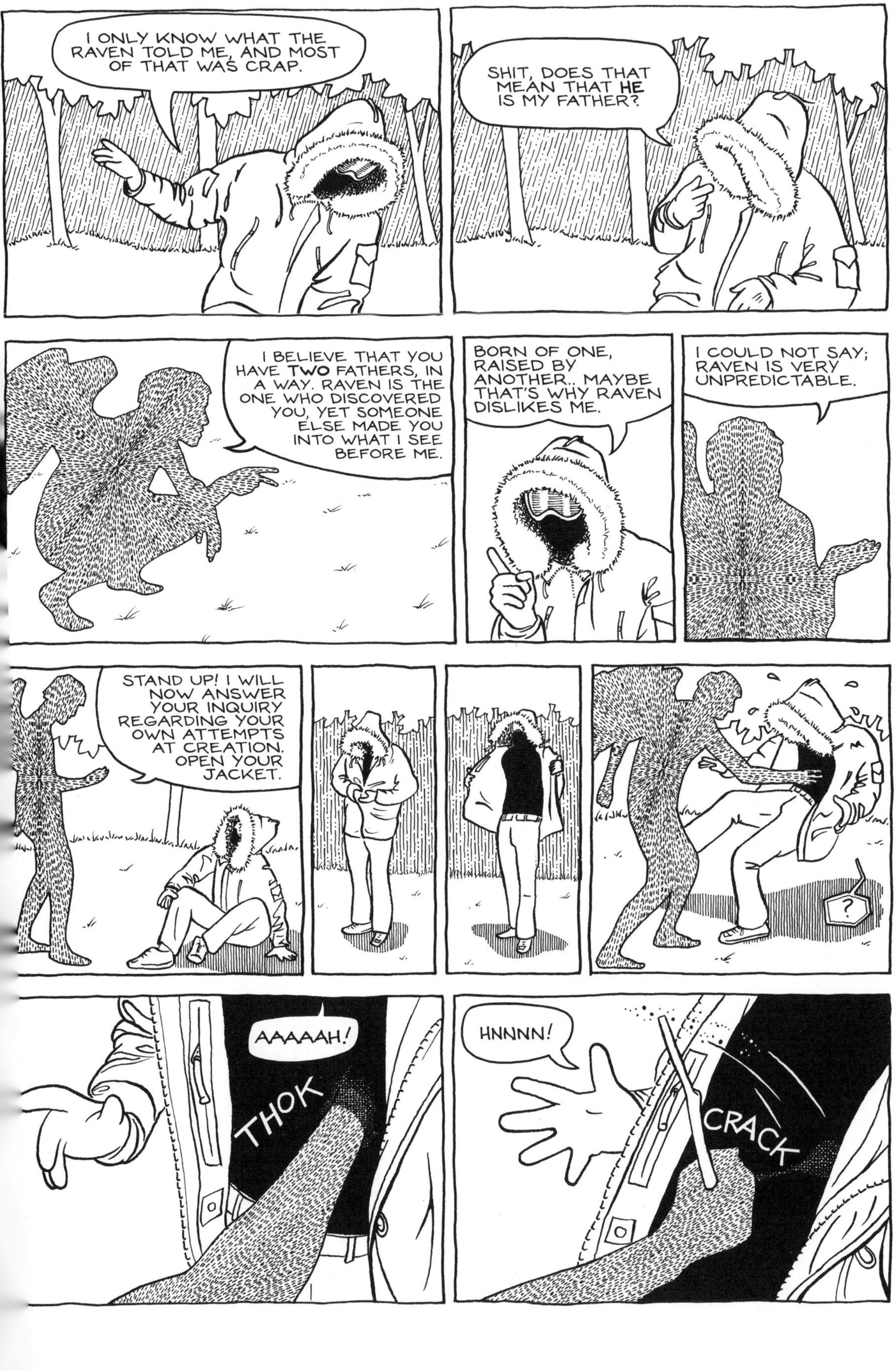
I ONLY KNOW WHAT THE RAVEN TOLD ME, AND MOST OF THAT WAS CRAP.
SHIT, DOES THAT MEAN THAT HE IS MY FATHER?
I BELIEVE THAT YOU HAVE TWO FATHERS, IN A WAY. RAVEN IS THE ONE WHO DISCOVERED YOU, YET SOMEONE ELSE MADE YOU INTO WHAT I SEE BEFORE ME.
BORN OF ONE, RAISED BY ANOTHER.. MAYBE THAT'S WHY RAVEN DISLIKES ME.
I COULD NOT SAY; RAVEN IS VERY UNPREDICTABLE.
STAND UP! I WILL NOW ANSWER YOUR INQUIRY REGARDING YOUR OWN ATTEMPTS AT CREATION. OPEN YOUR JACKET.
AAAAAH!
THOK
HNNNN!
CRACK

YOU SEE, YOU NEED TO START WITH A SEED.
AAAAAAHHHHHH!
LIFE IS EXTREMELY DIFFICULT TO MAKE FROM SCRATCH.
CHOK
PAT
PAT
FUCK!
OH MY GOD!
MOULD
MOULD
PAT
PATIENCE.
COUGH *COUGH*
MOUND
PAT

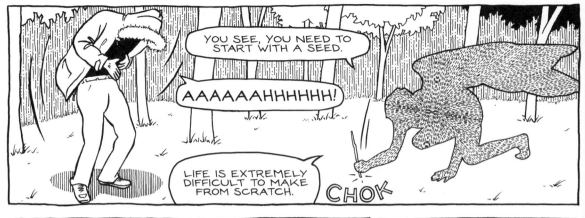

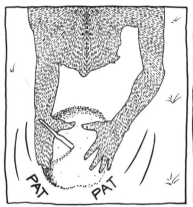

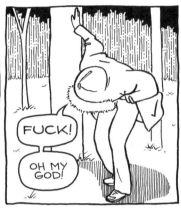

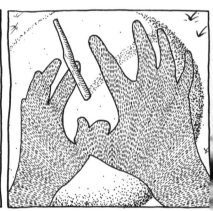

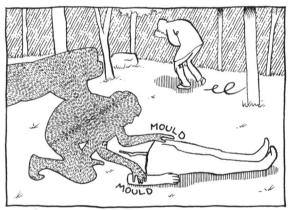

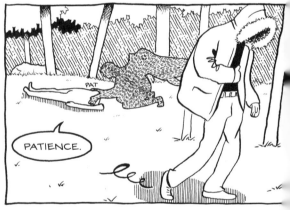

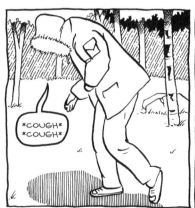

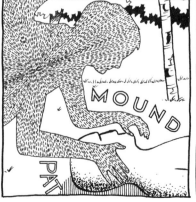

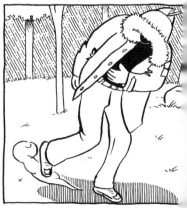

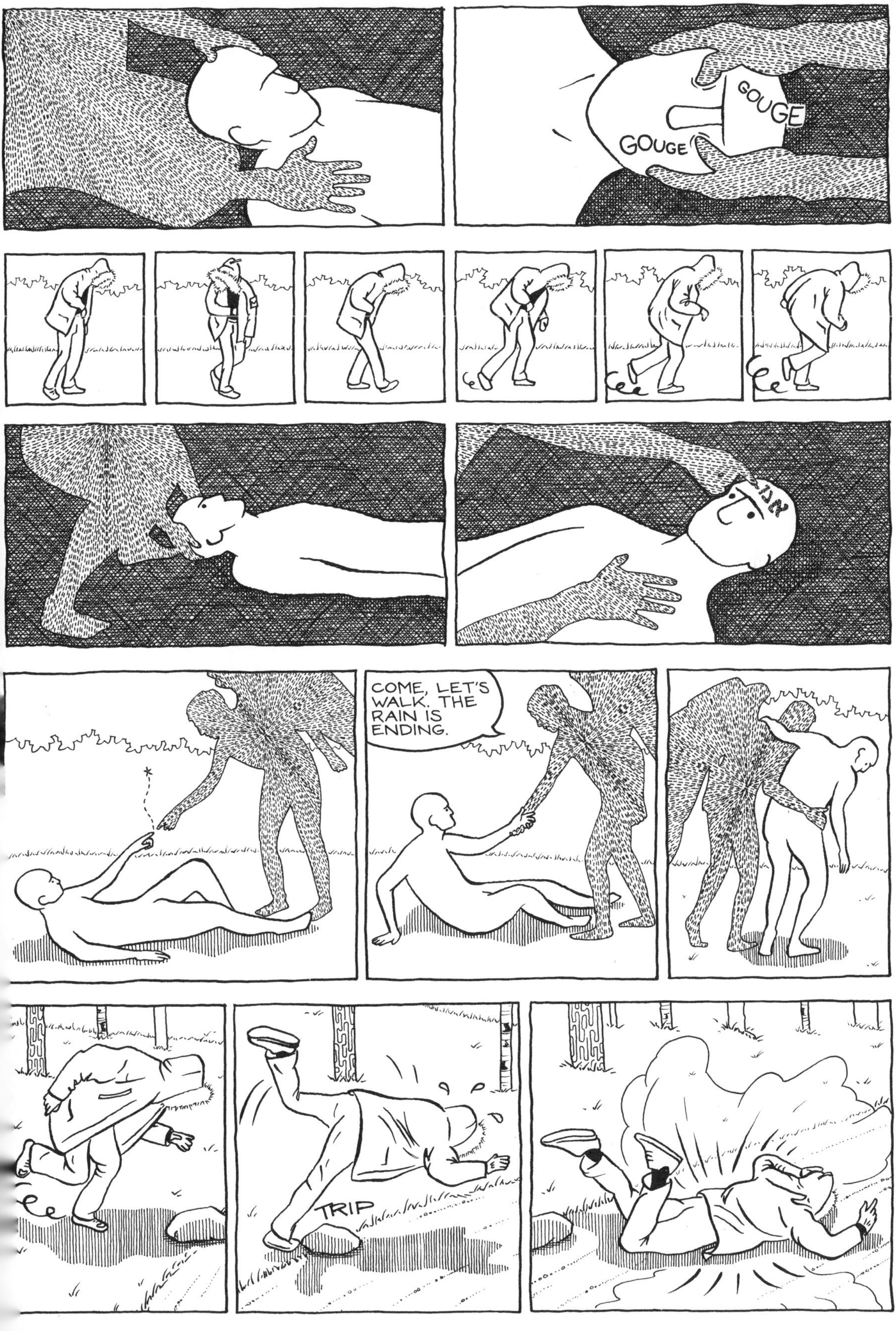
GOUGE
GOUGE
COME, LET'S WALK. THE RAIN IS ENDING.
TRIP

three

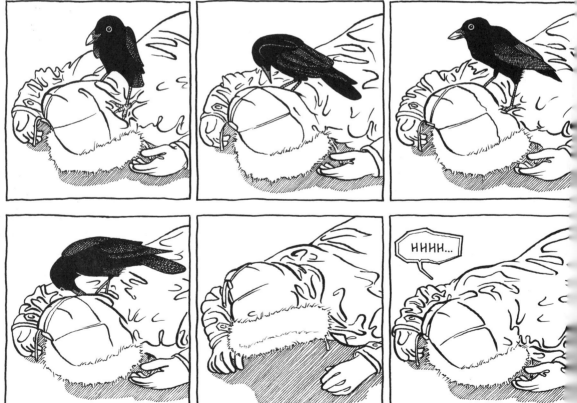

HHHH...

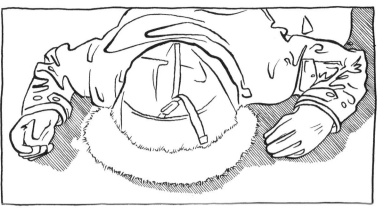

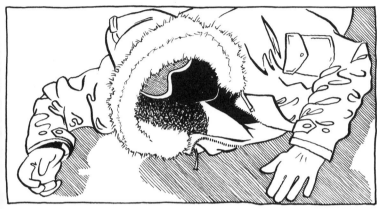

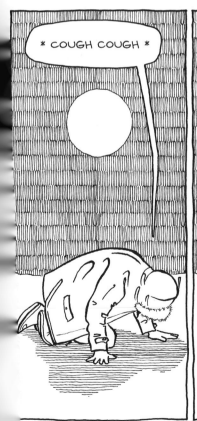

* COUGH COUGH *

UNNNNH!

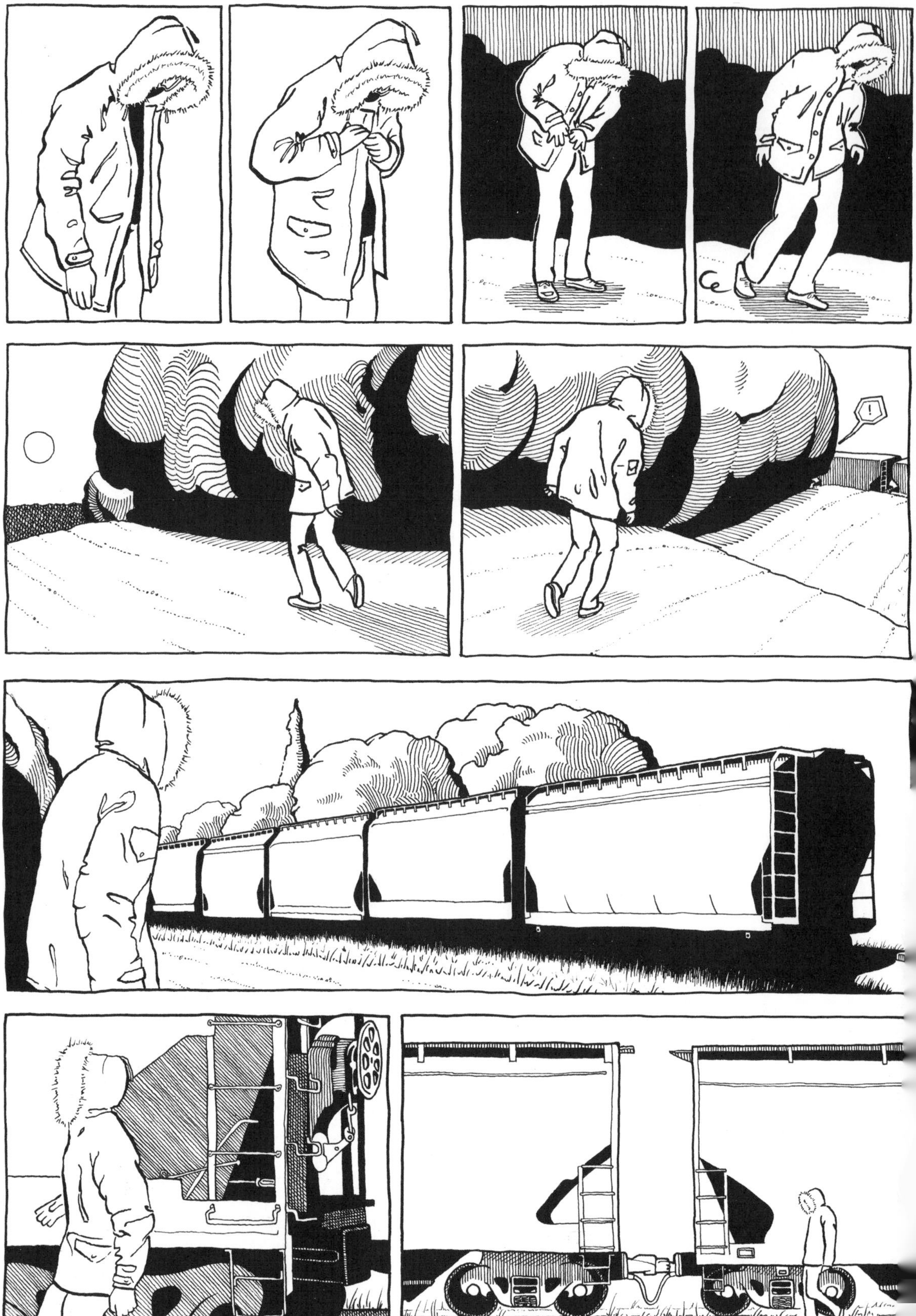
!

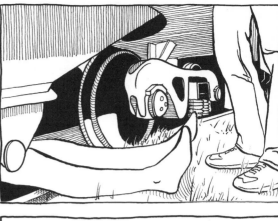

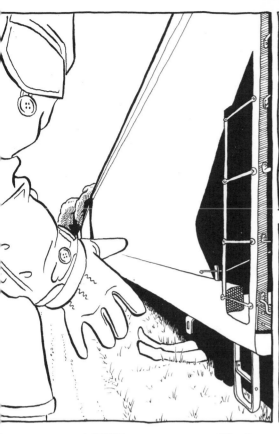

HEY MAN, YOU OK?

OK, C'MERE.

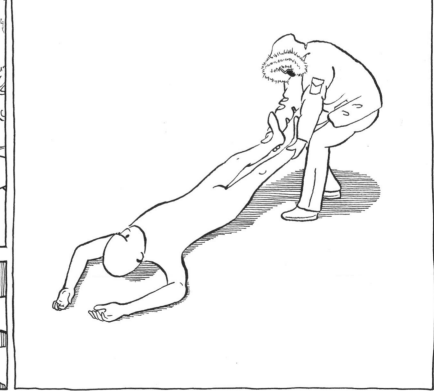

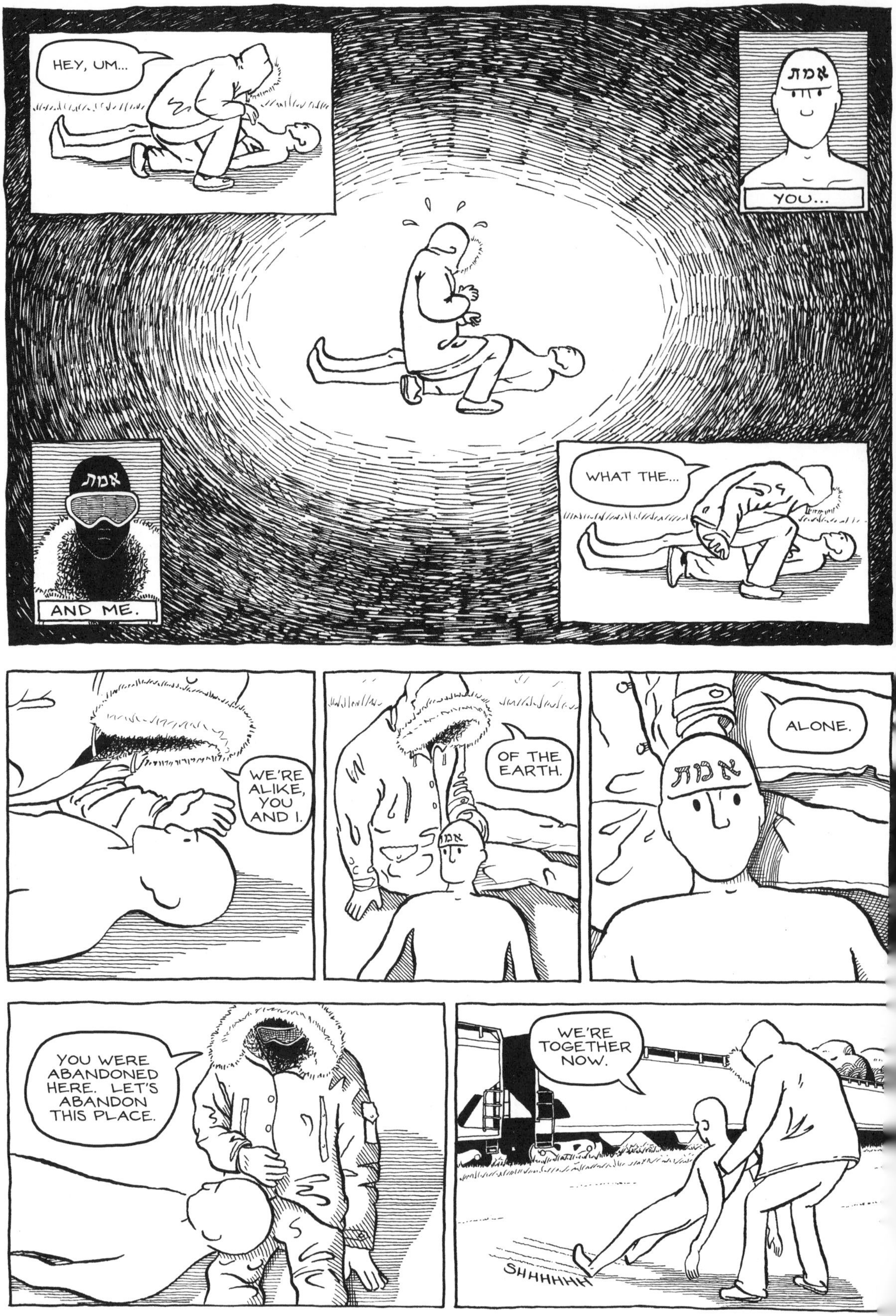

HEY, UM...
אמת
YOU...
אמת
AND ME.
WHAT THE...
WE'RE ALIKE, YOU AND I.
OF THE EARTH.
ALONE.
YOU WERE ABANDONED HERE. LET'S ABANDON THIS PLACE.
WE'RE TOGETHER NOW.
SHHHHHH

YOU KNOW, I FOUND MYSELF IN A SIMILAR SITUATION ONCE.
...DAMN, YOU'RE STIFF...
MY FIRST MEMORY IS WAKING UP UNDER AN ABANDONED RIG.
I WAS LOST, CONFUSED, NAKED.
I MADE A LOT OF FRIENDS IN THOSE DAYS.
CRAP
CRAP
CRAP
HEY GAVE ME THESE LOTHES.
LET'S SEE THOSE FUCKERS GET AT ME WITH ALL THIS ON!
ZIP
AND NOW WE NEED TO FIND YOU SOMETHING TO WEAR.
HUP! THERE YOU GO.

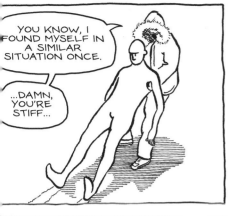

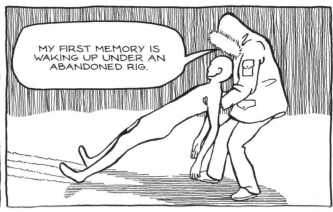

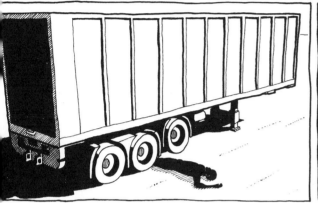

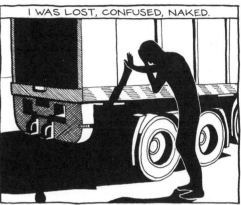

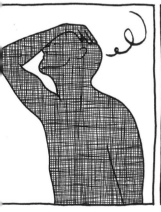

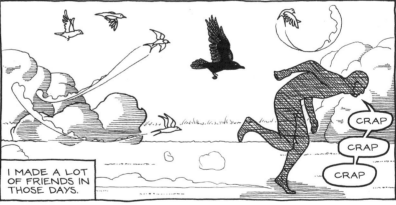

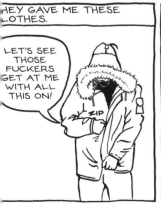

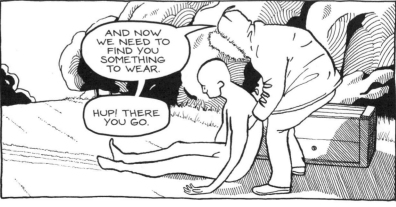

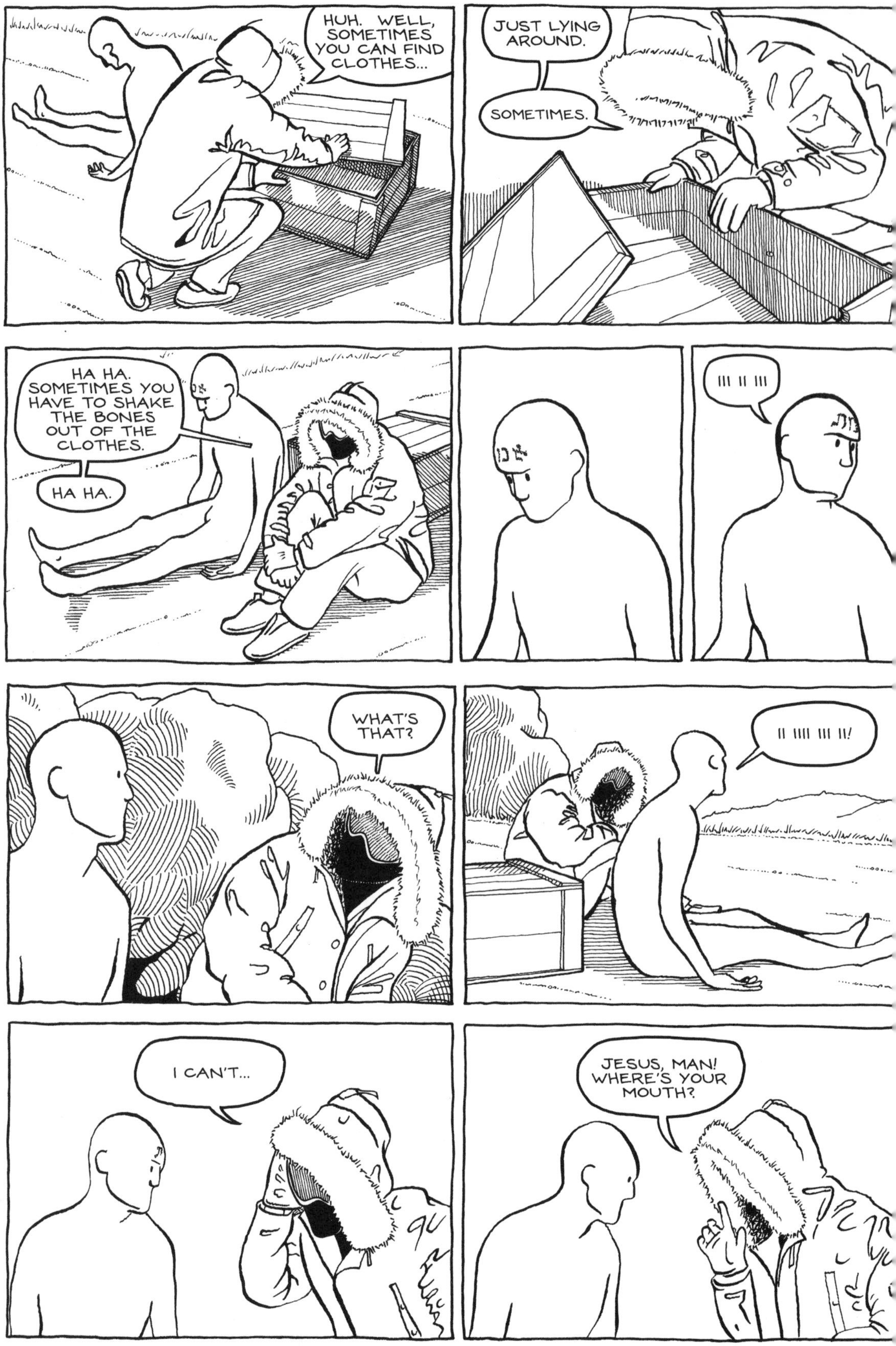
HUH. WELL, SOMETIMES YOU CAN FIND CLOTHES...
JUST LYING AROUND.
SOMETIMES.
HA HA. SOMETIMES YOU HAVE TO SHAKE THE BONES OUT OF THE CLOTHES.
HA HA.
III II III
WHAT'S THAT?
II IIII III II!
I CAN'T...
JESUS, MAN! WHERE'S YOUR MOUTH?

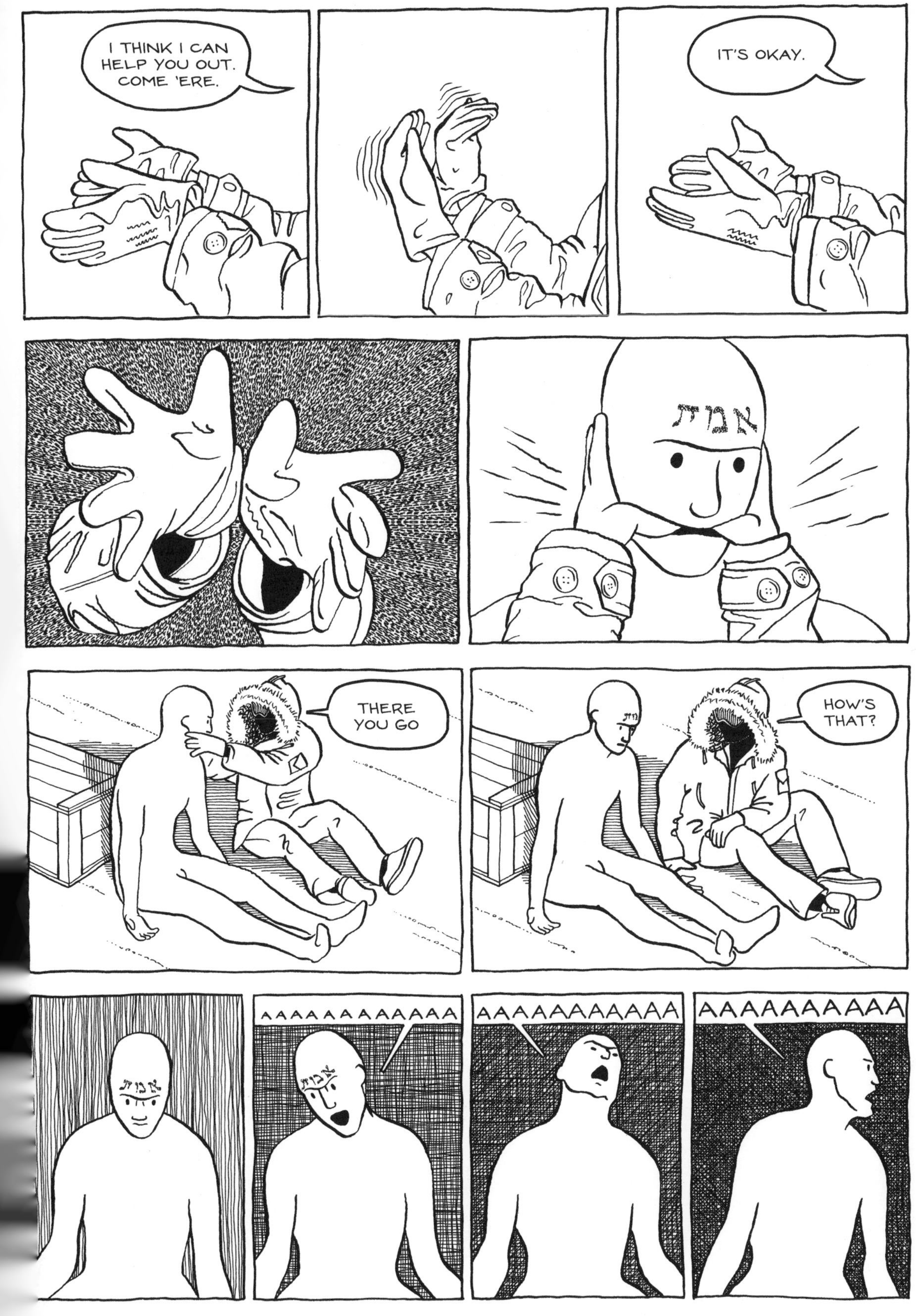
I THINK I CAN HELP YOU OUT. COME 'ERE.
IT'S OKAY.
THERE YOU GO
HOW'S THAT?
AAAAAAAAAAAA
AAAAAAAAAAA
AAAAAAAAAA

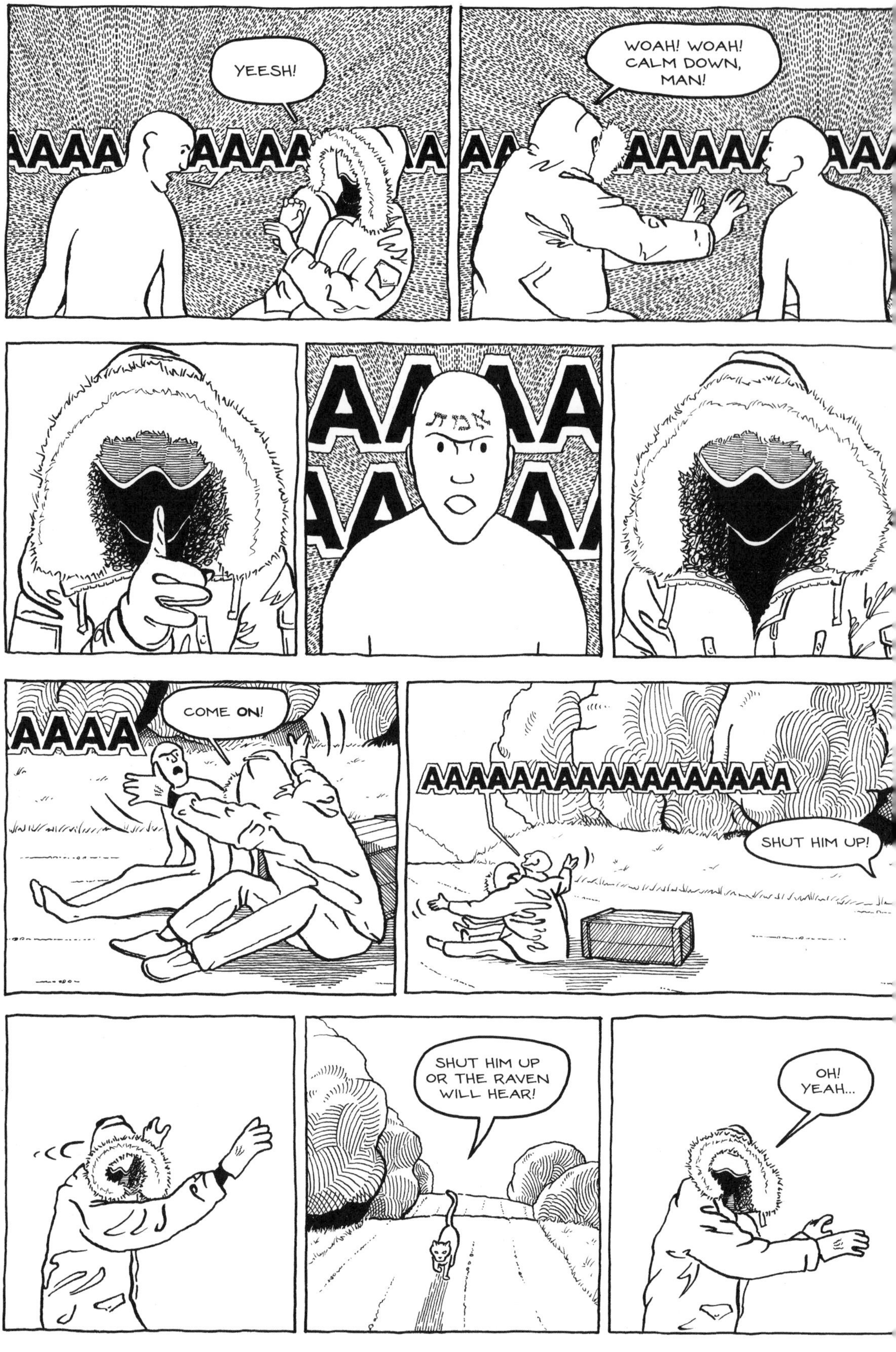
YEESH!
AAAAAAAAAAA
WOAH! WOAH! CALM DOWN, MAN!
AAAAAAAAAA
COME ON!
AAAA
AAAAAAAAAAAAAAAAAA
SHUT HIM UP!
SHUT HIM UP OR THE RAVEN WILL HEAR!
OH! YEAH...

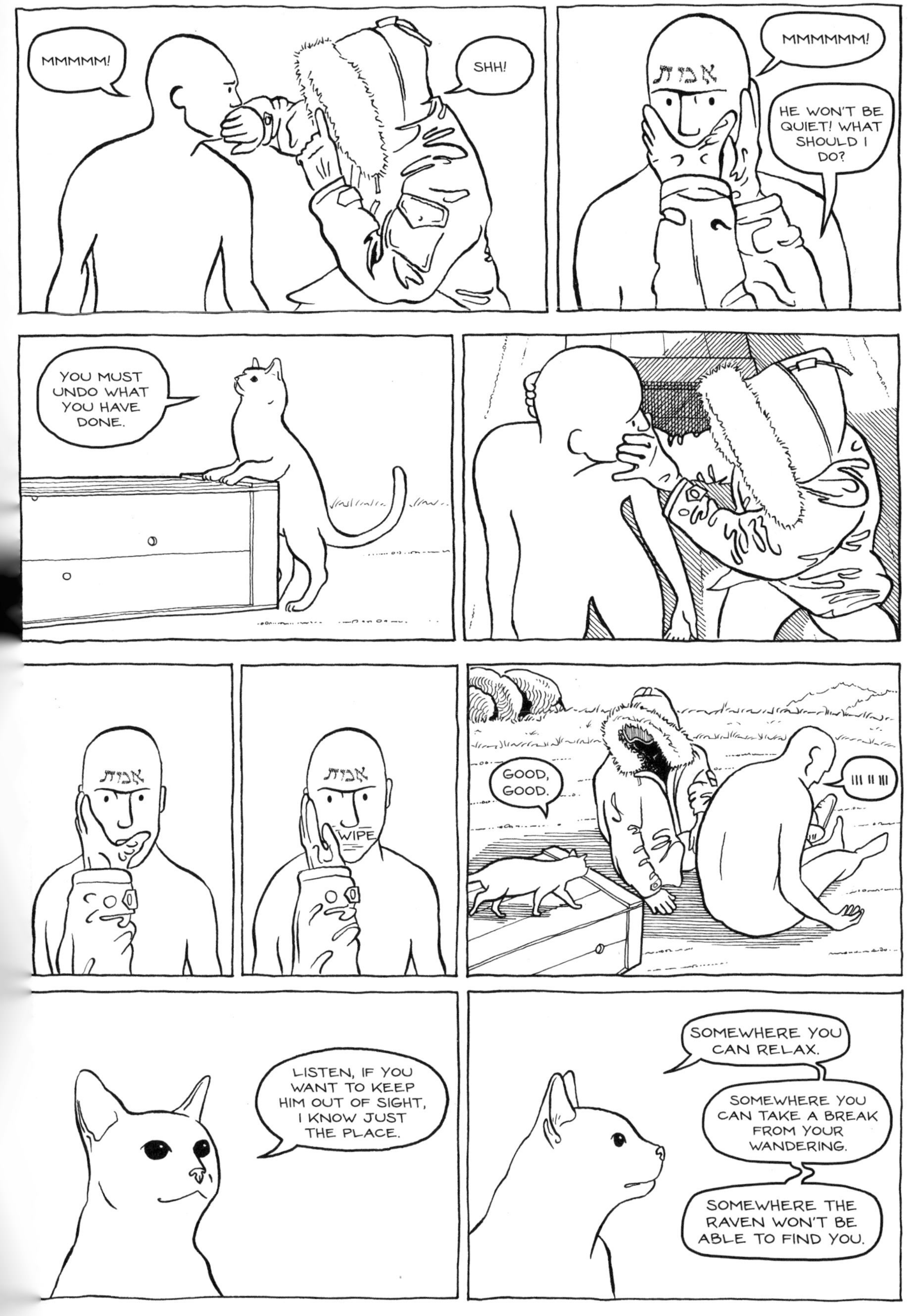
MMMMM!
SHH!
MMMMMM!
HE WON'T BE QUIET! WHAT SHOULD I DO?
YOU MUST UNDO WHAT YOU HAVE DONE.
WIPE
GOOD, GOOD.
LISTEN, IF YOU WANT TO KEEP HIM OUT OF SIGHT, I KNOW JUST THE PLACE.
SOMEWHERE YOU CAN RELAX.
SOMEWHERE YOU CAN TAKE A BREAK FROM YOUR WANDERING.
SOMEWHERE THE RAVEN WON'T BE ABLE TO FIND YOU.

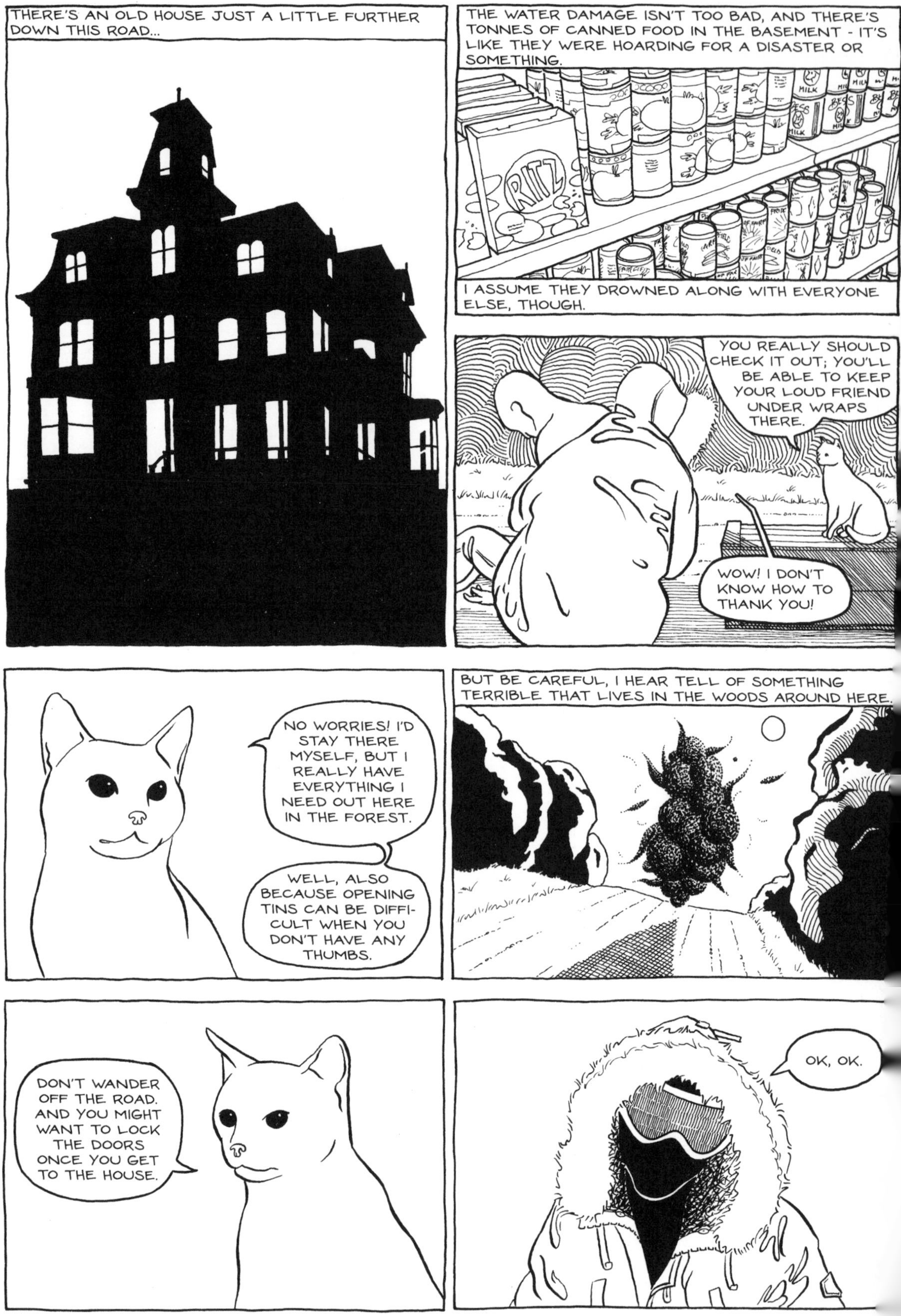
THERE'S AN OLD HOUSE JUST A LITTLE FURTHER DOWN THIS ROAD...
THE WATER DAMAGE ISN'T TOO BAD, AND THERE'S TONNES OF CANNED FOOD IN THE BASEMENT - IT'S LIKE THEY WERE HOARDING FOR A DISASTER OR SOMETHING.
RITZ
I ASSUME THEY DROWNED ALONG WITH EVERYONE ELSE, THOUGH.
YOU REALLY SHOULD CHECK IT OUT; YOU'LL BE ABLE TO KEEP YOUR LOUD FRIEND UNDER WRAPS THERE.
WOW! I DON'T KNOW HOW TO THANK YOU!
NO WORRIES! I'D STAY THERE MYSELF, BUT I REALLY HAVE EVERYTHING I NEED OUT HERE IN THE FOREST.
WELL, ALSO BECAUSE OPENING TINS CAN BE DIFFI-CULT WHEN YOU DON'T HAVE ANY THUMBS.
BUT BE CAREFUL, I HEAR TELL OF SOMETHING TERRIBLE THAT LIVES IN THE WOODS AROUND HERE.
DON'T WANDER OFF THE ROAD. AND YOU MIGHT WANT TO LOCK THE DOORS ONCE YOU GET TO THE HOUSE.
OK, OK.

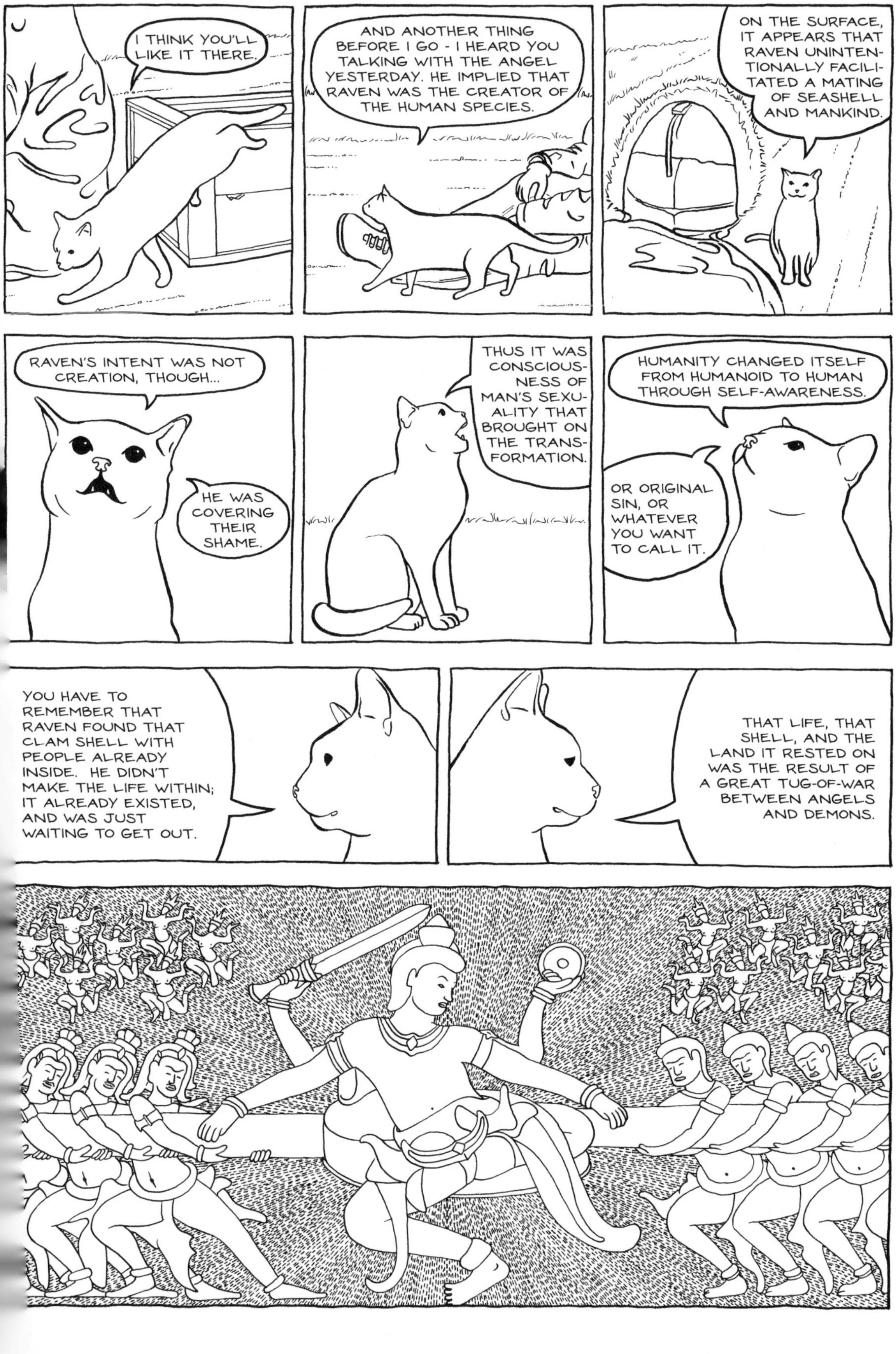
I THINK YOU'LL LIKE IT THERE.
AND ANOTHER THING BEFORE I GO - I HEARD YOU TALKING WITH THE ANGEL YESTERDAY. HE IMPLIED THAT RAVEN WAS THE CREATOR OF THE HUMAN SPECIES.
ON THE SURFACE, IT APPEARS THAT RAVEN UNINTENTIONALLY FACILITATED A MATING OF SEASHELL AND MANKIND.
RAVEN'S INTENT WAS NOT CREATION, THOUGH...
HE WAS COVERING THEIR SHAME.
THUS IT WAS CONSCIOUSNESS OF MAN'S SEXUALITY THAT BROUGHT ON THE TRANSFORMATION.
HUMANITY CHANGED ITSELF FROM HUMANOID TO HUMAN THROUGH SELF-AWARENESS.
OR ORIGINAL SIN, OR WHATEVER YOU WANT TO CALL IT.
YOU HAVE TO REMEMBER THAT RAVEN FOUND THAT CLAM SHELL WITH PEOPLE ALREADY INSIDE. HE DIDN'T MAKE THE LIFE WITHIN; IT ALREADY EXISTED, AND WAS JUST WAITING TO GET OUT.
THAT LIFE, THAT SHELL, AND THE LAND IT RESTED ON WAS THE RESULT OF A GREAT TUG-OF-WAR BETWEEN ANGELS AND DEMONS.

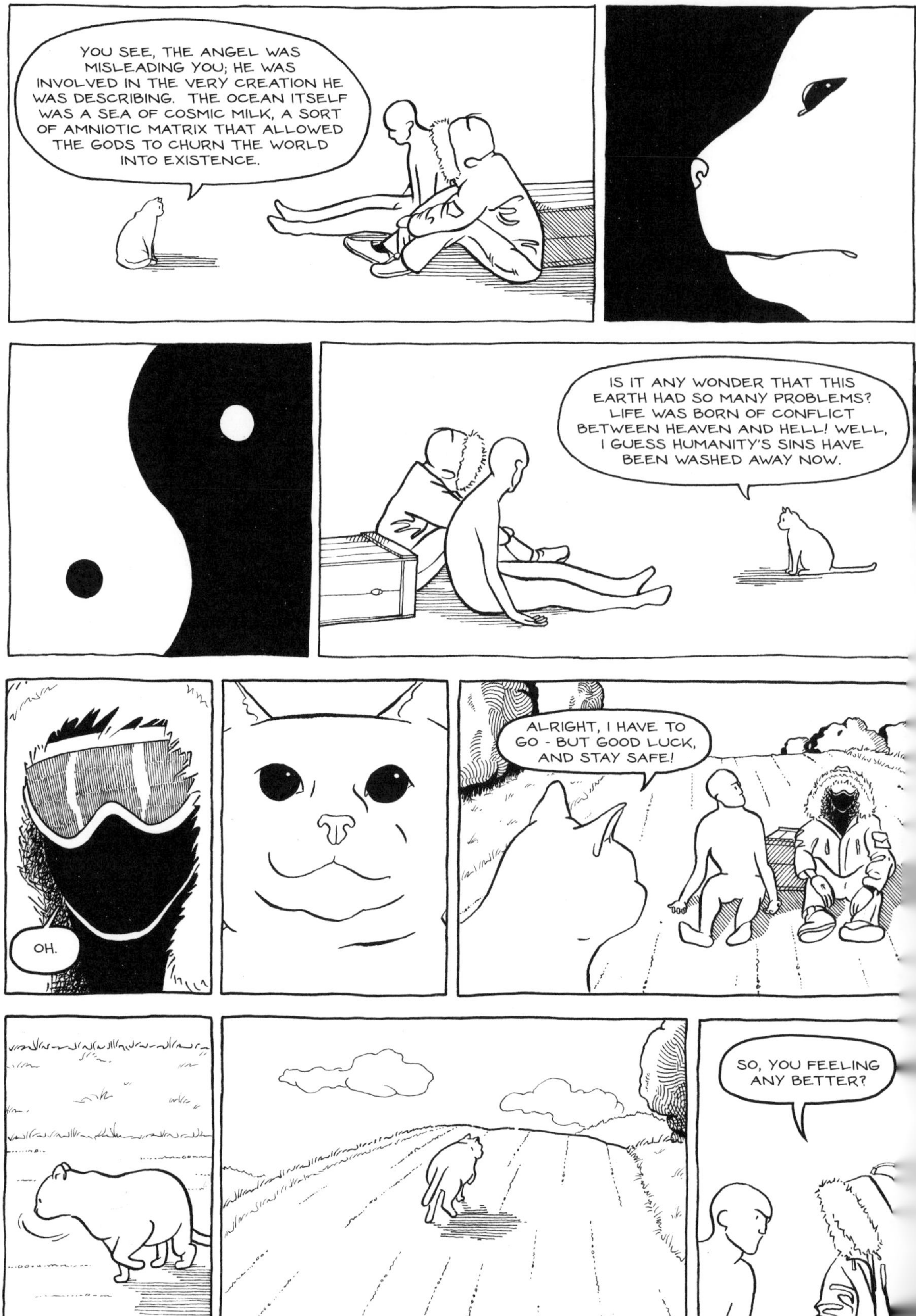
YOU SEE, THE ANGEL WAS MISLEADING YOU; HE WAS INVOLVED IN THE VERY CREATION HE WAS DESCRIBING. THE OCEAN ITSELF WAS A SEA OF COSMIC MILK, A SORT OF AMNIOTIC MATRIX THAT ALLOWED THE GODS TO CHURN THE WORLD INTO EXISTENCE.
IS IT ANY WONDER THAT THIS EARTH HAD SO MANY PROBLEMS? LIFE WAS BORN OF CONFLICT BETWEEN HEAVEN AND HELL! WELL, I GUESS HUMANITY'S SINS HAVE BEEN WASHED AWAY NOW.
OH.
ALRIGHT, I HAVE TO GO - BUT GOOD LUCK, AND STAY SAFE!
SO, YOU FEELING ANY BETTER?

LET'S TRY AND FIND THAT PLACE.
C'MON.
THAT'S IT! THERE IT IS!
IT'S, UH, A BIT SMALLER THAN I IMAGINED.

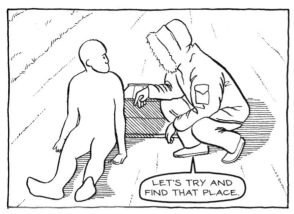

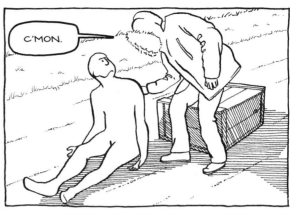

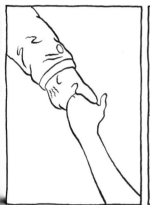

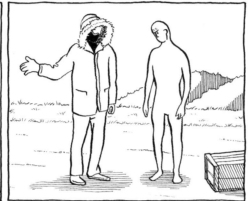

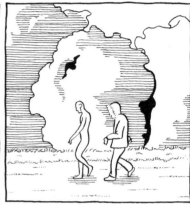

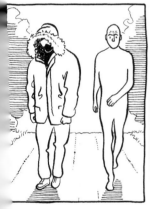

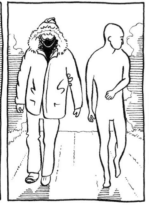

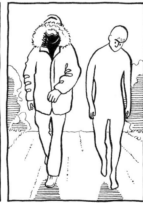

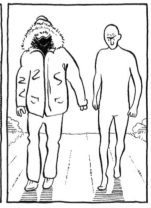

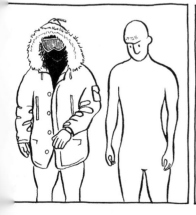

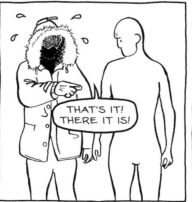

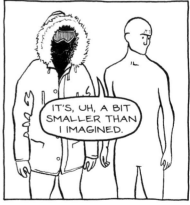

four

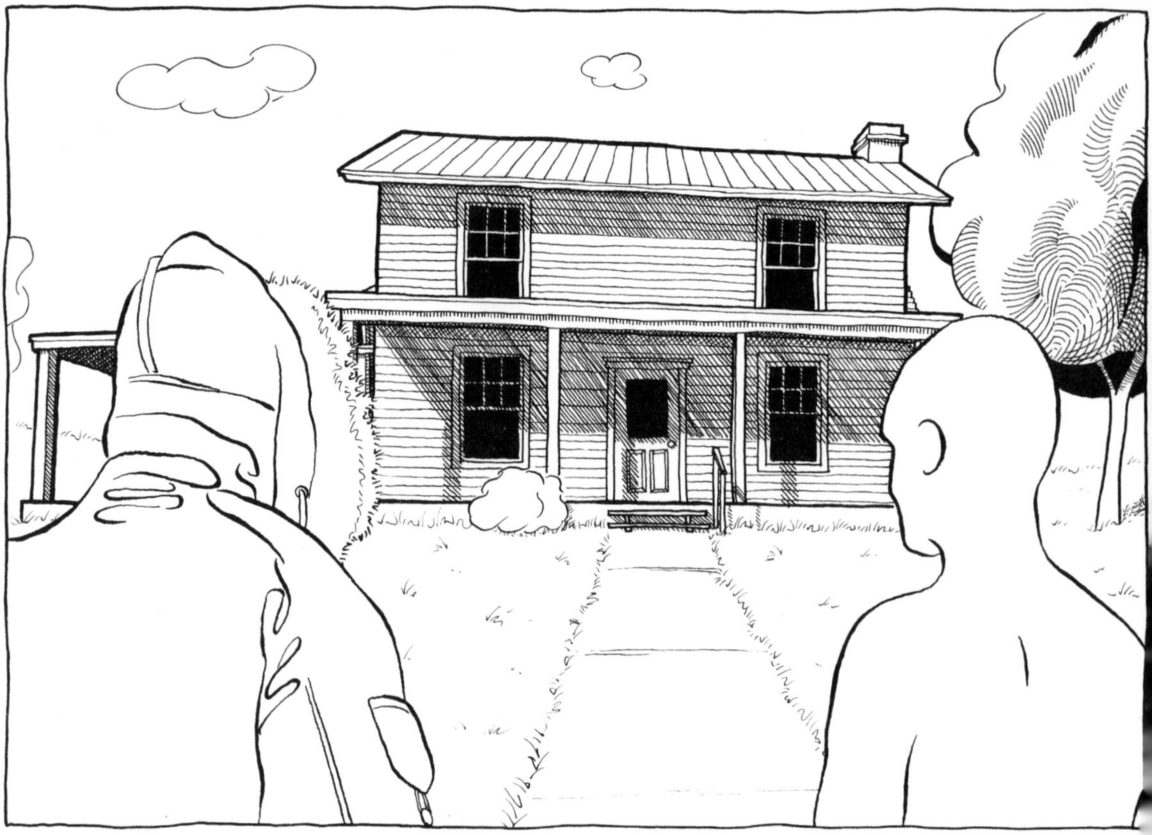

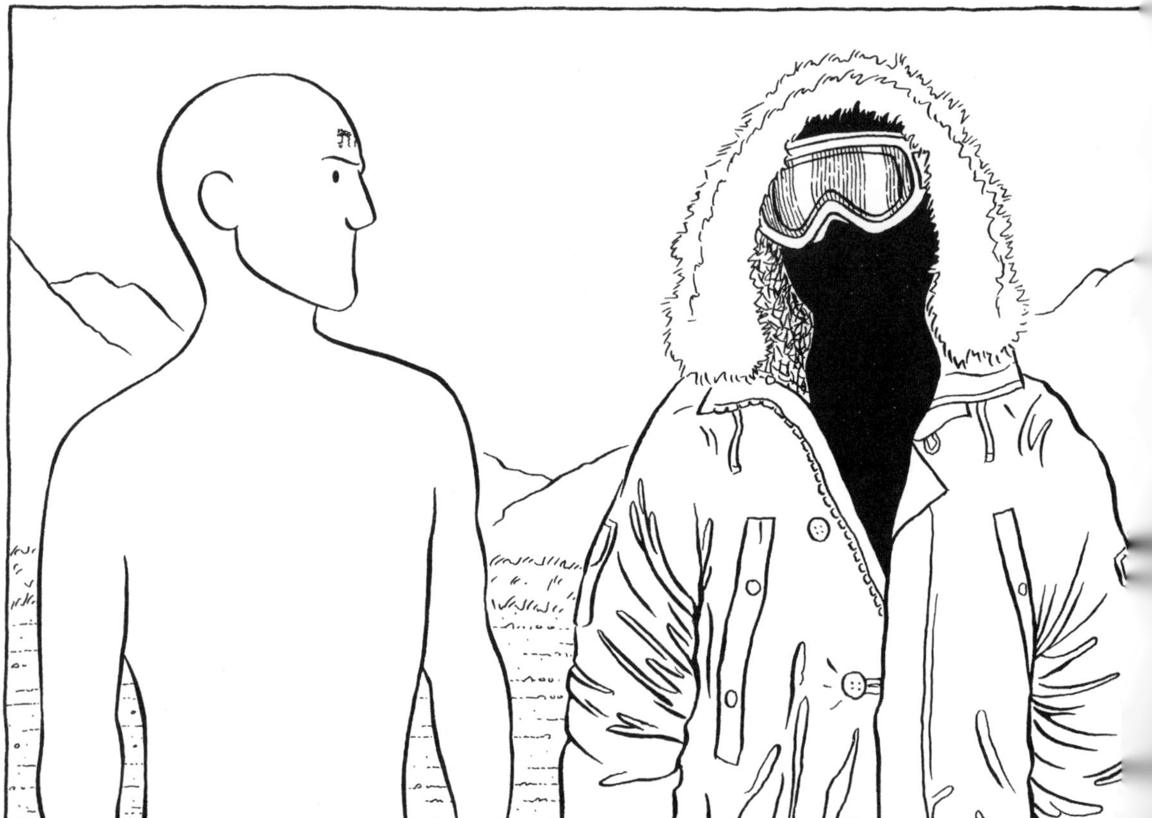

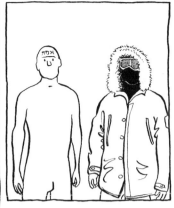

TELL YOU WHAT - YOU STAY HERE.

I'LL GO IN AND CHECK IT OUT - SEE IF IT'S SAFE.

. . .

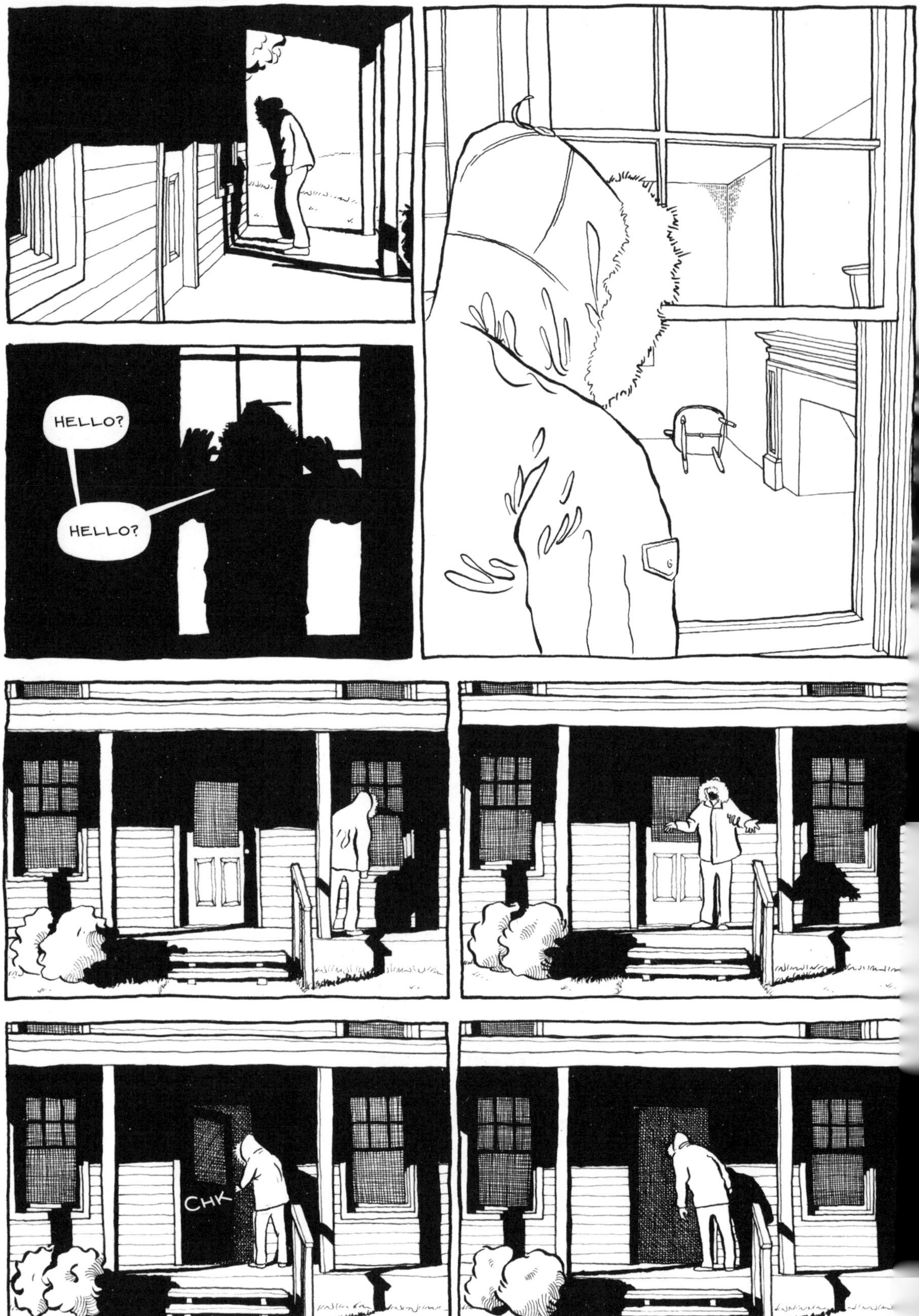
HELLO?
HELLO?
CHK

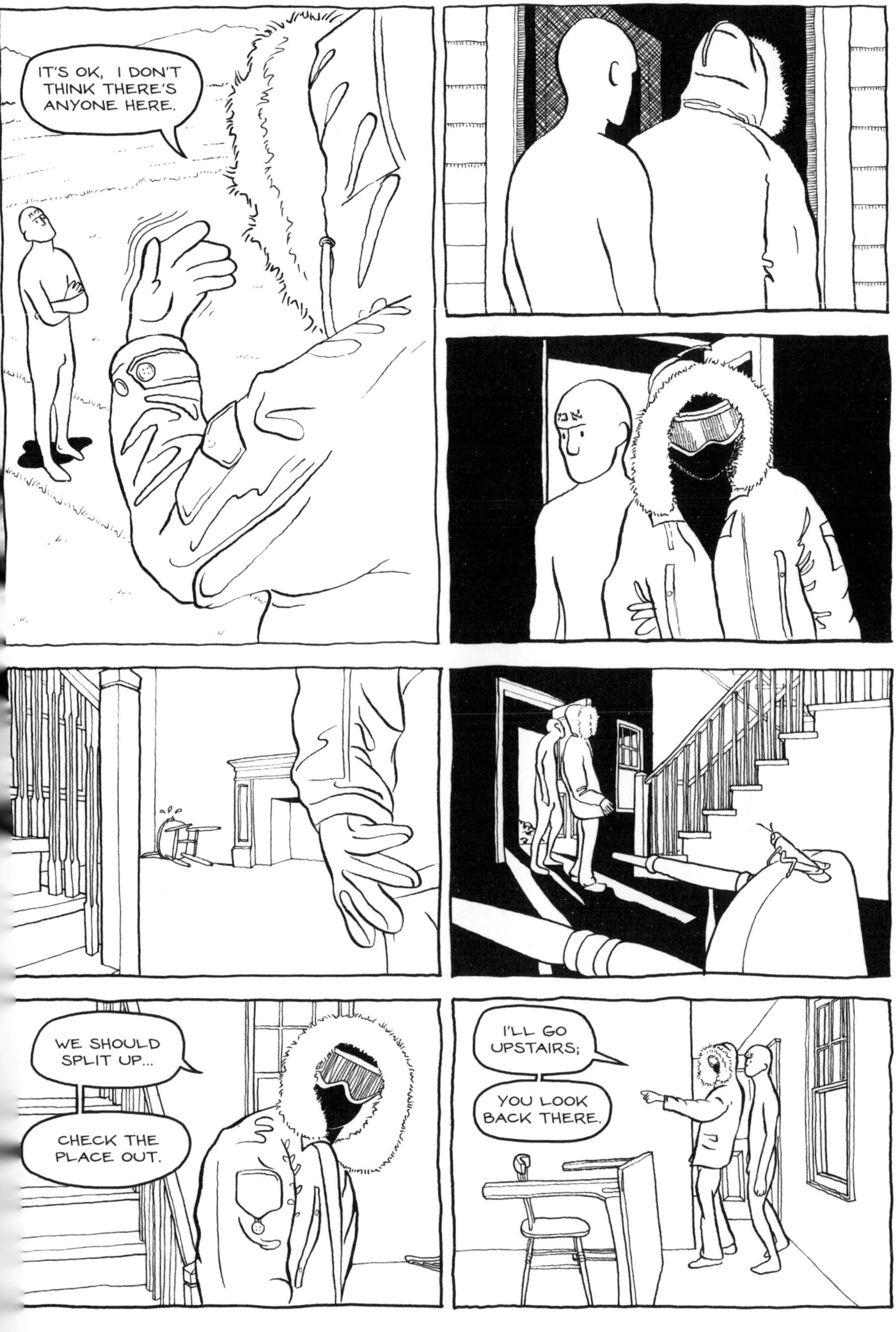
IT'S OK, I DON'T THINK THERE'S ANYONE HERE.
WE SHOULD SPLIT UP...
CHECK THE PLACE OUT.
I'LL GO UPSTAIRS;
YOU LOOK BACK THERE.

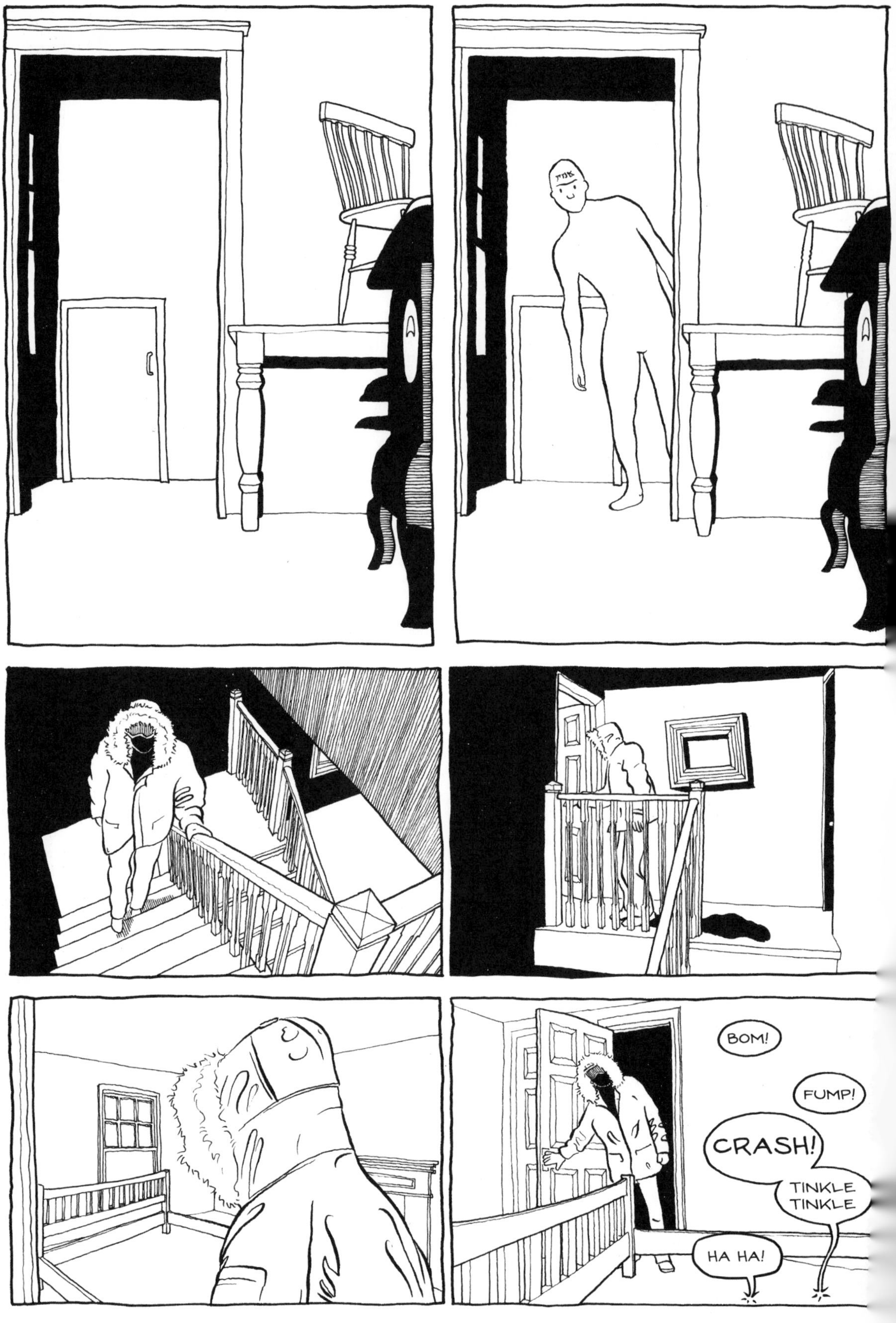
BOM!
FUMP!
CRASH!
TINKLE TINKLE
HA HA!

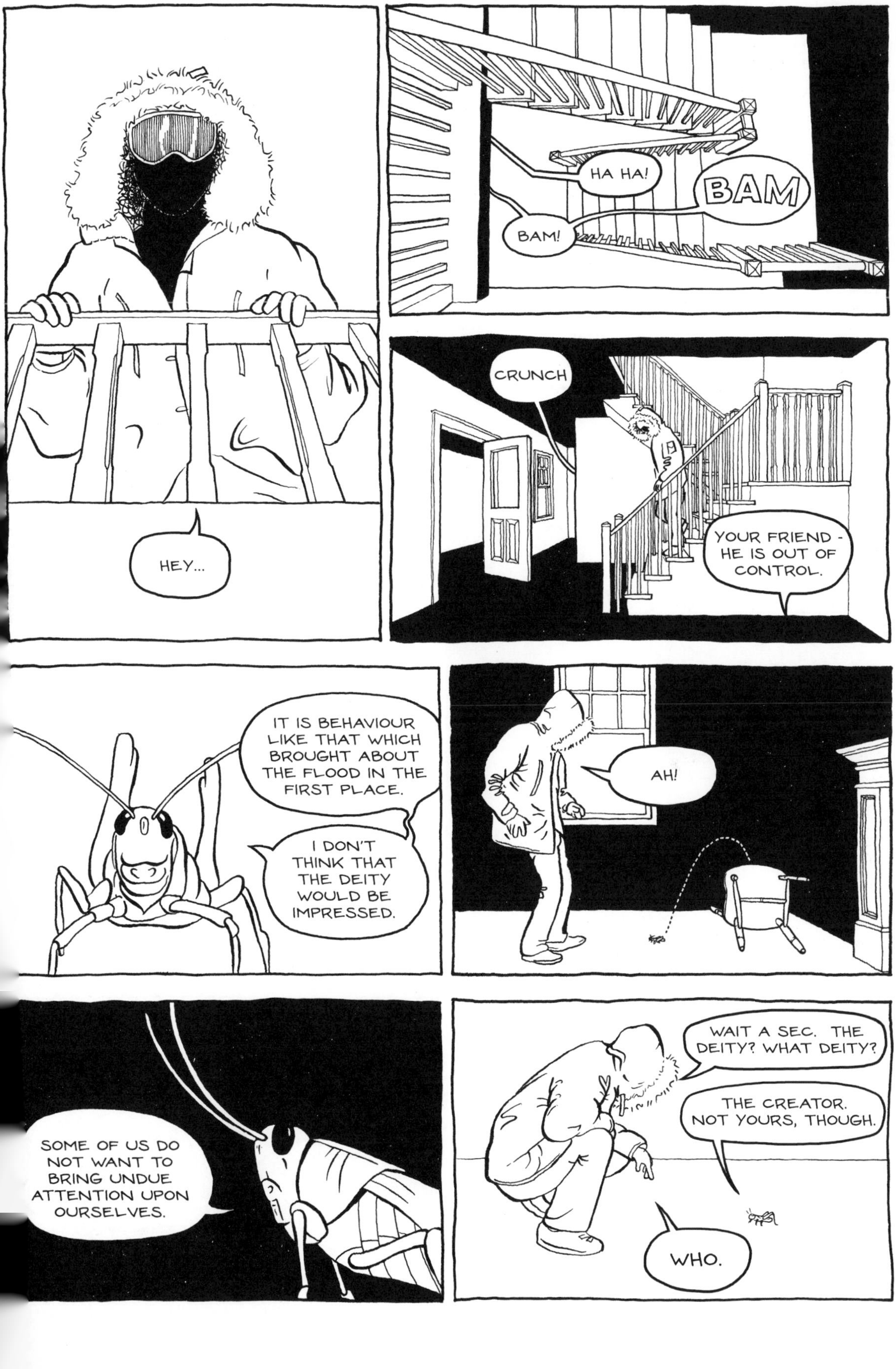
HEY...
HA HA!
BAM!
BAM
CRUNCH
YOUR FRIEND - HE IS OUT OF CONTROL.
IT IS BEHAVIOUR LIKE THAT WHICH BROUGHT ABOUT THE FLOOD IN THE FIRST PLACE.
I DON'T THINK THAT THE DEITY WOULD BE IMPRESSED.
AH!
SOME OF US DO NOT WANT TO BRING UNDUE ATTENTION UPON OURSELVES.
WAIT A SEC. THE DEITY? WHAT DEITY?
THE CREATOR. NOT YOURS, THOUGH.
WHO.

I'M NOT SURE I SHOULD SAY.

THE LAST GUY WHO CROSSED HIM WOUND UP CHAINED TO A ROCK...

A BIRD EATING HIS LIVER FOR ETERNITY.

LOOK, EVERYONE ELSE AROUND HERE FEELS THE NEED TO DUMP THEIR SHIT ON ME.

JUST TELL ME WHO YOU'RE TALKING ABOUT. WHO'S GONNA KNOW?

JUST THINK OF ME AS A REPOSITORY OF MYTHOLOGY.

WOAH THERE! MYTHOLOGY? WATCH YOUR MOUTH!

THIS IS **TRUTH**, NOT SOME SUPERSTIOUS BULLSHIT LIKE SOME OF THOSE OTHER CRANKS BELIEVE.

OK THEN. WHO?

WHO IS THE DEITY?

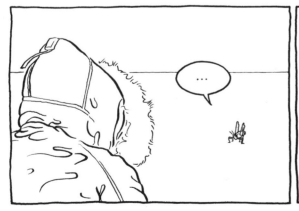

...

HE IS A PETTY AND VINDICTIVE GOD.

HE WOULD HAVE SCOURED THE EARTH BARE OF CIVILISATION, IF HE HAD HAD HIS WAY.

YOU KNOW, YOUR CREATOR IS AT LEAST PARTIALLY RESPONSIBLE FOR THIS DELUGE.

IT WASN'T ENOUGH TO SIMPLY MAKE MAN FROM CLAY.

HE HAD TO BESTOW UPON HIM THE DUBIOUS GIFTS OF KNOWLEDGE.

PROMETHIUS, YOU SNAKE!

HE BROUGHT UPON US THE WRATH OF A MALICIOUS AND CONTROLLING GOD!

HE IS ALSO OUR SAVIOUR, THOUGH.

NO ONE AND NOTHING WOULD HAVE SURVIVED THE FLOOD IF HE HAD NOT INTERVENED.

HE IMPLORED HIS SON TO BUILD AN ARK TO FERRY CIVILISA-TION FROM ONE AGE TO THE NEXT.

THIS IS A POST-HUMAN WORLD NOW.

KNOWLEDGE IS NO LONGER THE SOLE DOMAIN OF MAN.

HIS WORLD IS GONE; HIS TECHNOL-OGY IS OBSOLETE; THE FINAL MANIFESTA-TIONS OF HUMANITY'S SUPREMACY OVER NATURE ARE SUC-CUMBING TO THE EFFECTS OF ENTROPY

YOU AREN'T ANSWERING MY QUESTION.

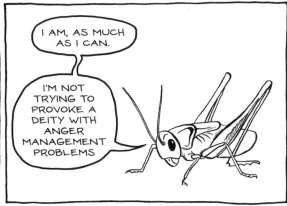

I AM, AS MUCH AS I CAN.

I'M NOT TRYING TO PROVOKE A DEITY WITH ANGER MANAGEMENT PROBLEMS

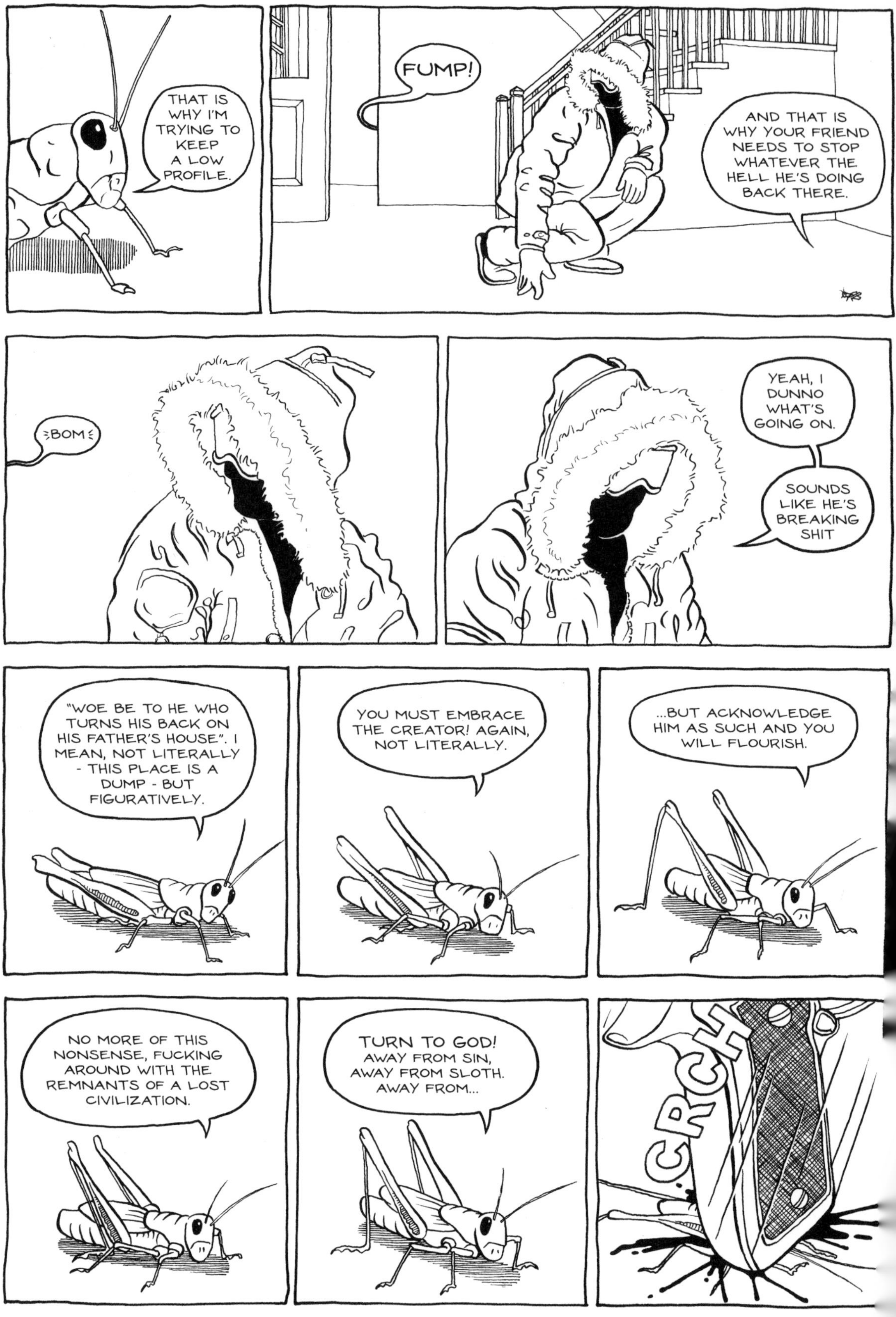
THAT IS WHY I'M TRYING TO KEEP A LOW PROFILE.
FUMP!
AND THAT IS WHY YOUR FRIEND NEEDS TO STOP WHATEVER THE HELL HE'S DOING BACK THERE.
BOM
YEAH, I DUNNO WHAT'S GOING ON.
SOUNDS LIKE HE'S BREAKING SHIT
"WOE BE TO HE WHO TURNS HIS BACK ON HIS FATHER'S HOUSE". I MEAN, NOT LITERALLY - THIS PLACE IS A DUMP - BUT FIGURATIVELY.
YOU MUST EMBRACE THE CREATOR! AGAIN, NOT LITERALLY.
...BUT ACKNOWLEDGE HIM AS SUCH AND YOU WILL FLOURISH.
NO MORE OF THIS NONSENSE, FUCKING AROUND WITH THE REMNANTS OF A LOST CIVILIZATION.
TURN TO GOD! AWAY FROM SIN, AWAY FROM SLOTH. AWAY FROM...
CRCH

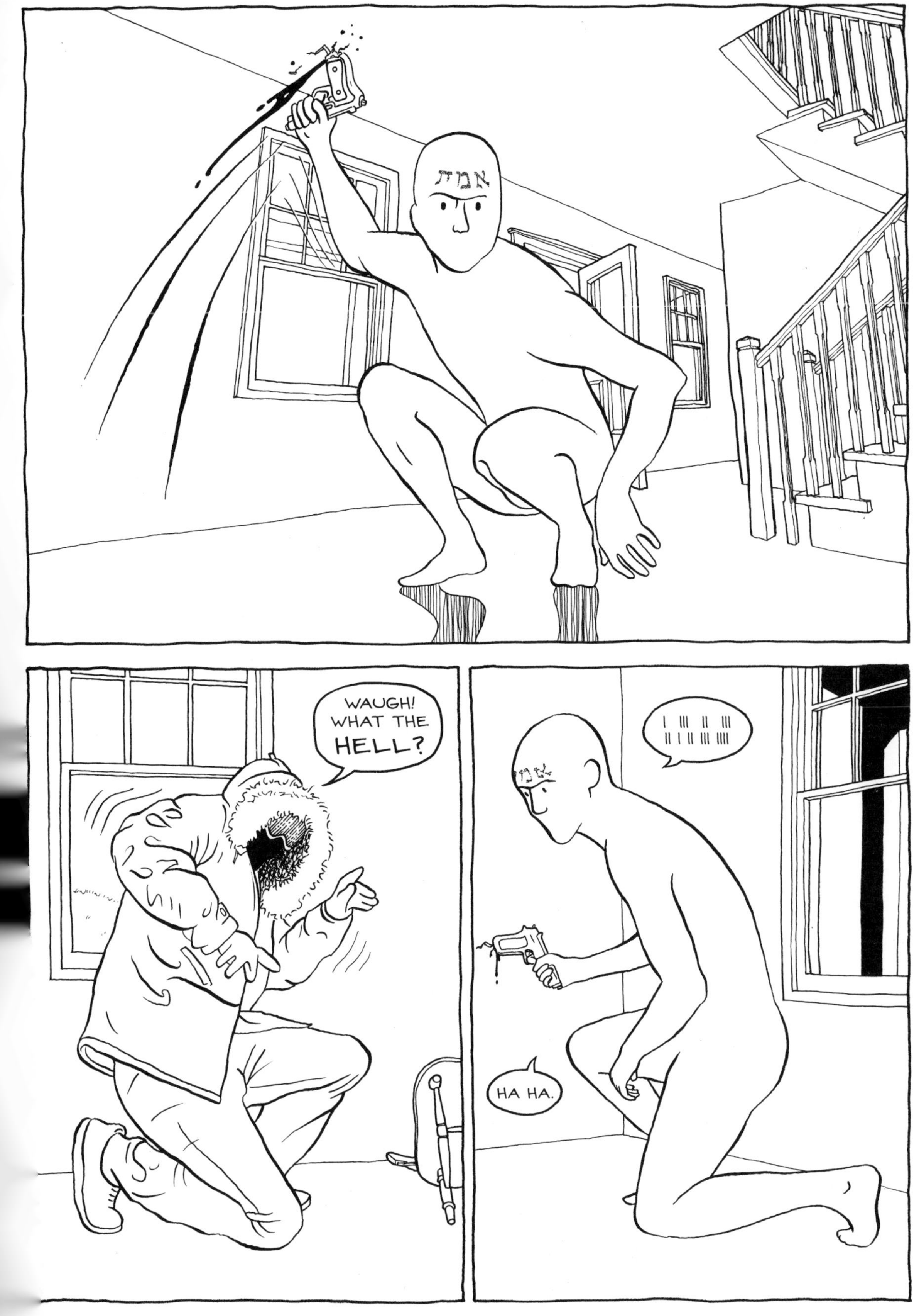
אמת
WAUGH! WHAT THE HELL?
HA HA.

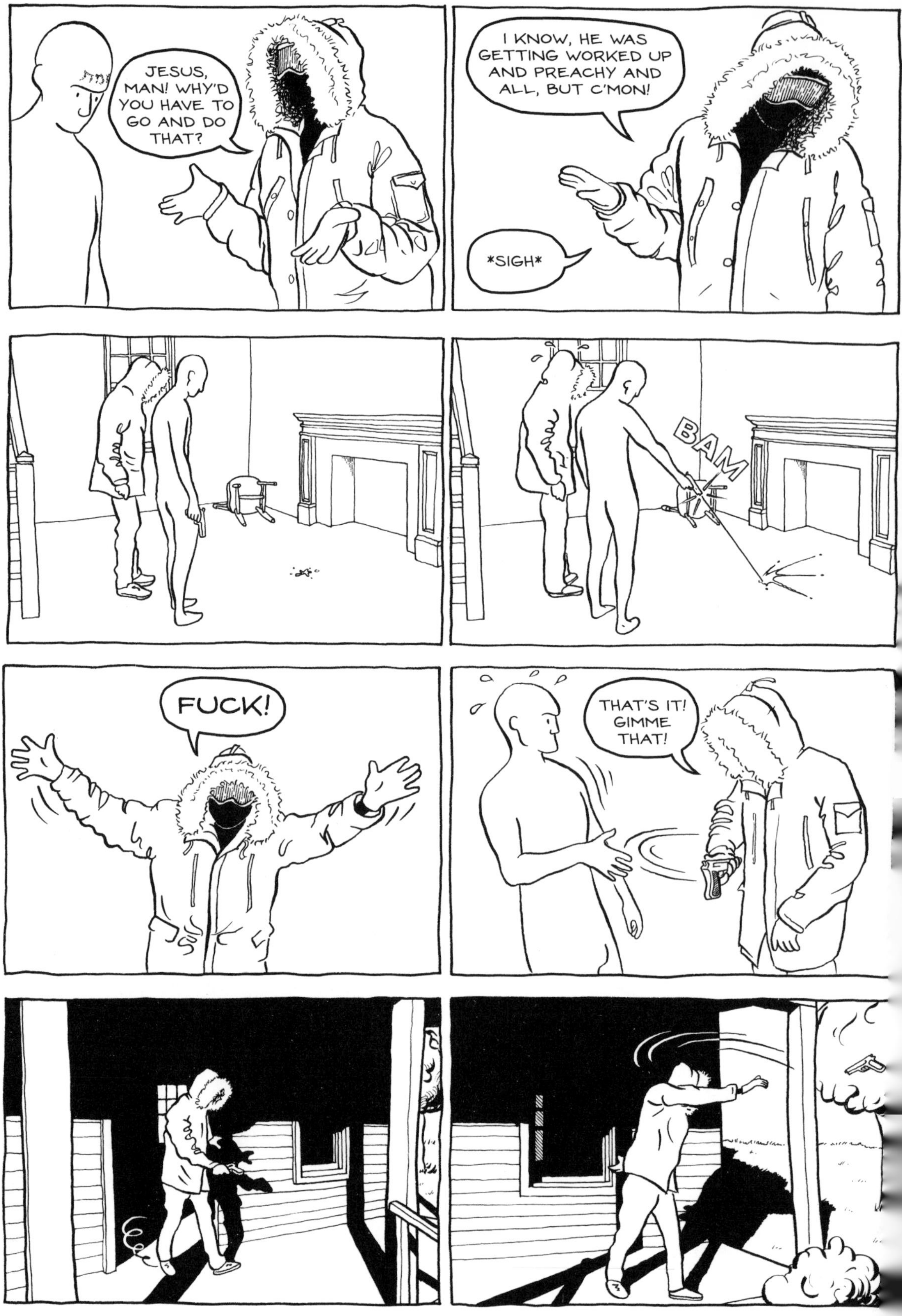
JESUS, MAN! WHY'D YOU HAVE TO GO AND DO THAT?
I KNOW, HE WAS GETTING WORKED UP AND PREACHY AND ALL, BUT C'MON!
SIGH
BAM
FUCK!
THAT'S IT! GIMME THAT!

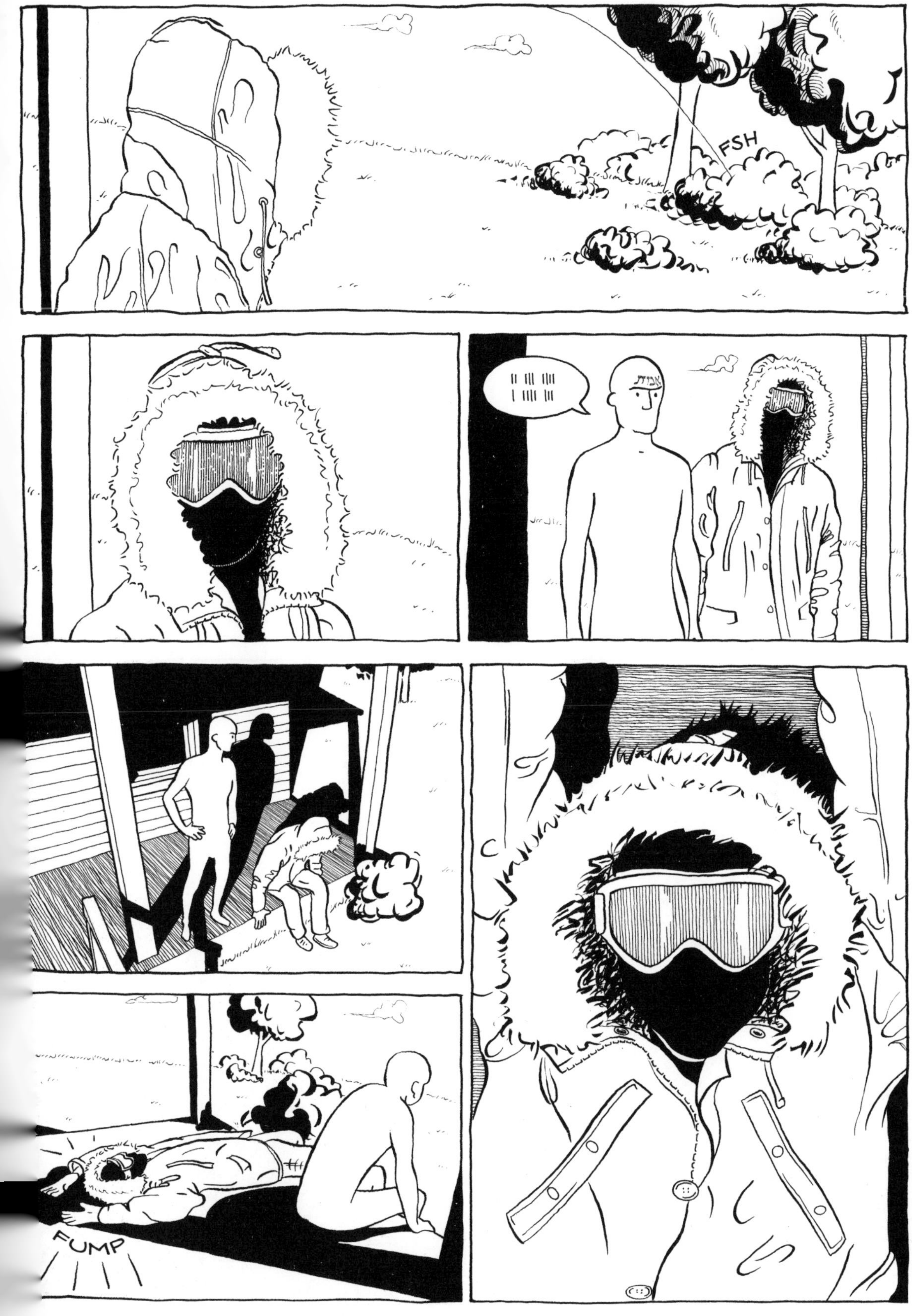
FSH
FUMP

OH MY GOD.
I'M SO TIRED THAT I FEEL LIKE I COULD THROW UP.

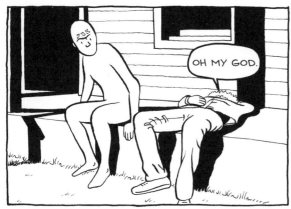

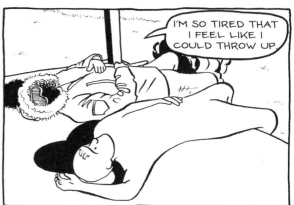

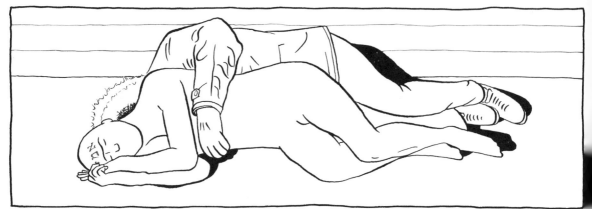

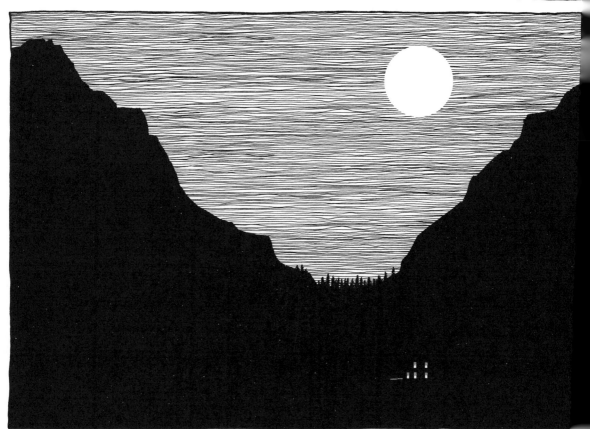

five

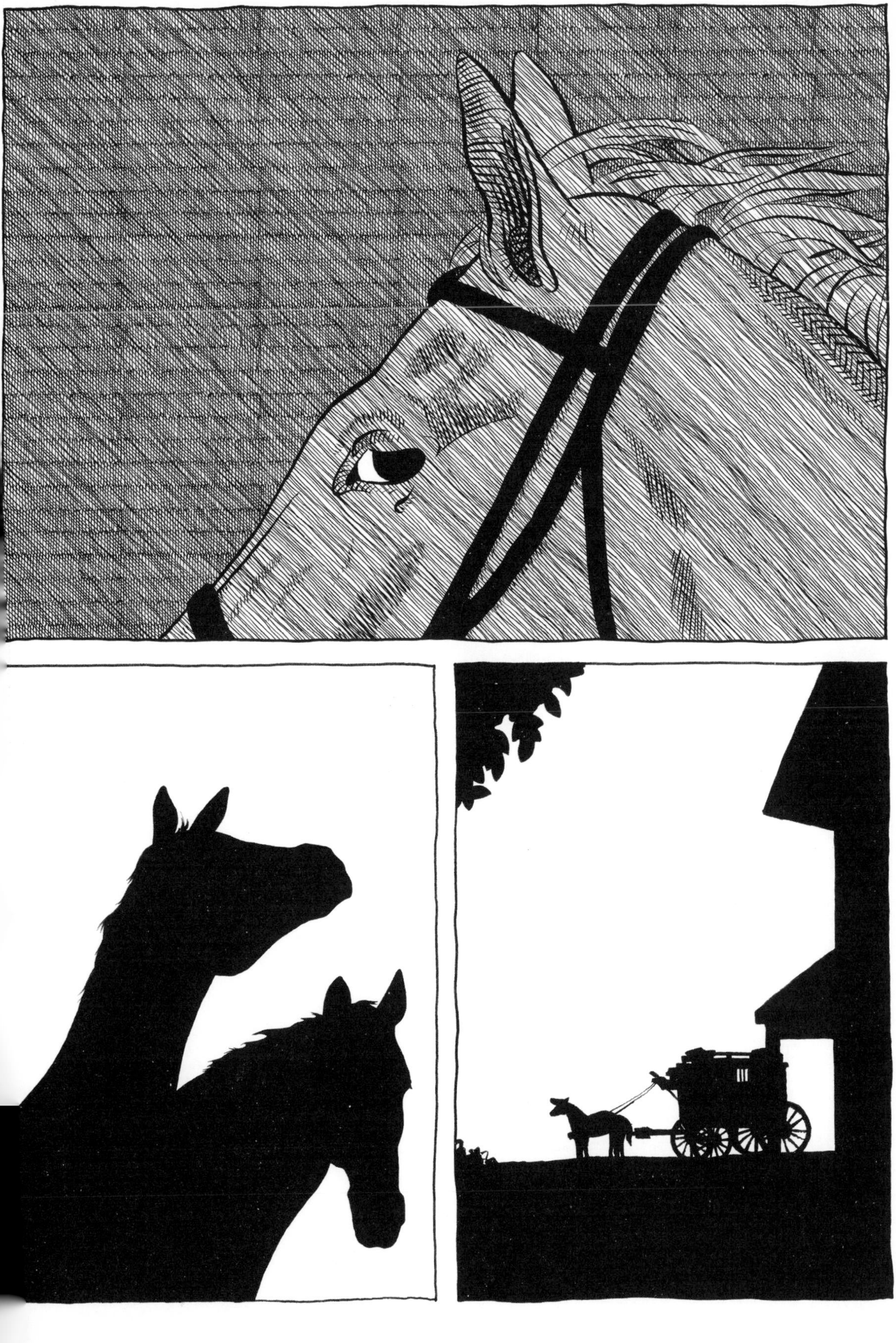

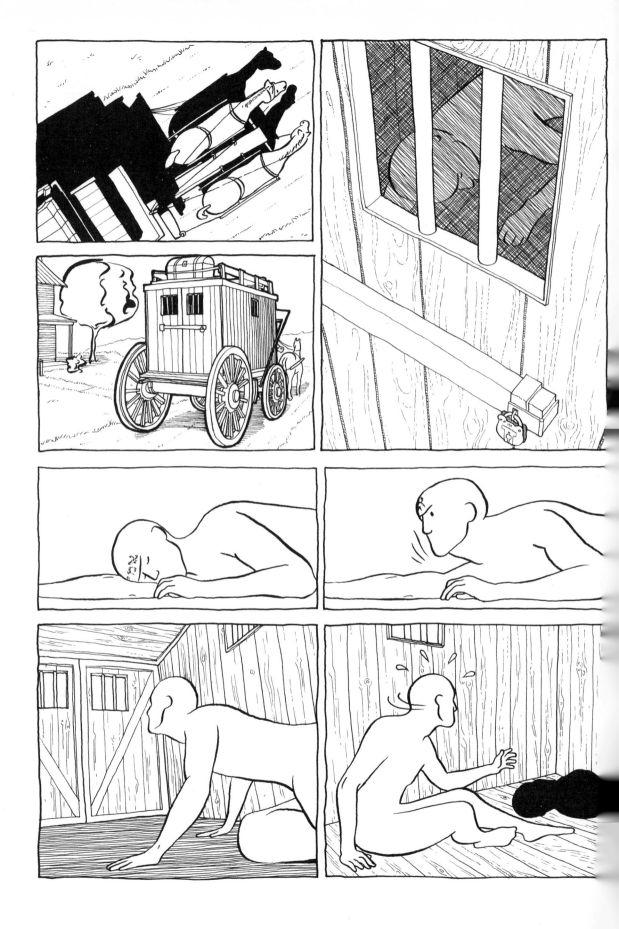

WHA...
WHAT...
WHERE ARE WE?
אמת

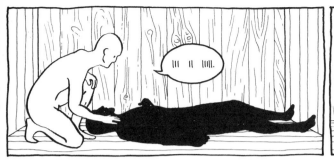

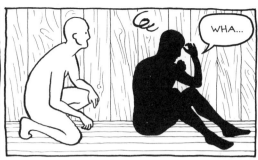

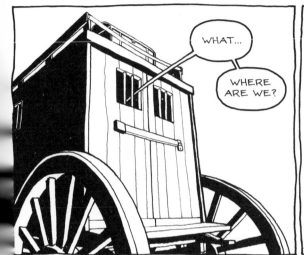

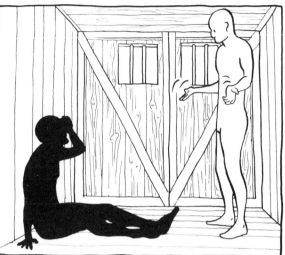

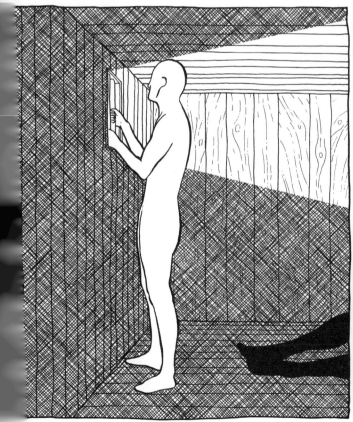

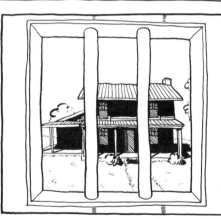

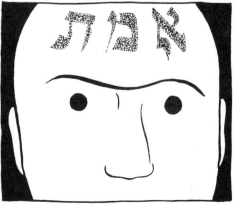

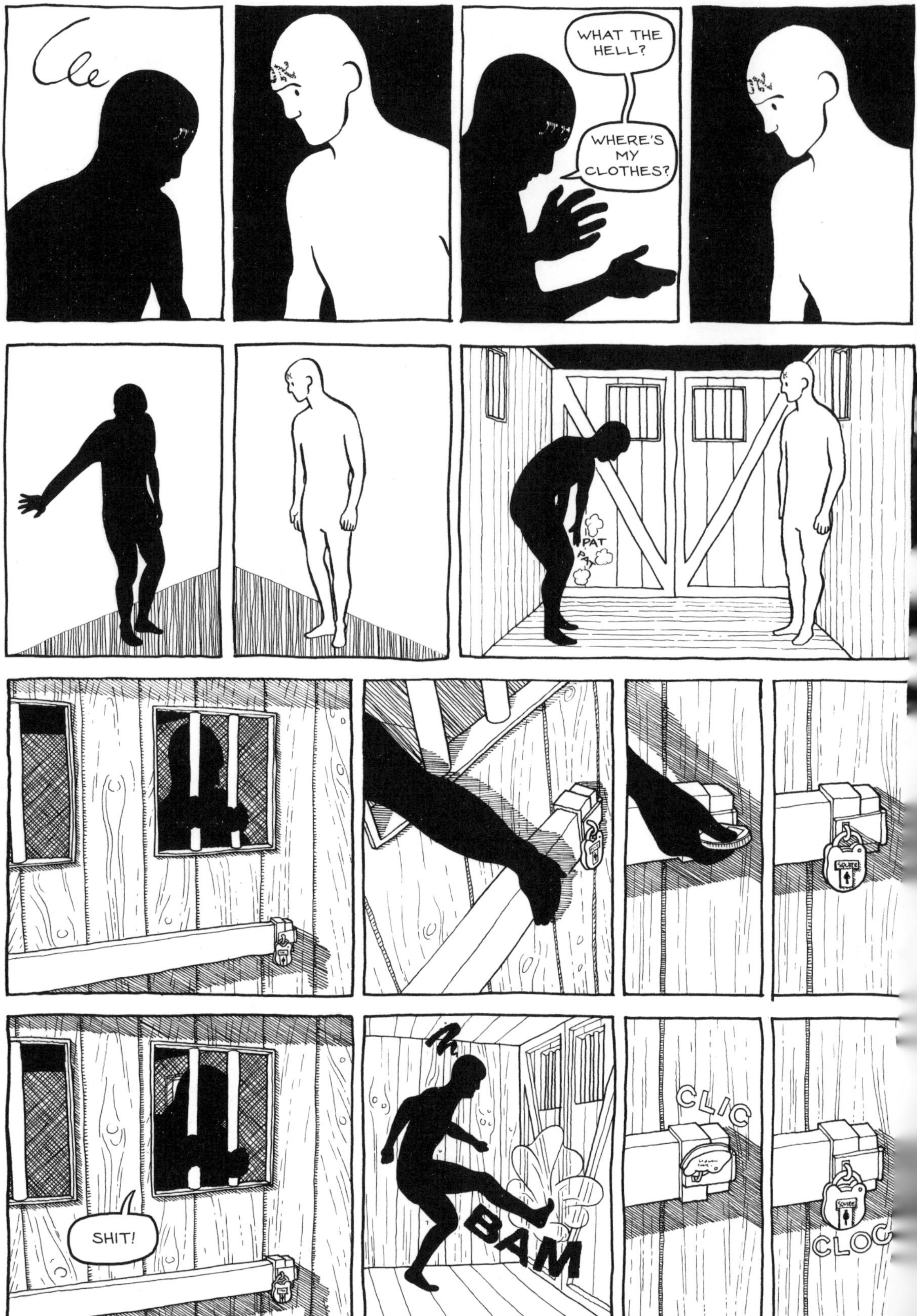
WHAT THE HELL?
WHERE'S MY CLOTHES?
PAT
PAT
SHIT!
BAM
CLIC
CLOC

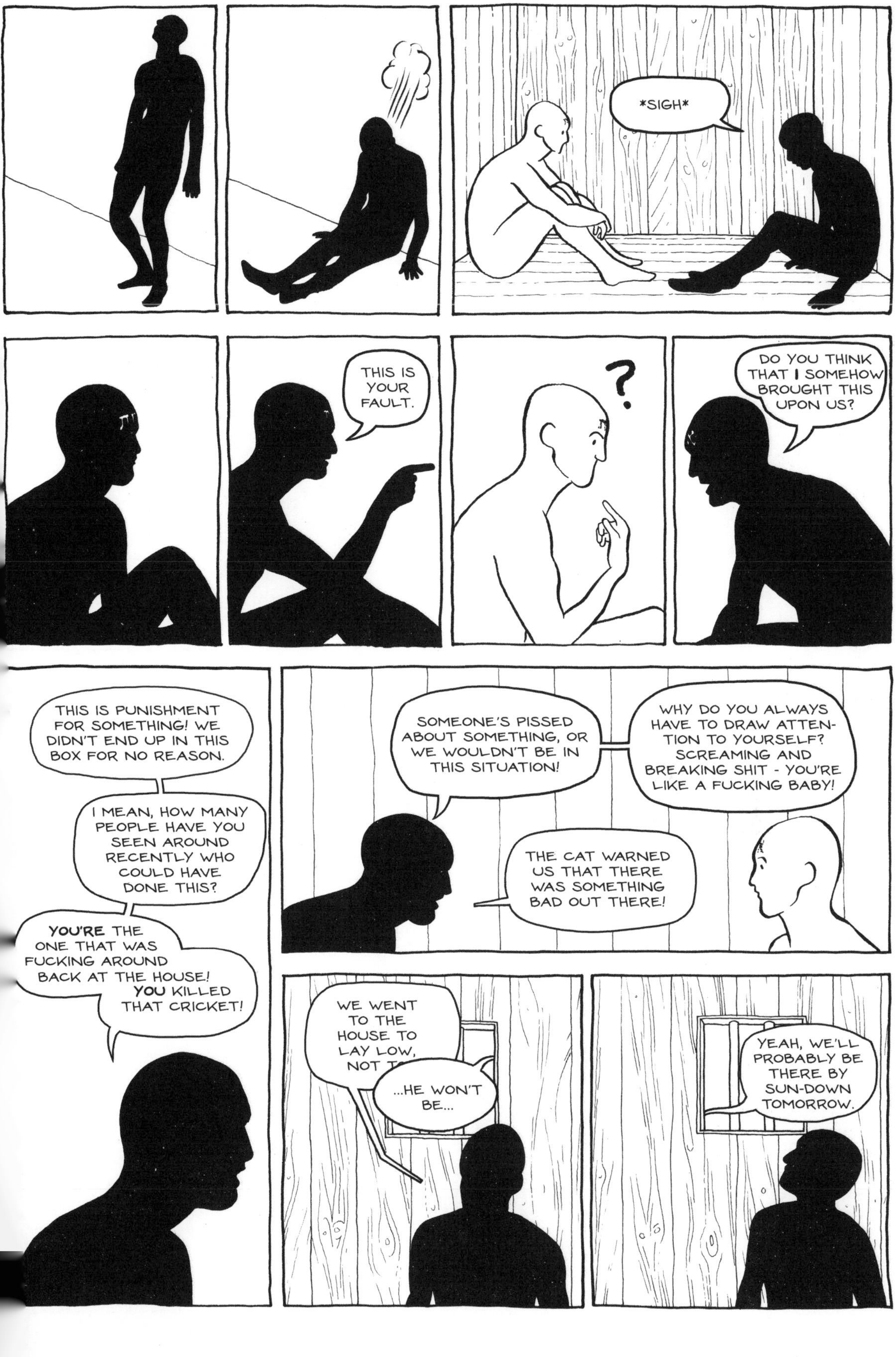
SIGH
THIS IS YOUR FAULT.
?
DO YOU THINK THAT I SOMEHOW BROUGHT THIS UPON US?
THIS IS PUNISHMENT FOR SOMETHING! WE DIDN'T END UP IN THIS BOX FOR NO REASON.
I MEAN, HOW MANY PEOPLE HAVE YOU SEEN AROUND RECENTLY WHO COULD HAVE DONE THIS?
YOU'RE THE ONE THAT WAS FUCKING AROUND BACK AT THE HOUSE! YOU KILLED THAT CRICKET!
SOMEONE'S PISSED ABOUT SOMETHING, OR WE WOULDN'T BE IN THIS SITUATION!
WHY DO YOU ALWAYS HAVE TO DRAW ATTENTION TO YOURSELF? SCREAMING AND BREAKING SHIT - YOU'RE LIKE A FUCKING BABY!
THE CAT WARNED US THAT THERE WAS SOMETHING BAD OUT THERE!
WE WENT TO THE HOUSE TO LAY LOW, NOT
...HE WON'T BE...
YEAH, WE'LL PROBABLY BE THERE BY SUN-DOWN TOMORROW.

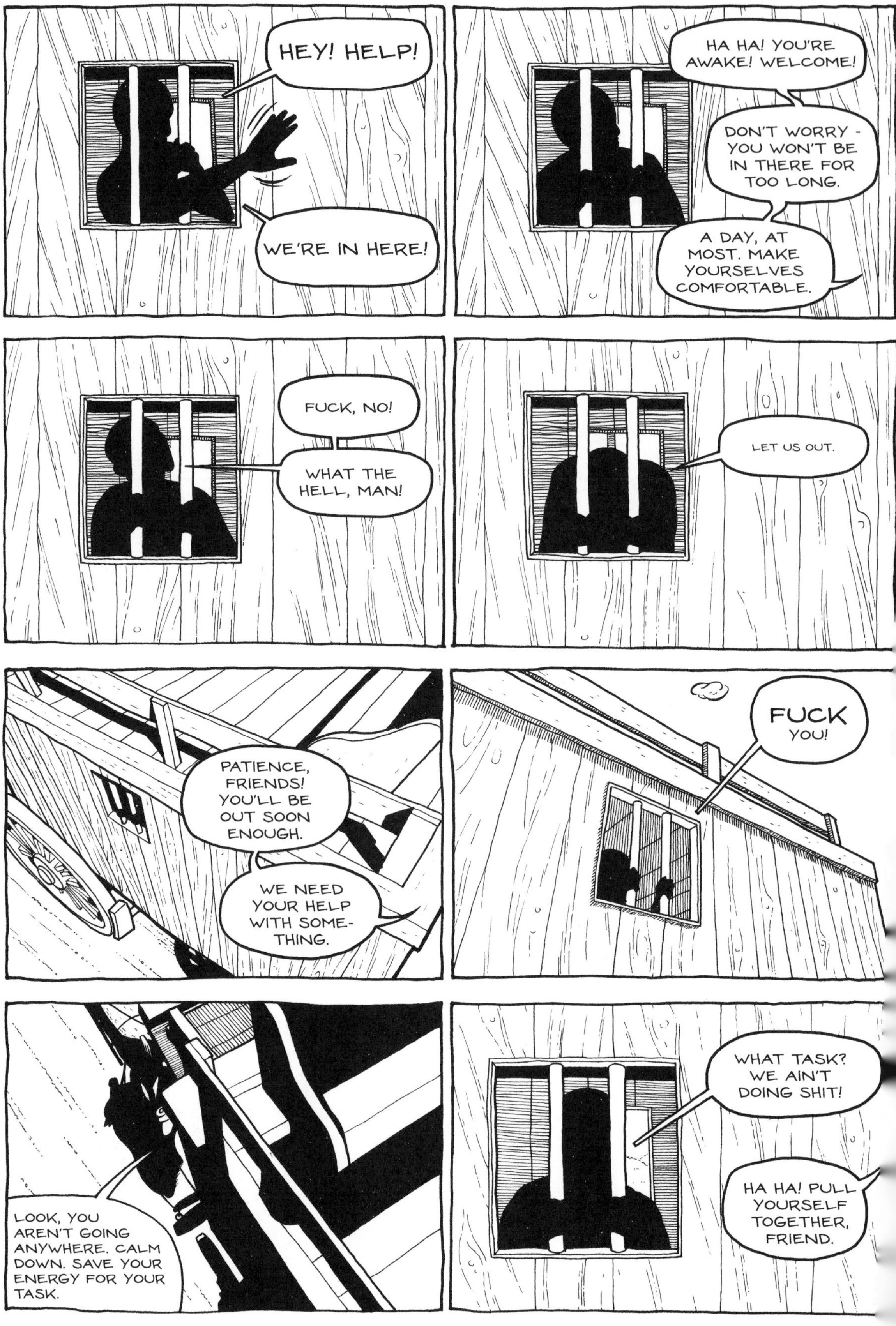
HEY! HELP!
WE'RE IN HERE!
HA HA! YOU'RE AWAKE! WELCOME!
DON'T WORRY - YOU WON'T BE IN THERE FOR TOO LONG.
A DAY, AT MOST. MAKE YOURSELVES COMFORTABLE.
FUCK, NO!
WHAT THE HELL, MAN!
LET US OUT.
PATIENCE, FRIENDS! YOU'LL BE OUT SOON ENOUGH.
WE NEED YOUR HELP WITH SOME-THING.
FUCK YOU!
LOOK, YOU AREN'T GOING ANYWHERE. CALM DOWN. SAVE YOUR ENERGY FOR YOUR TASK.
WHAT TASK? WE AIN'T DOING SHIT!
HA HA! PULL YOURSELF TOGETHER, FRIEND.

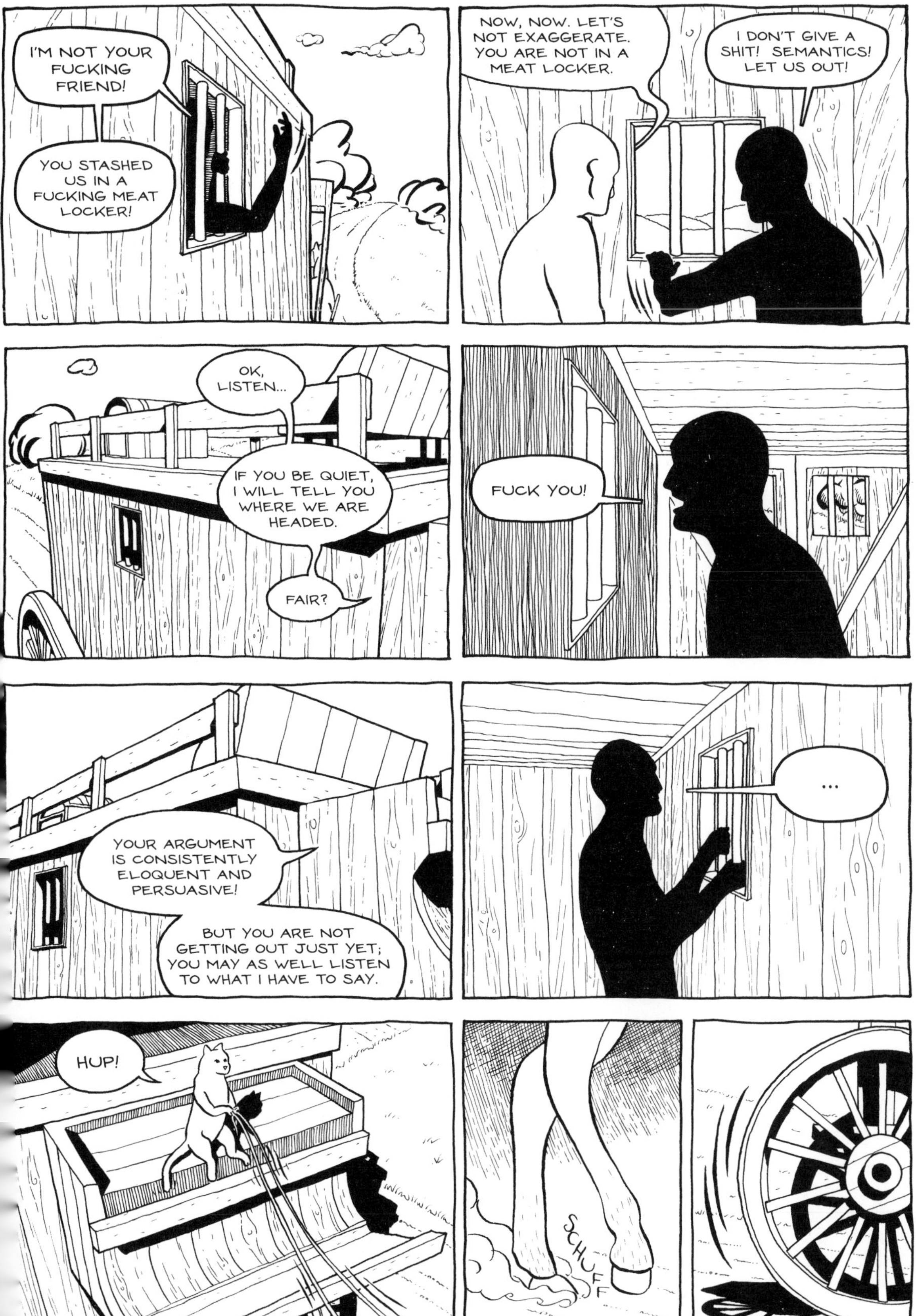
I'M NOT YOUR FUCKING FRIEND!
YOU STASHED US IN A FUCKING MEAT LOCKER!
NOW, NOW. LET'S NOT EXAGGERATE. YOU ARE NOT IN A MEAT LOCKER.
I DON'T GIVE A SHIT! SEMANTICS! LET US OUT!
OK, LISTEN...
IF YOU BE QUIET, I WILL TELL YOU WHERE WE ARE HEADED.
FAIR?
FUCK YOU!
YOUR ARGUMENT IS CONSISTENTLY ELOQUENT AND PERSUASIVE!
BUT YOU ARE NOT GETTING OUT JUST YET; YOU MAY AS WELL LISTEN TO WHAT I HAVE TO SAY.
...
HUP!
SCHUFF

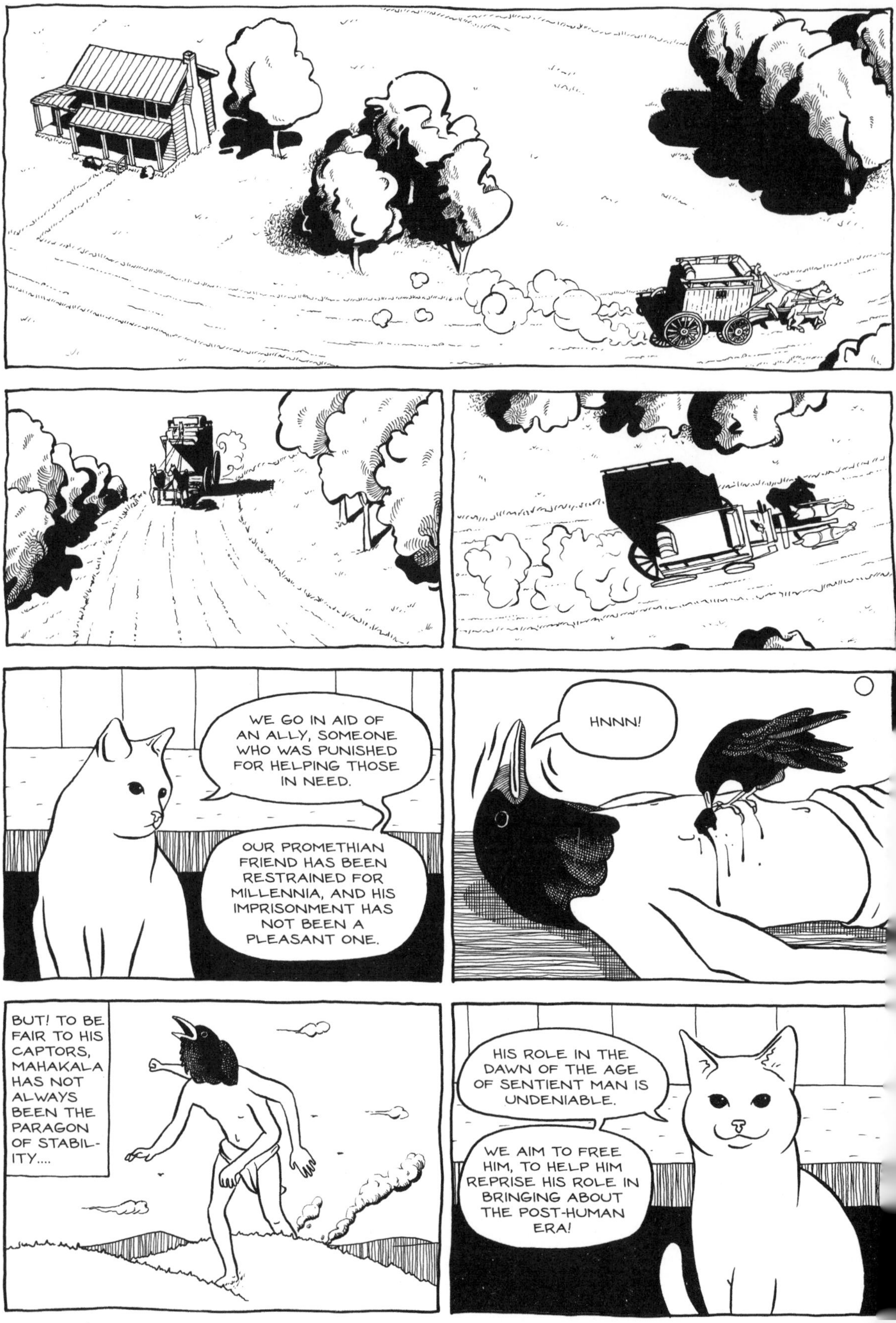
WE GO IN AID OF AN ALLY, SOMEONE WHO WAS PUNISHED FOR HELPING THOSE IN NEED.
OUR PROMETHIAN FRIEND HAS BEEN RESTRAINED FOR MILLENNIA, AND HIS IMPRISONMENT HAS NOT BEEN A PLEASANT ONE.
HNNN!
BUT! TO BE FAIR TO HIS CAPTORS, MAHAKALA HAS NOT ALWAYS BEEN THE PARAGON OF STABIL-ITY....
HIS ROLE IN THE DAWN OF THE AGE OF SENTIENT MAN IS UNDENIABLE.
WE AIM TO FREE HIM, TO HELP HIM REPRISE HIS ROLE IN BRINGING ABOUT THE POST-HUMAN ERA!

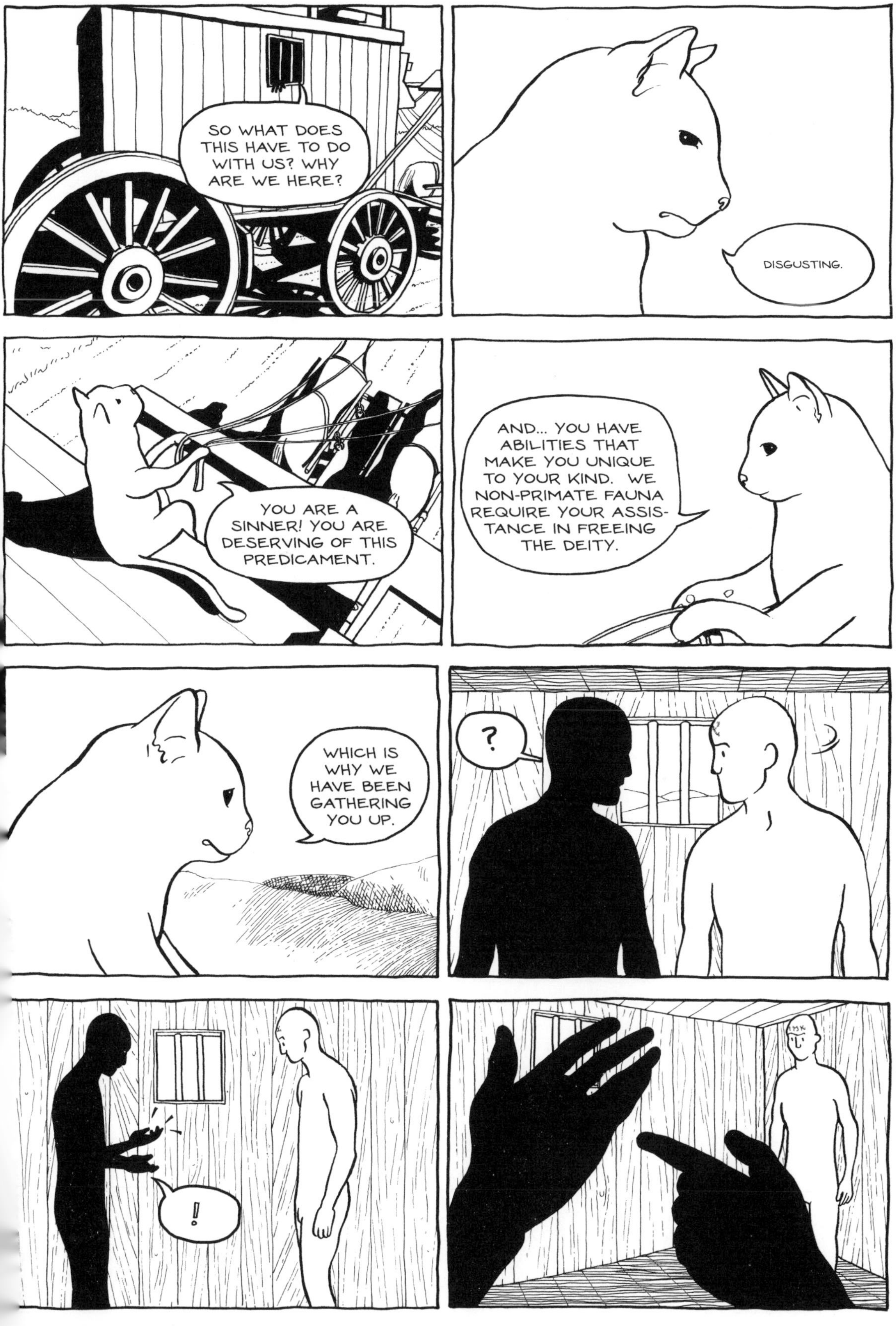
SO WHAT DOES THIS HAVE TO DO WITH US? WHY ARE WE HERE?
DISGUSTING.
YOU ARE A SINNER! YOU ARE DESERVING OF THIS PREDICAMENT.
AND... YOU HAVE ABILITIES THAT MAKE YOU UNIQUE TO YOUR KIND. WE NON-PRIMATE FAUNA REQUIRE YOUR ASSISTANCE IN FREEING THE DEITY.
WHICH IS WHY WE HAVE BEEN GATHERING YOU UP.
?
!

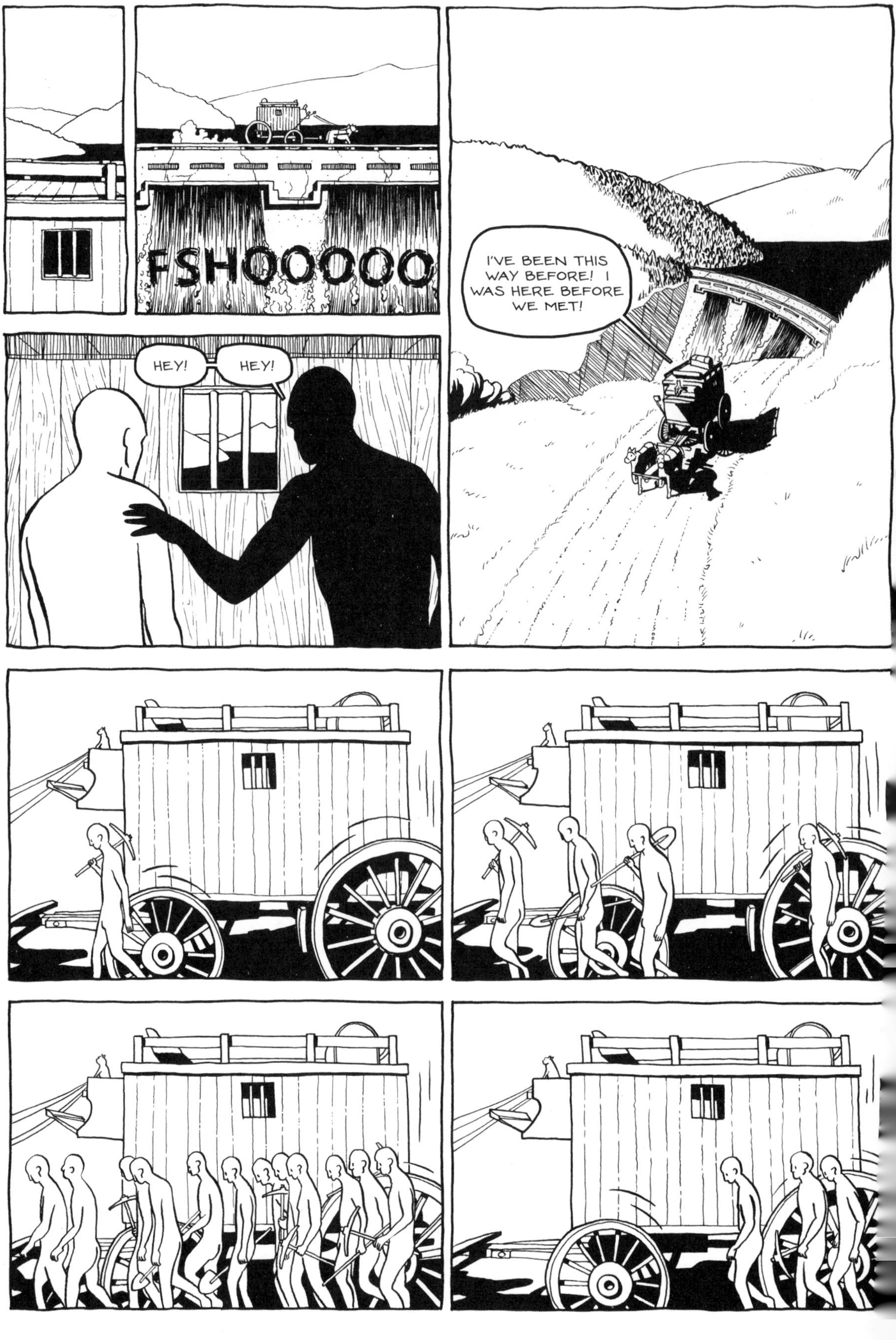
FSHOOOOO
HEY!
HEY!
I'VE BEEN THIS WAY BEFORE! I WAS HERE BEFORE WE MET!

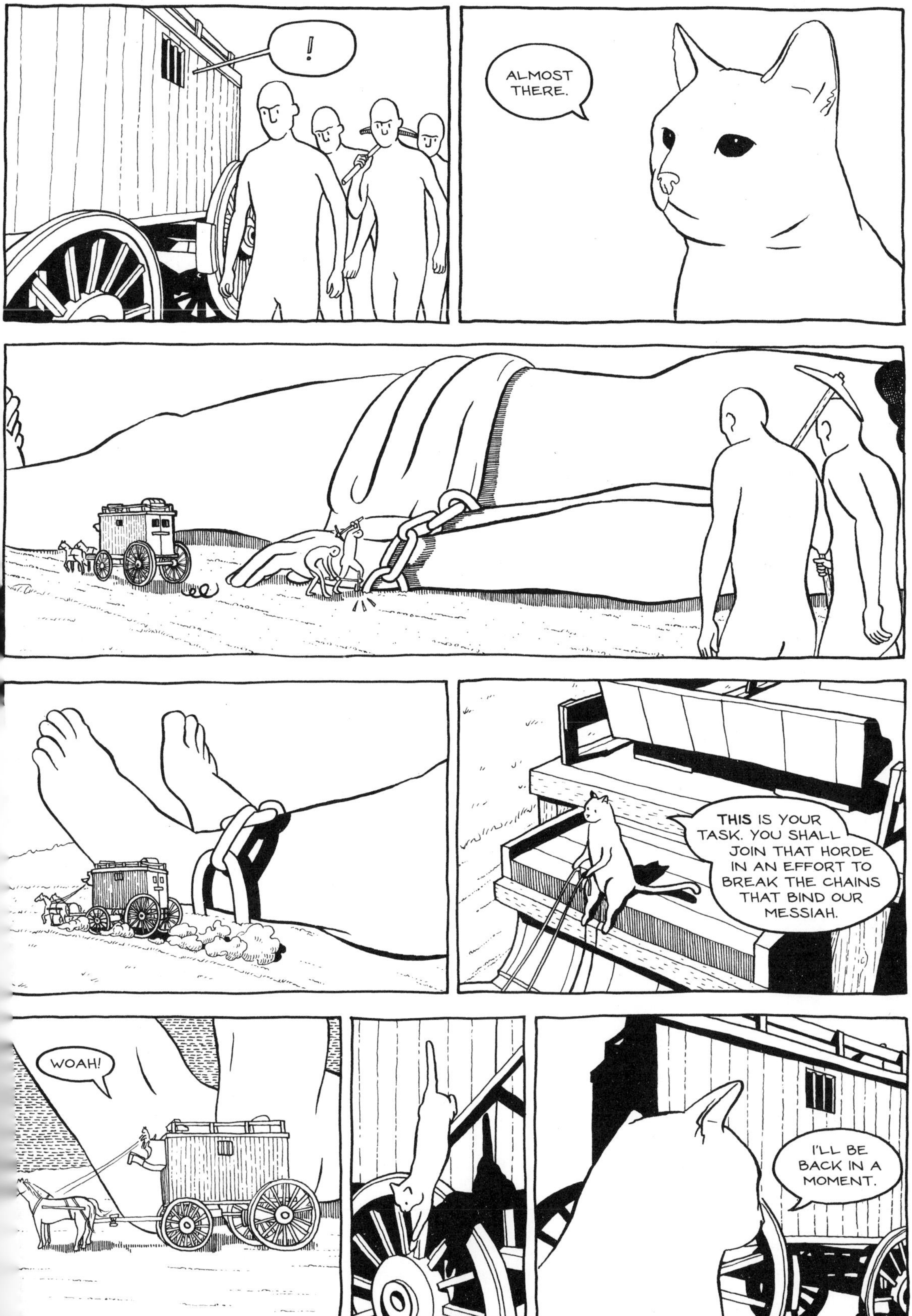
!
ALMOST THERE.
THIS IS YOUR TASK. YOU SHALL JOIN THAT HORDE IN AN EFFORT TO BREAK THE CHAINS THAT BIND OUR MESSIAH.
WOAH!
I'LL BE BACK IN A MOMENT.

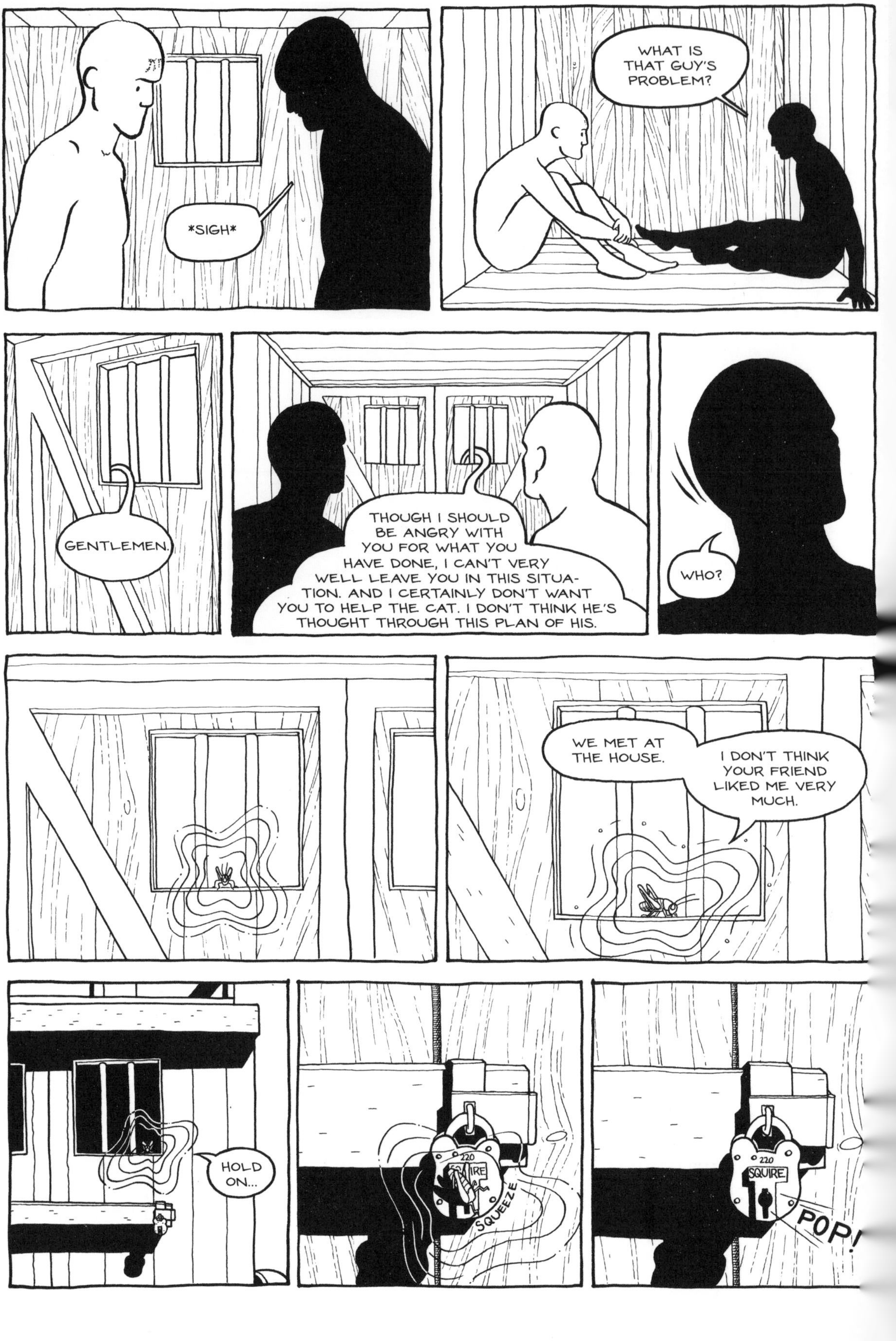
SIGH
WHAT IS THAT GUY'S PROBLEM?
GENTLEMEN.
THOUGH I SHOULD BE ANGRY WITH YOU FOR WHAT YOU HAVE DONE, I CAN'T VERY WELL LEAVE YOU IN THIS SITUATION. AND I CERTAINLY DON'T WANT YOU TO HELP THE CAT. I DON'T THINK HE'S THOUGHT THROUGH THIS PLAN OF HIS.
WHO?
WE MET AT THE HOUSE.
I DON'T THINK YOUR FRIEND LIKED ME VERY MUCH.
HOLD ON...
220
SQUEEZE
220
SQUIRE
POP!

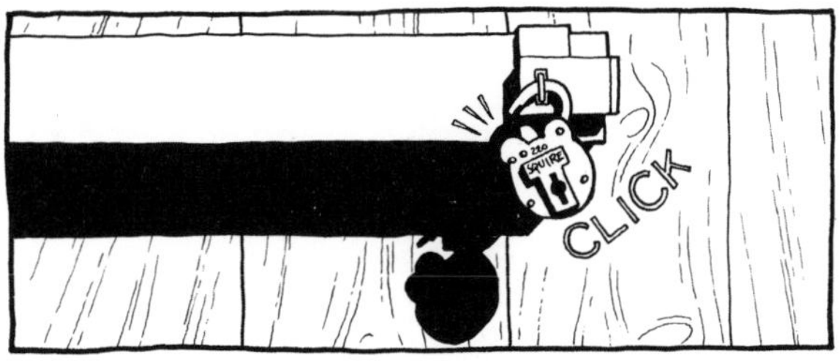
220
SQUIRE
CLICK

six

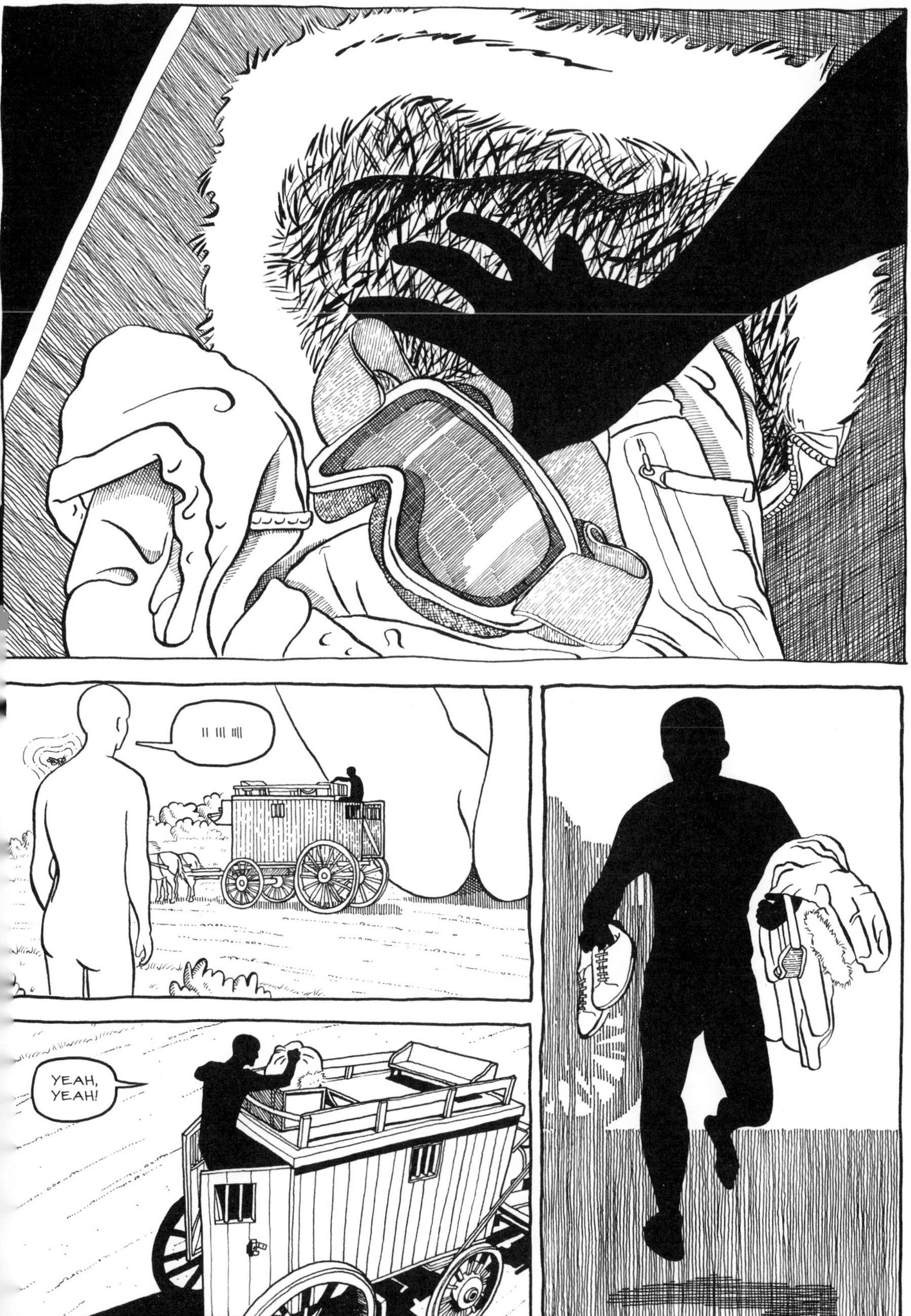
YEAH, YEAH!

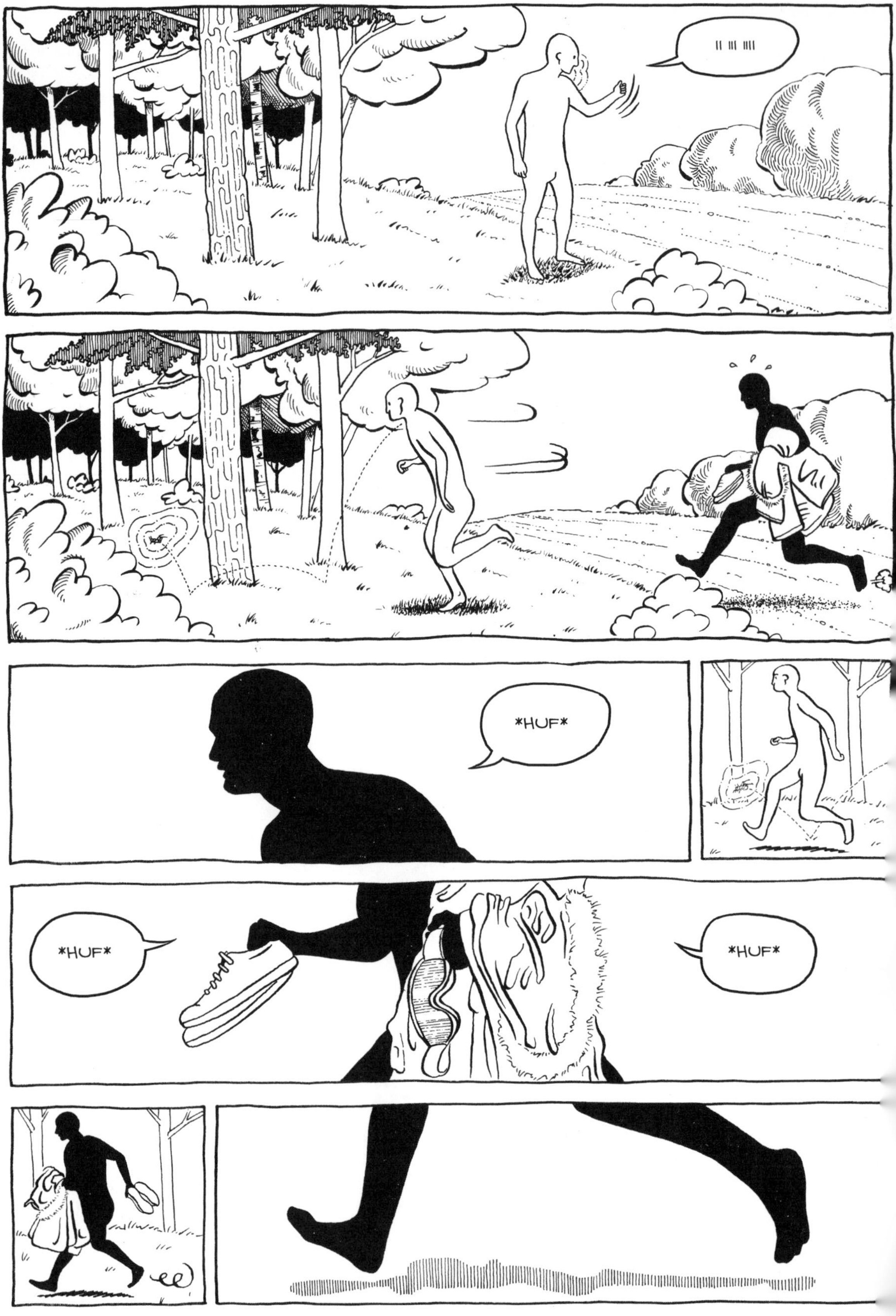

|| ||| ||||
HUF
HUF
HUF

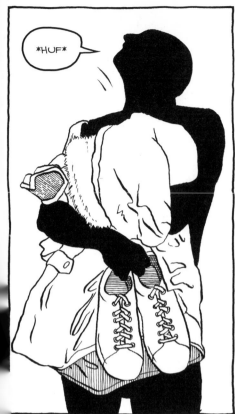

HUF

HUF

LISTEN MAN, GO ON IF YOU HAVE TO, BUT I'M FEELING A BIT VULNERABLE HERE.

I'M GETTING DRESSED.

YES, GOOD. PROTECT YOURSELF.

HUF

THOUGH I DON'T THINK THERE'S ANYTHING TO WORRY ABOUT - WE'RE NOT BEING FOLLOWED.

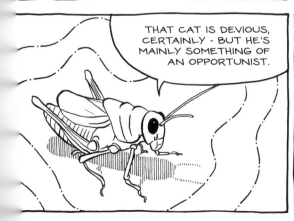

THAT CAT IS DEVIOUS, CERTAINLY - BUT HE'S MAINLY SOMETHING OF AN OPPORTUNIST.

WHAT ARE YOU TALKING ABOUT? HE TOTALLY SET ME UP!

HE SENT US TO THAT HOUSE - HE KNEW EXACTLY WHERE WE WERE.

I'M NOT SO SURE ABOUT THAT. BUT GET DRESSED AND LET'S BE ON OUR WAY IF YOU FEEL LIKE WE'RE BEING PURSUED.

DON'T PANDER TO ME.

YOU WEREN'T LOCKED IN A BOX BY A FUCKING CAT!

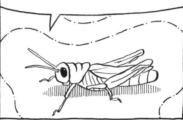

AND **YOU** WEREN'T CRUSHED UNDER THE BUTT OF A GUN BY SOME IMMATURE ASSHOLE WHO DOESN'T THINK ABOUT THE CONSEQUENCES OF HIS ACTIONS!

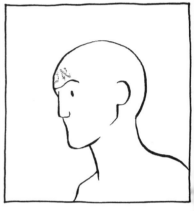

WOAH, DON'T LOOK AT ME!

IT WASN'T ME...

I DIDN'T...

I DIDN'T SQUISH YOU...

I'M...

IT WAS...

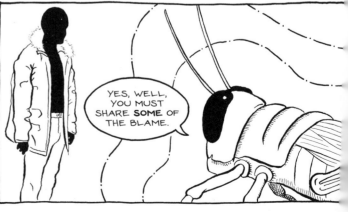

YES, WELL, YOU MUST SHARE **SOME** OF THE BLAME.

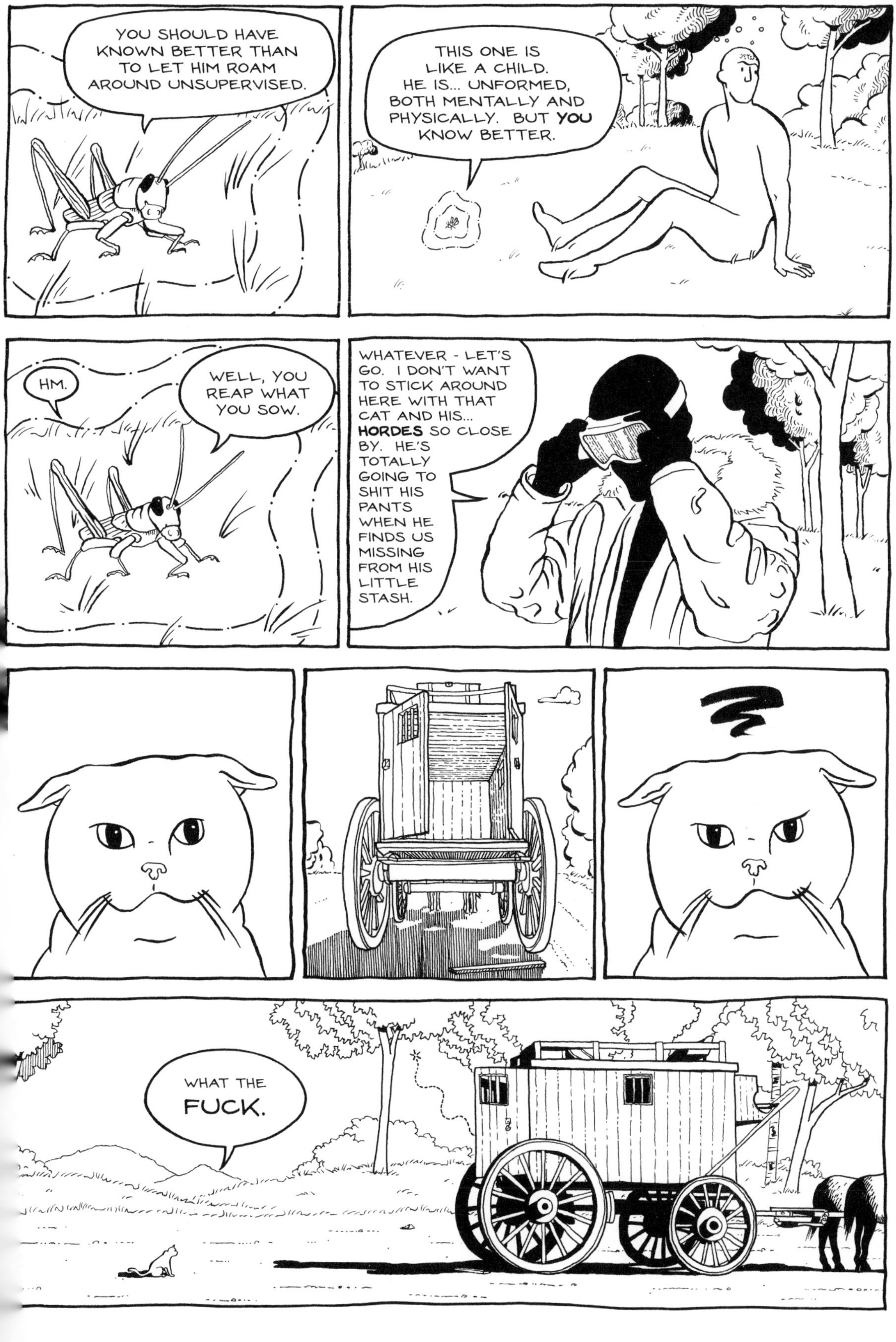

YOU SHOULD HAVE KNOWN BETTER THAN TO LET HIM ROAM AROUND UNSUPERVISED.
THIS ONE IS LIKE A CHILD. HE IS... UNFORMED, BOTH MENTALLY AND PHYSICALLY. BUT **YOU** KNOW BETTER.
HM.
WELL, YOU REAP WHAT YOU SOW.
WHATEVER - LET'S GO. I DON'T WANT TO STICK AROUND HERE WITH THAT CAT AND HIS... **HORDES** SO CLOSE BY. HE'S TOTALLY GOING TO SHIT HIS PANTS WHEN HE FINDS US MISSING FROM HIS LITTLE STASH.
WHAT THE **FUCK.**

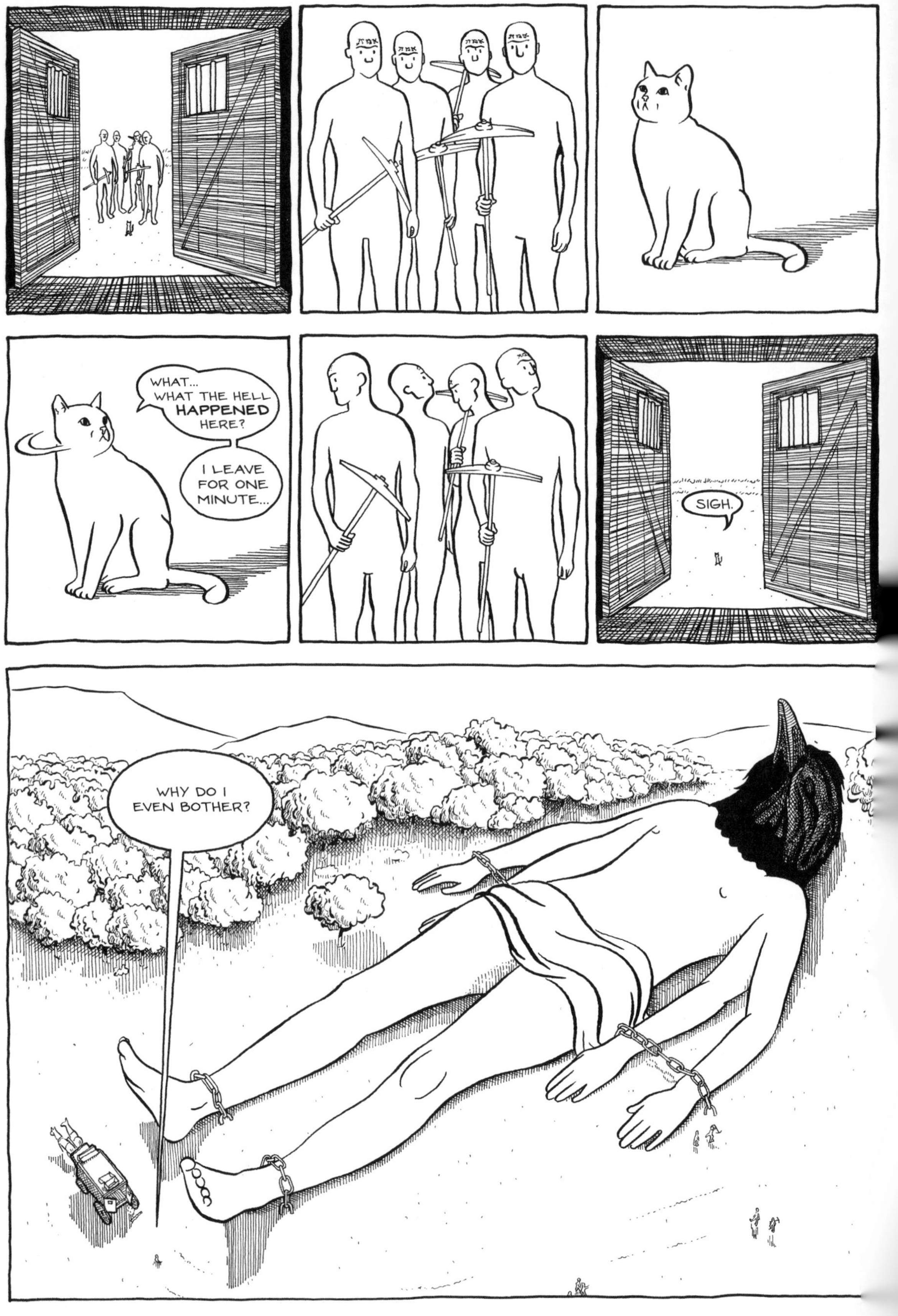
WHAT... WHAT THE HELL **HAPPENED** HERE?
I LEAVE FOR ONE MINUTE...
SIGH.
WHY DO I EVEN BOTHER?

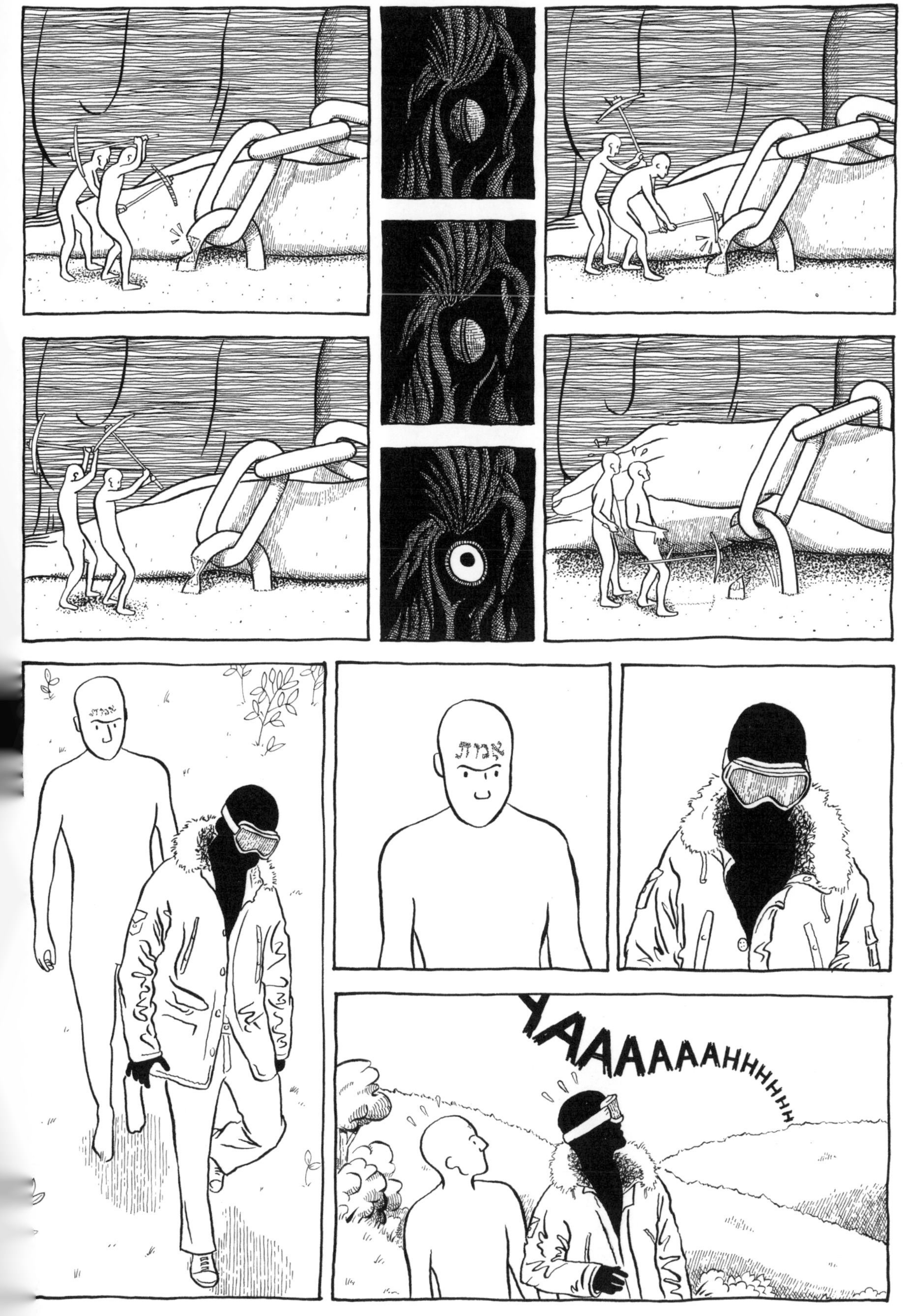
YAAAAAAHHHHHHH

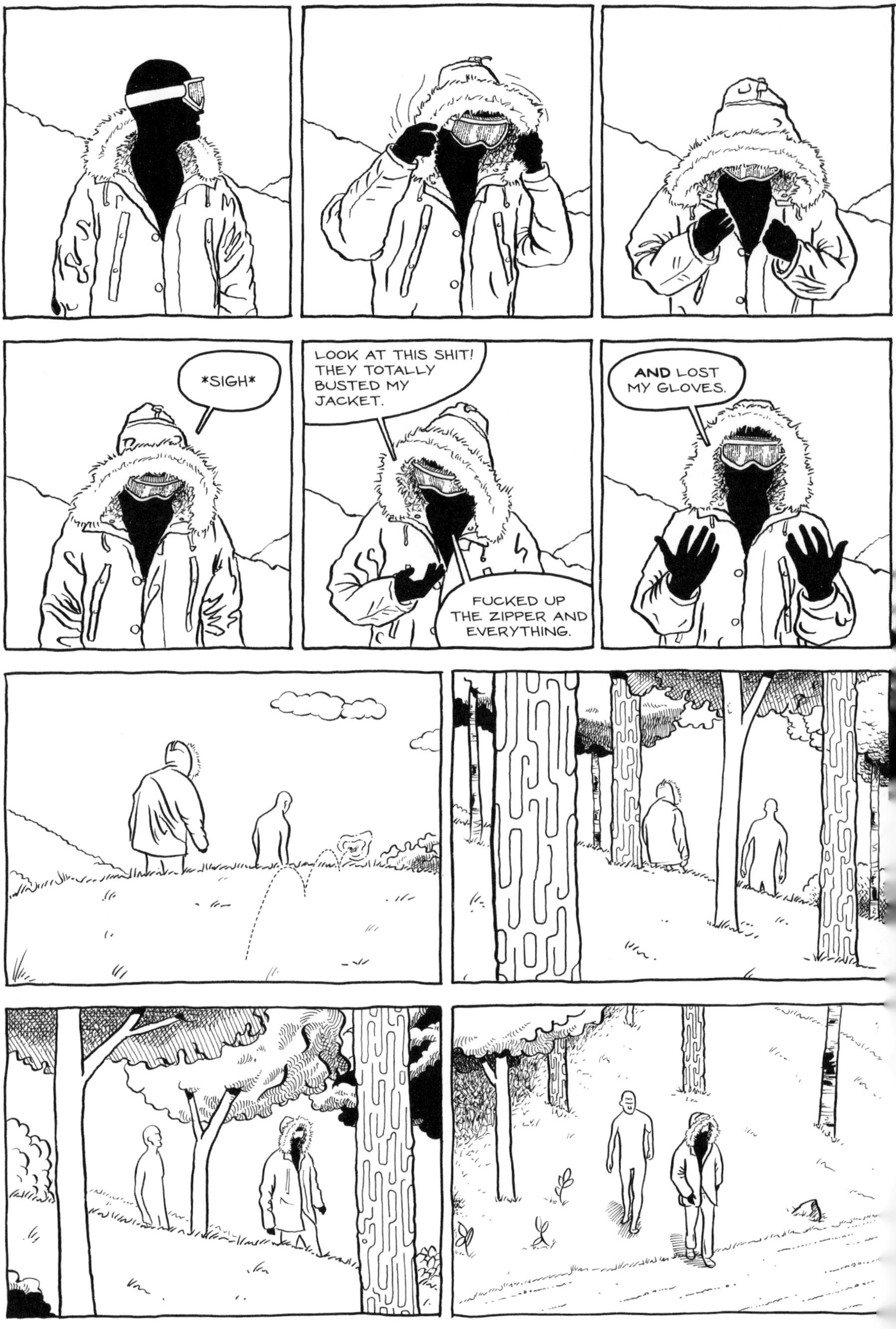
SIGH
LOOK AT THIS SHIT! THEY TOTALLY BUSTED MY JACKET.
FUCKED UP THE ZIPPER AND EVERYTHING.
AND LOST MY GLOVES.

I THINK WE WANT TO GO THIS WAY.

WAIT!

UM, LISTEN - BEFORE WE GO ON, I JUST WANTED TO APOLOGISE FOR PROSELYTISING.

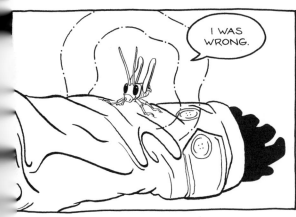

I WAS WRONG.

WELL, UM, YOU KNOW, YOU'RE RIGHT - YOU SHOULD GO THAT WAY IF YOU WANT TO HEAD BACK IN THE DIRECTION YOU CAME FROM.

THAT IS WHERE YOU'RE GOING, ISN'T IT?

APOLOGY ACCEPTED.

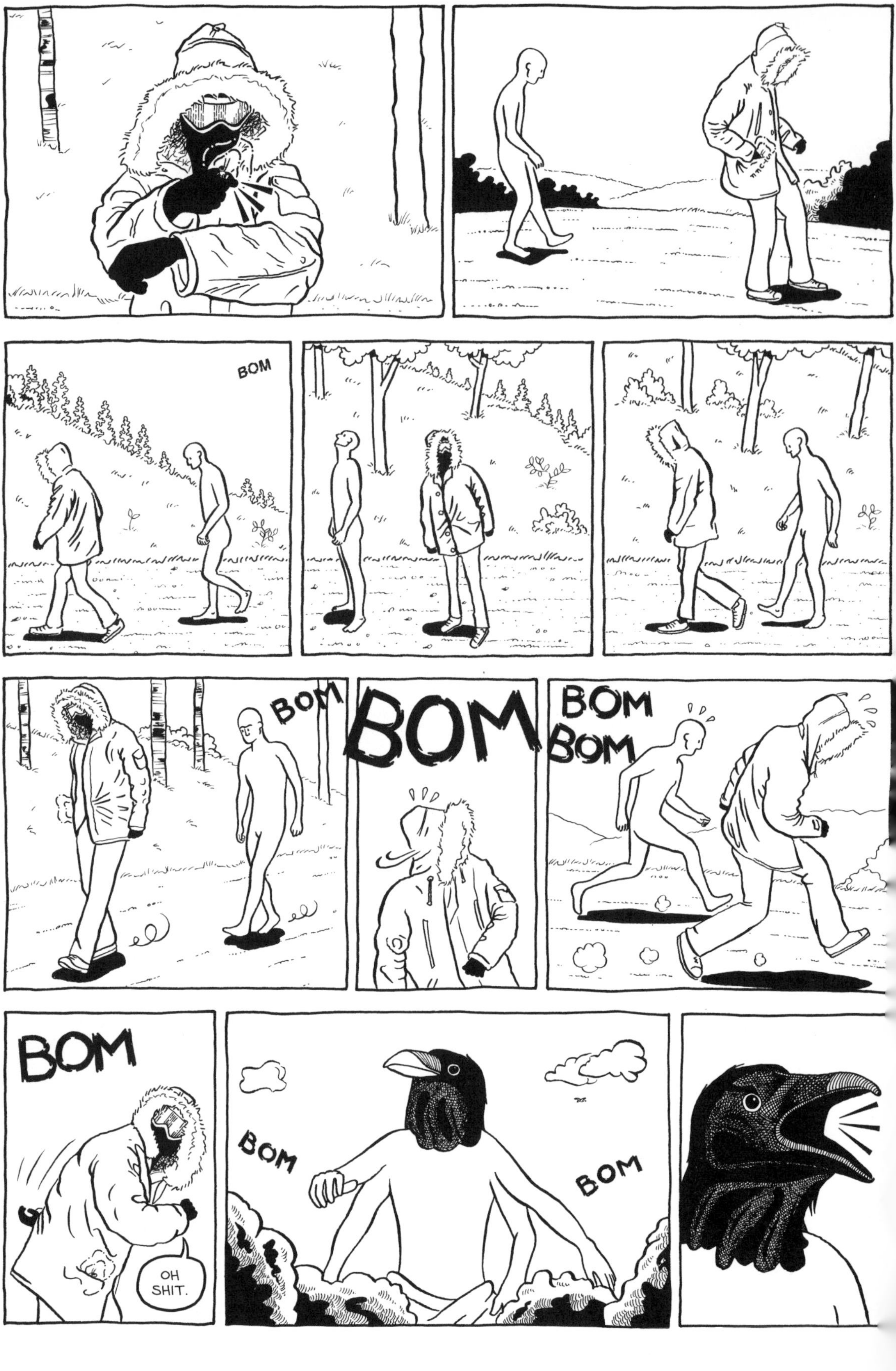
BOM
BOM
BOM
BOM
BOM
BOM
OH SHIT.
BOM
BOM

אמת

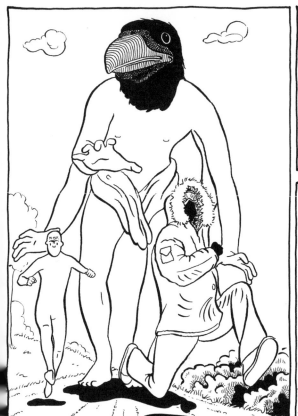

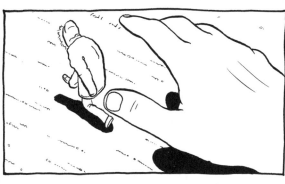

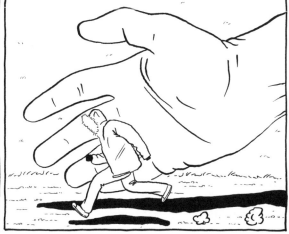

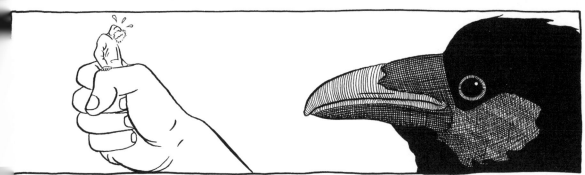

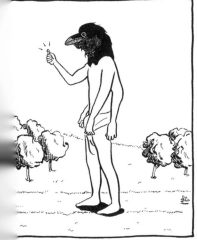

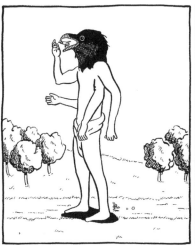

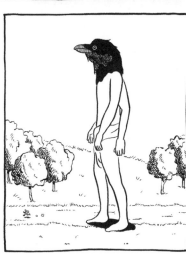

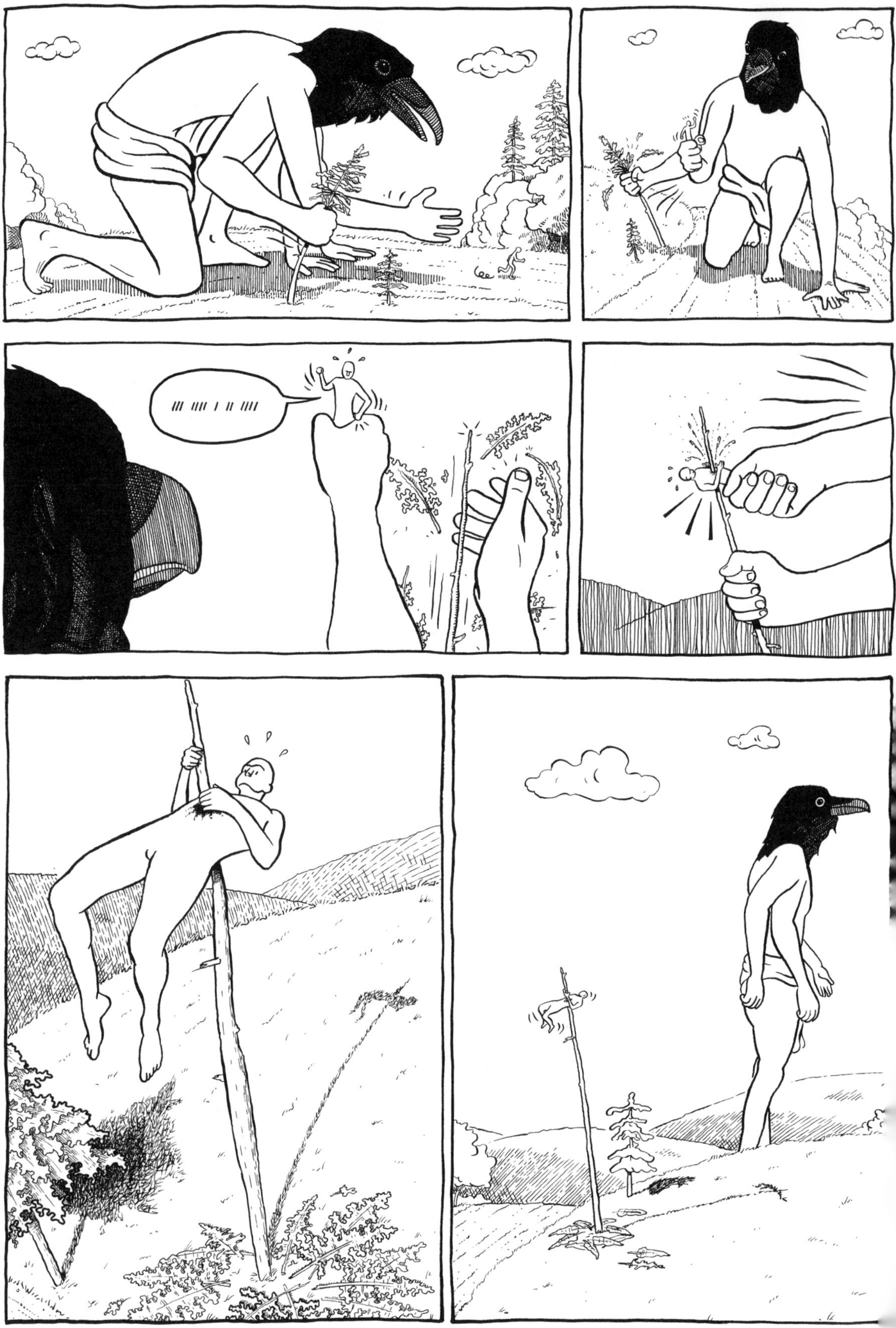

seven

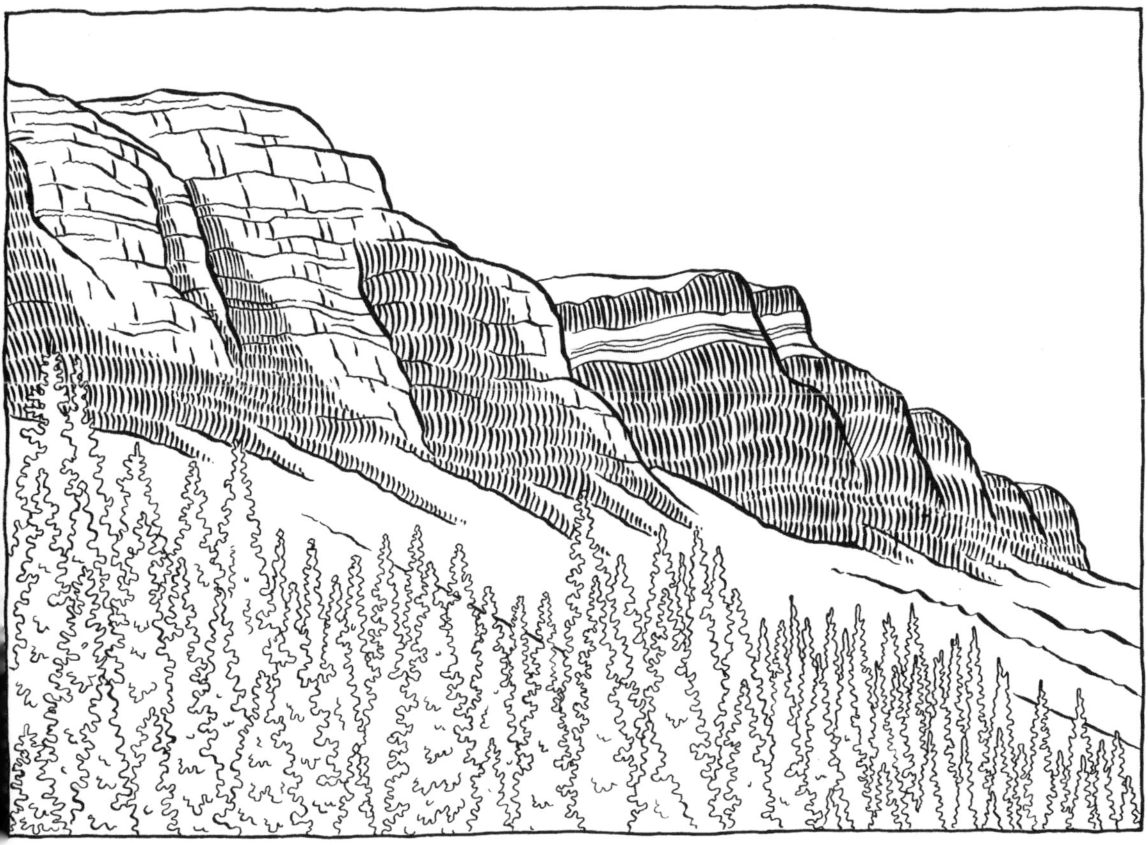

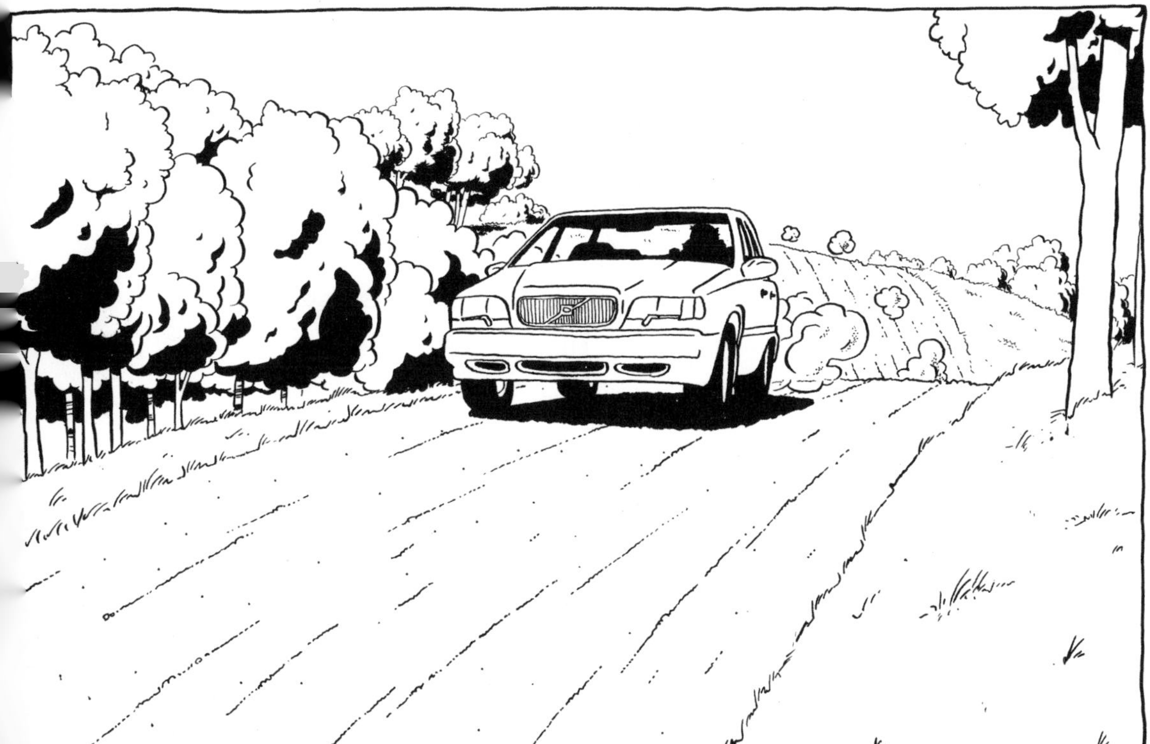

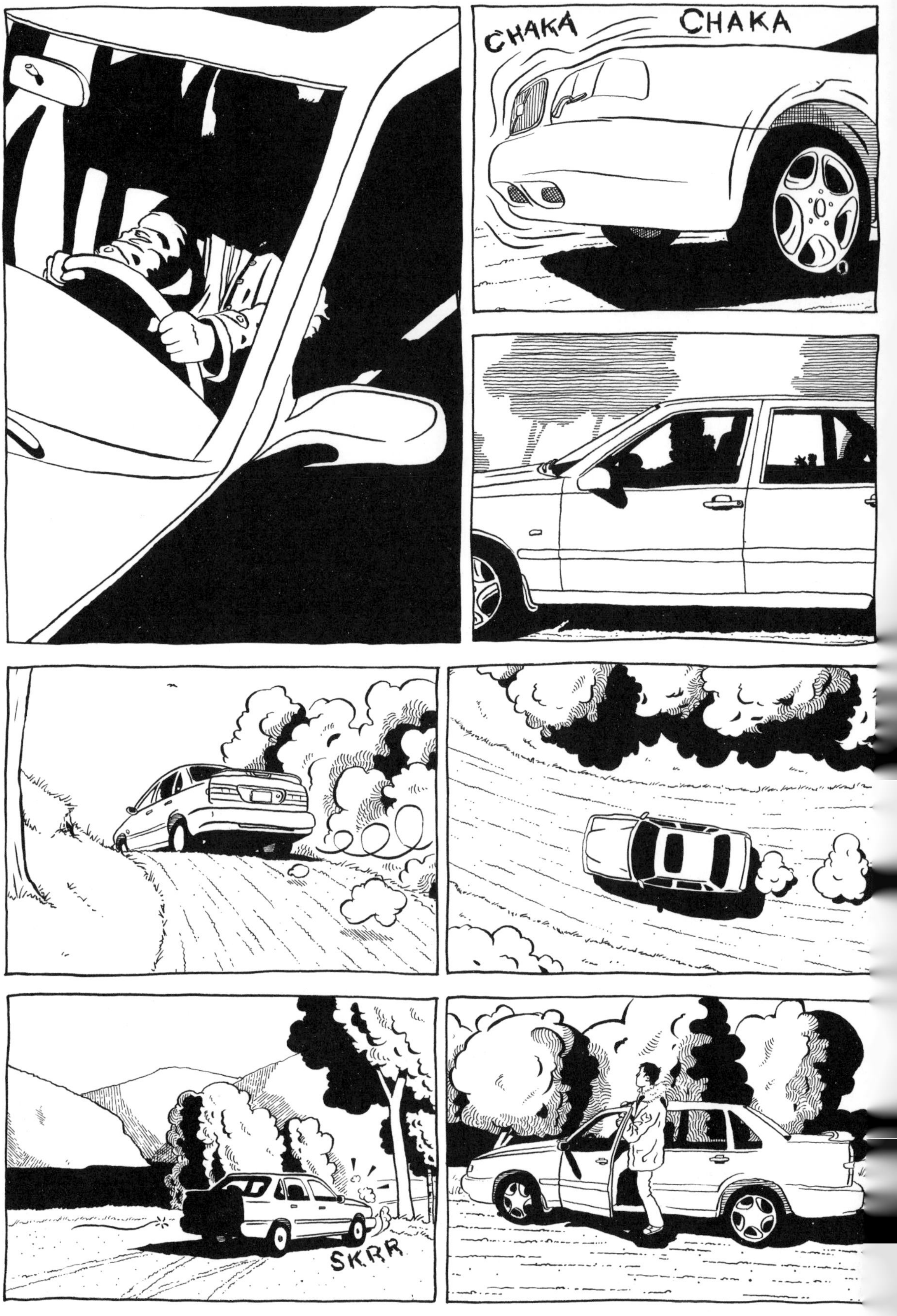
CHAKA
CHAKA
SKRR

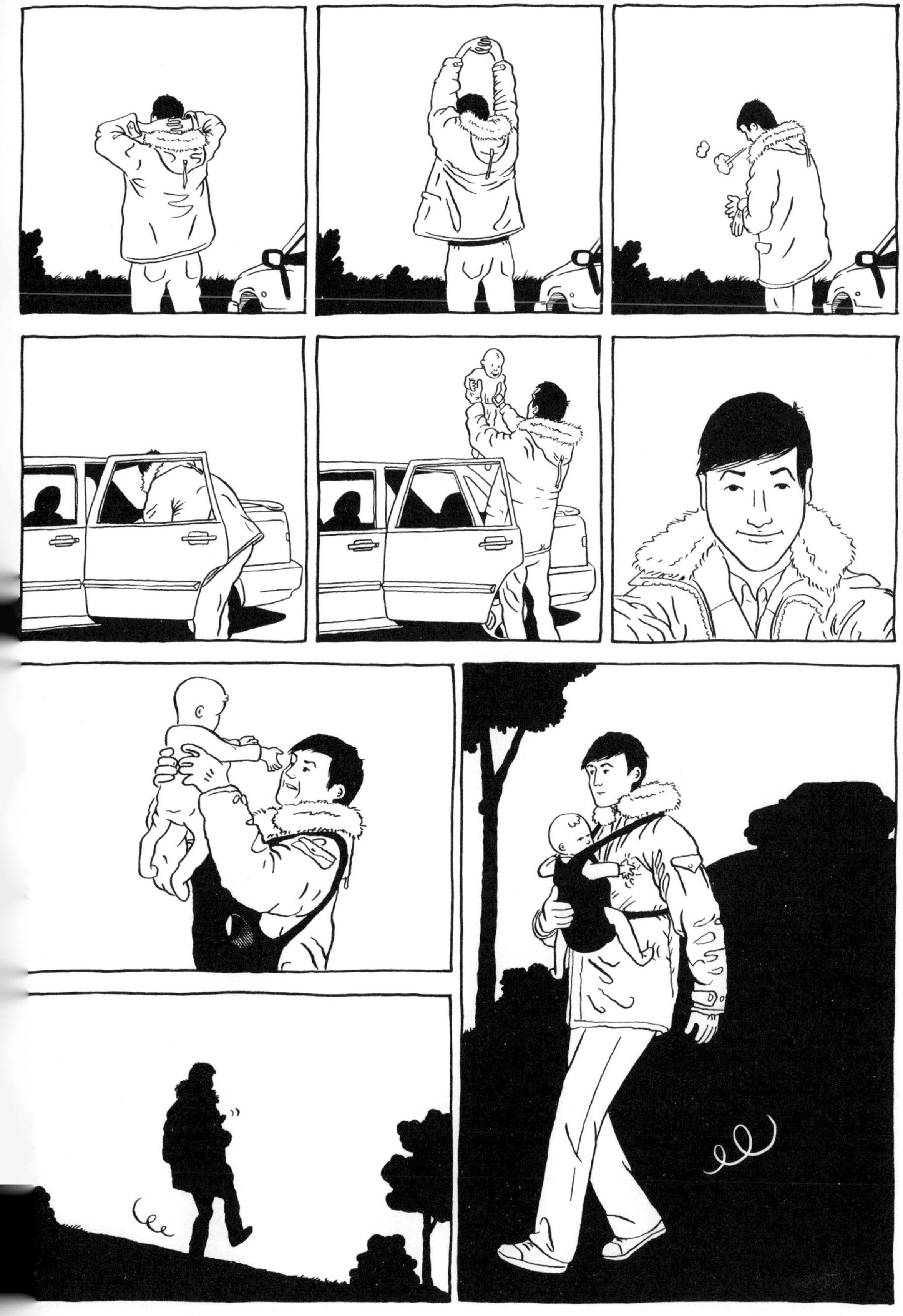

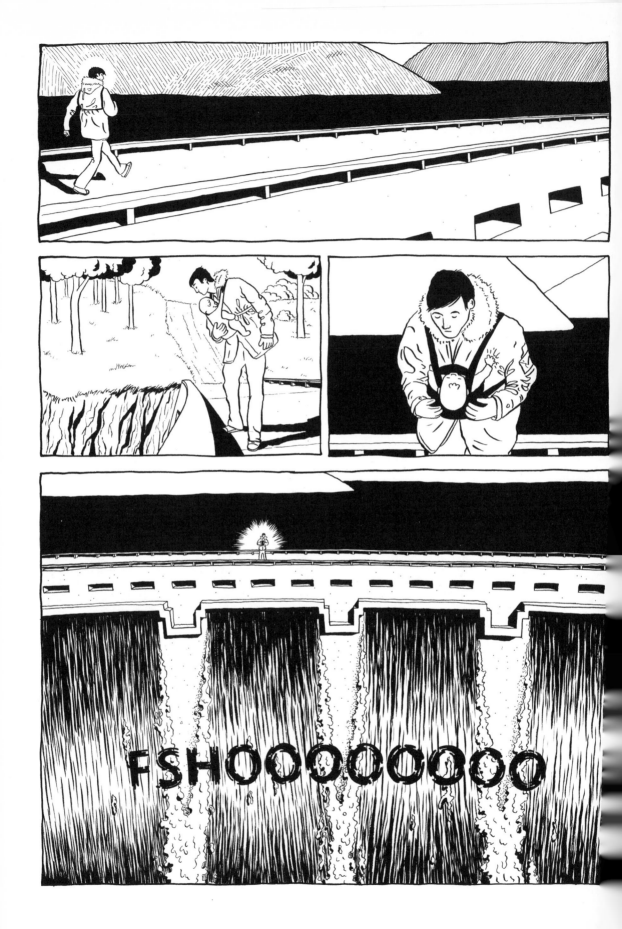

FSHOOOOOOOOO

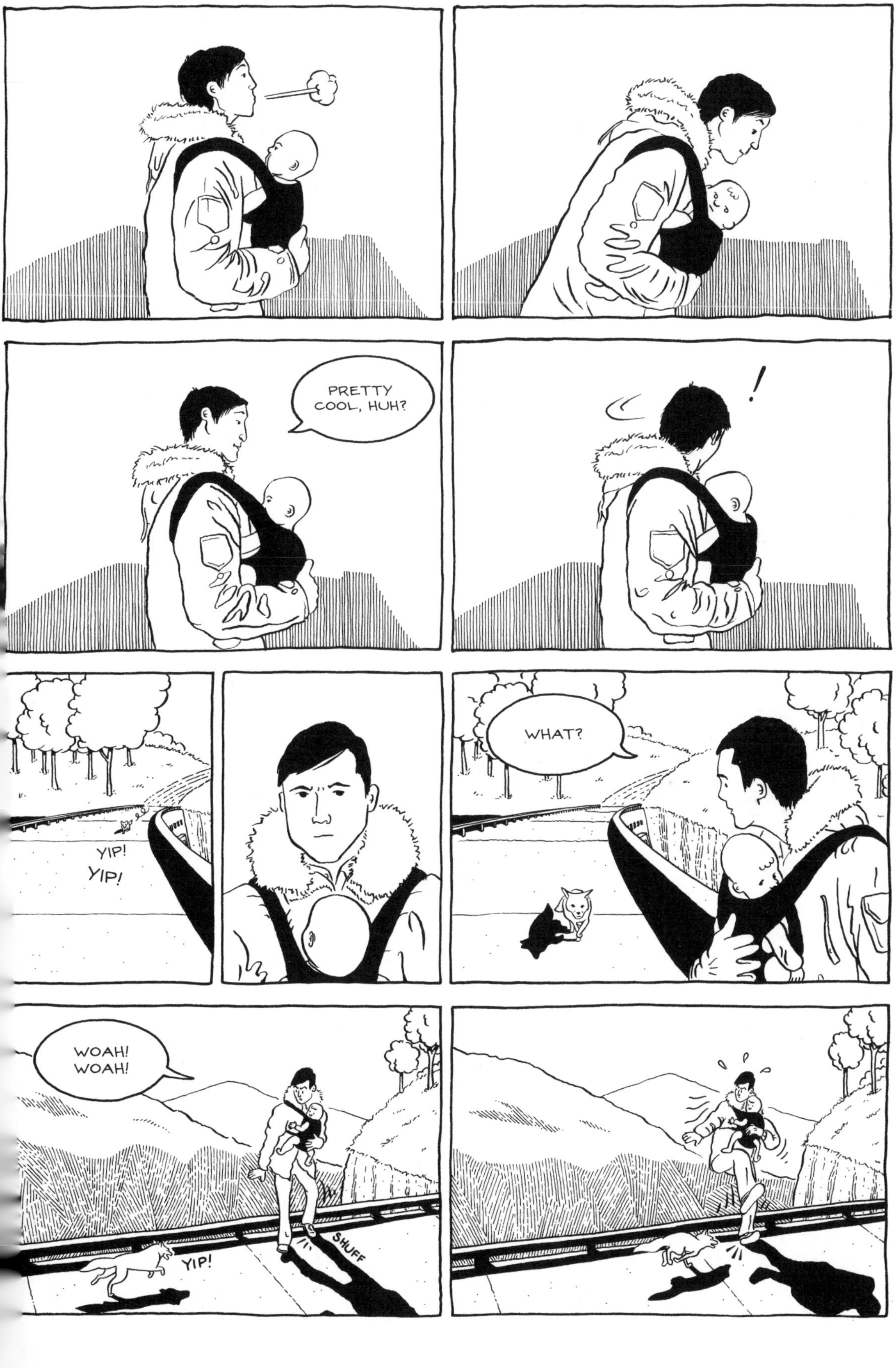
PRETTY COOL, HUH?
!
YIP!
YIP!
WHAT?
WOAH! WOAH!
YIP!
SHUFF

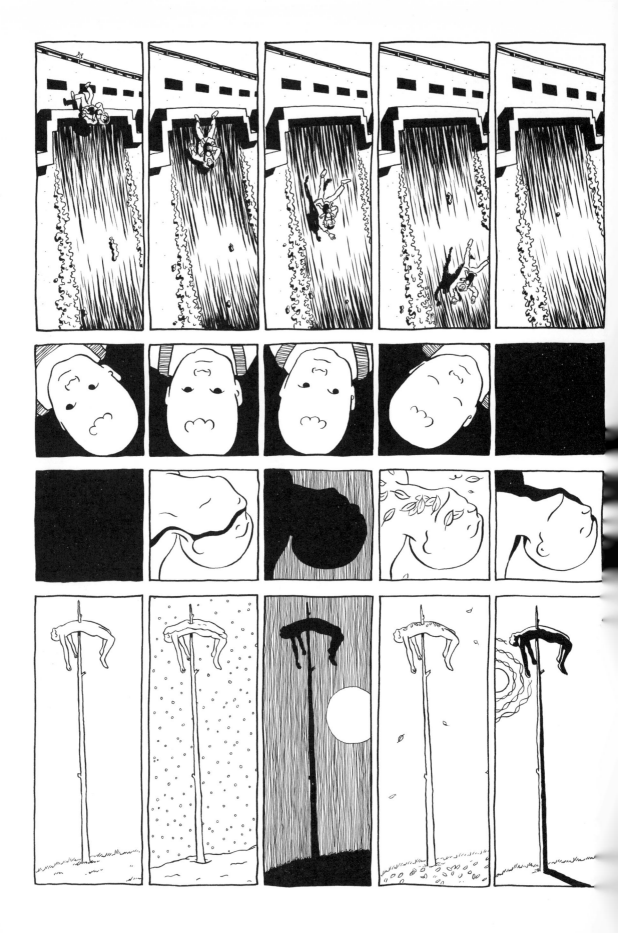

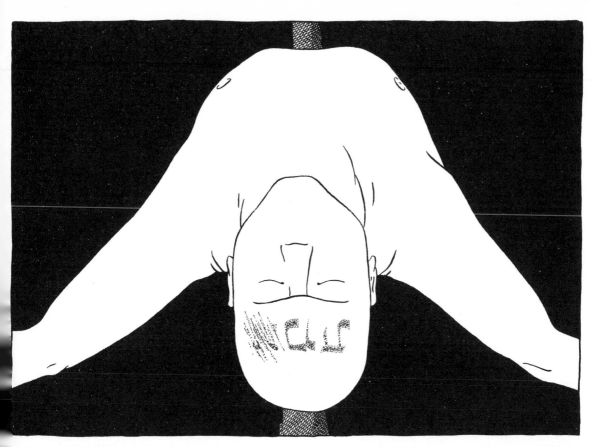

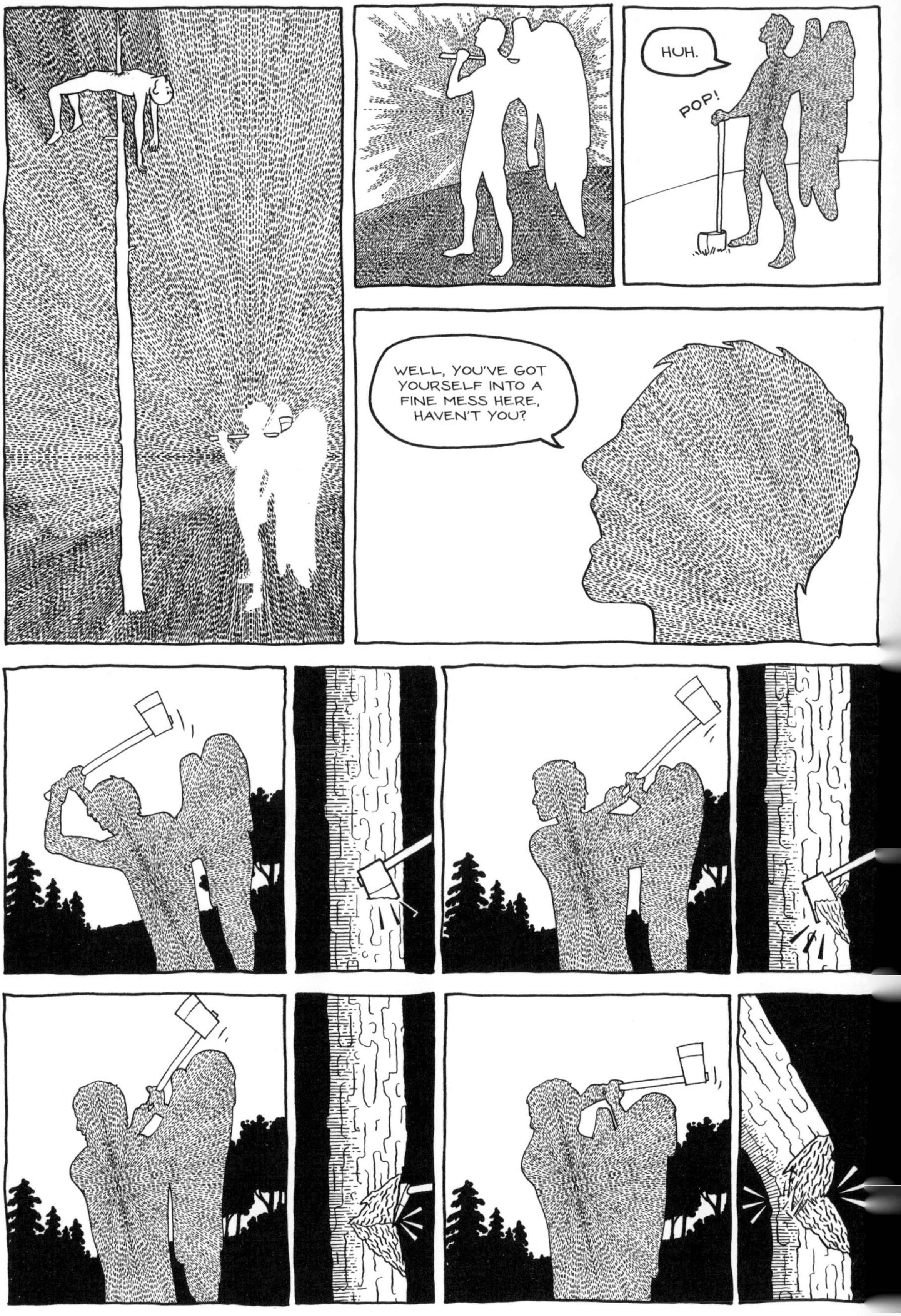
HUH.
POP!
WELL, YOU'VE GOT YOURSELF INTO A FINE MESS HERE, HAVEN'T YOU?

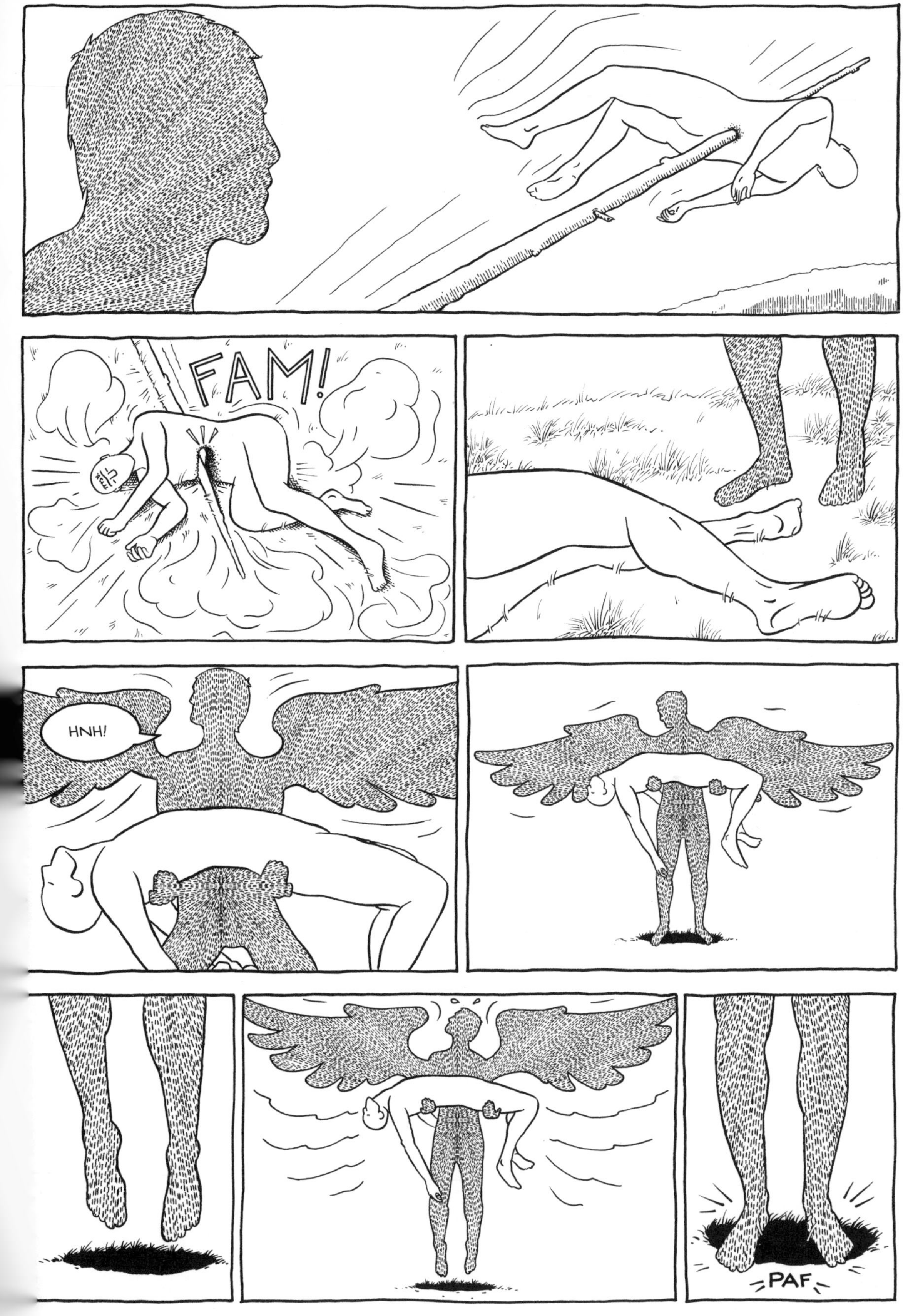
FAM!
HNH!
PAF

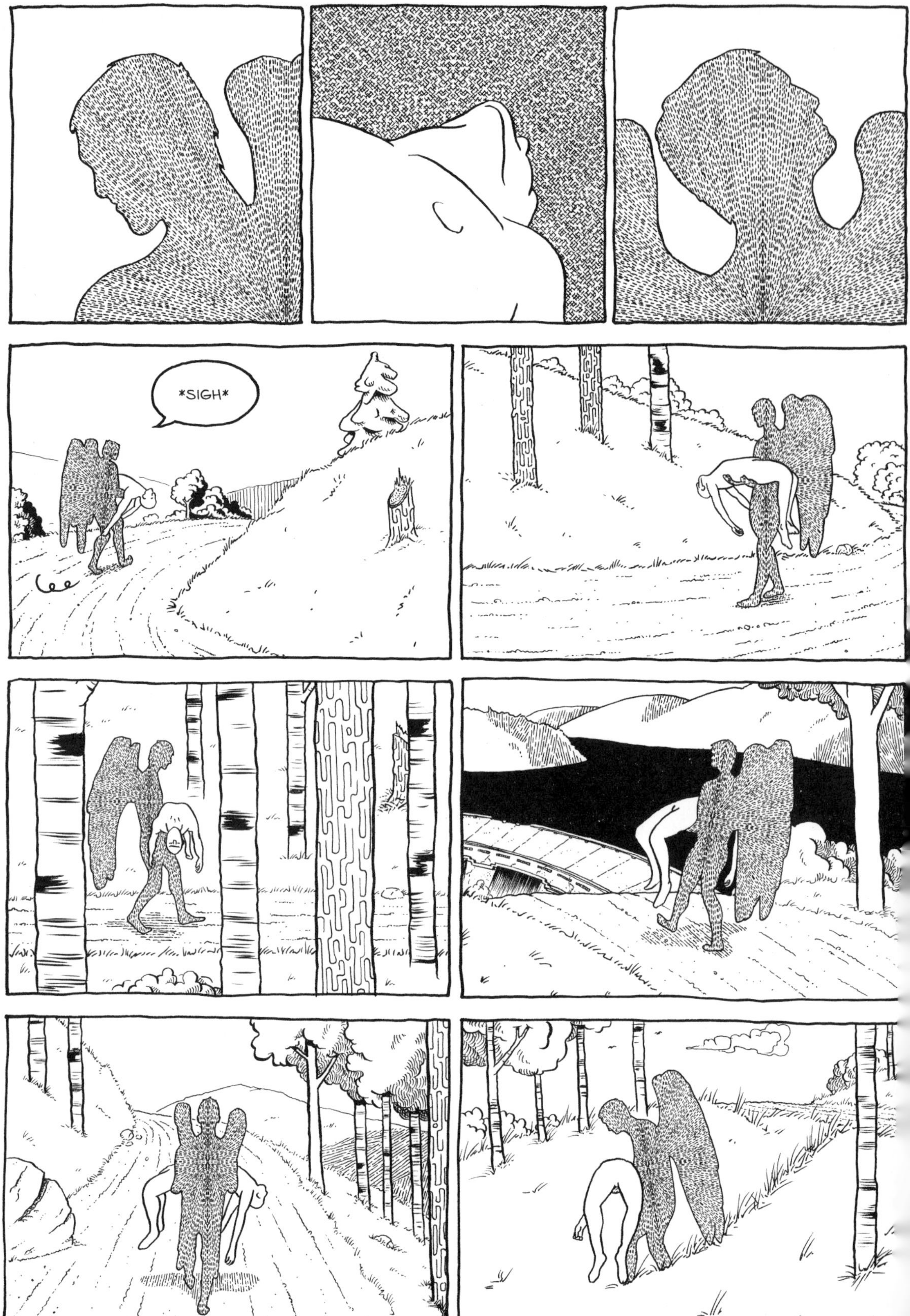
SIGH

SPLISH
SPLISH
HM.
PAT
PAT

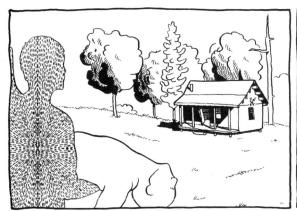

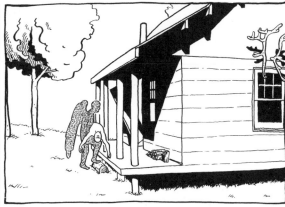

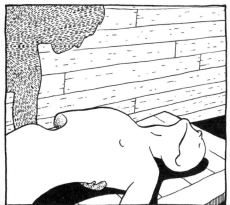

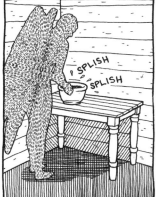

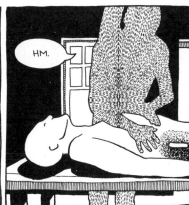

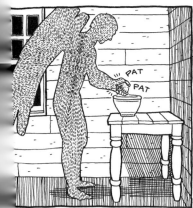

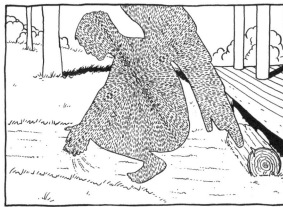

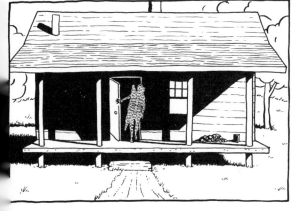

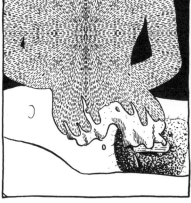

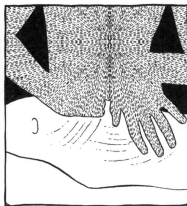

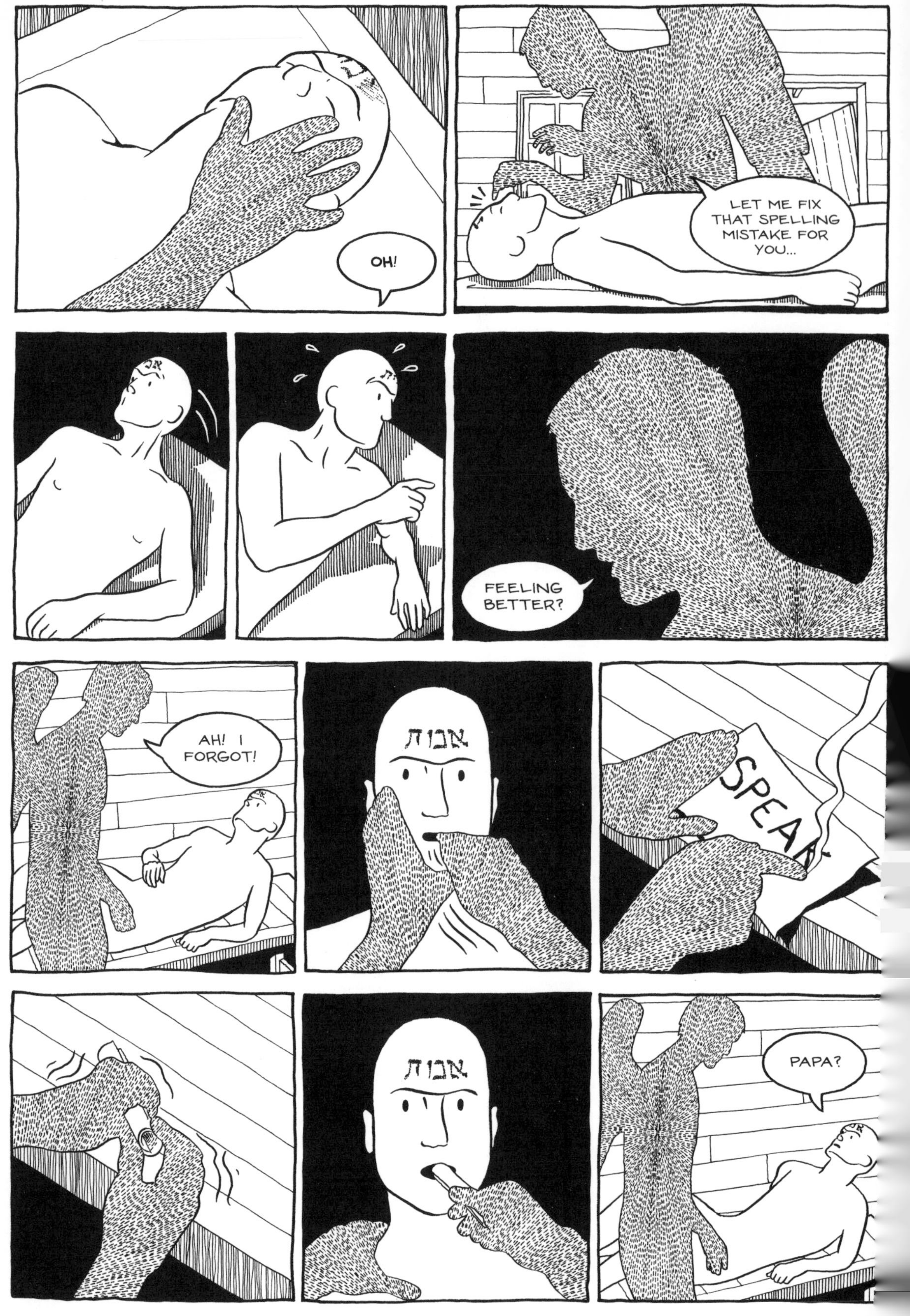
OH!
LET ME FIX THAT SPELLING MISTAKE FOR YOU...
FEELING BETTER?
AH! I FORGOT!
אבות
אבות
PAPA?

eight

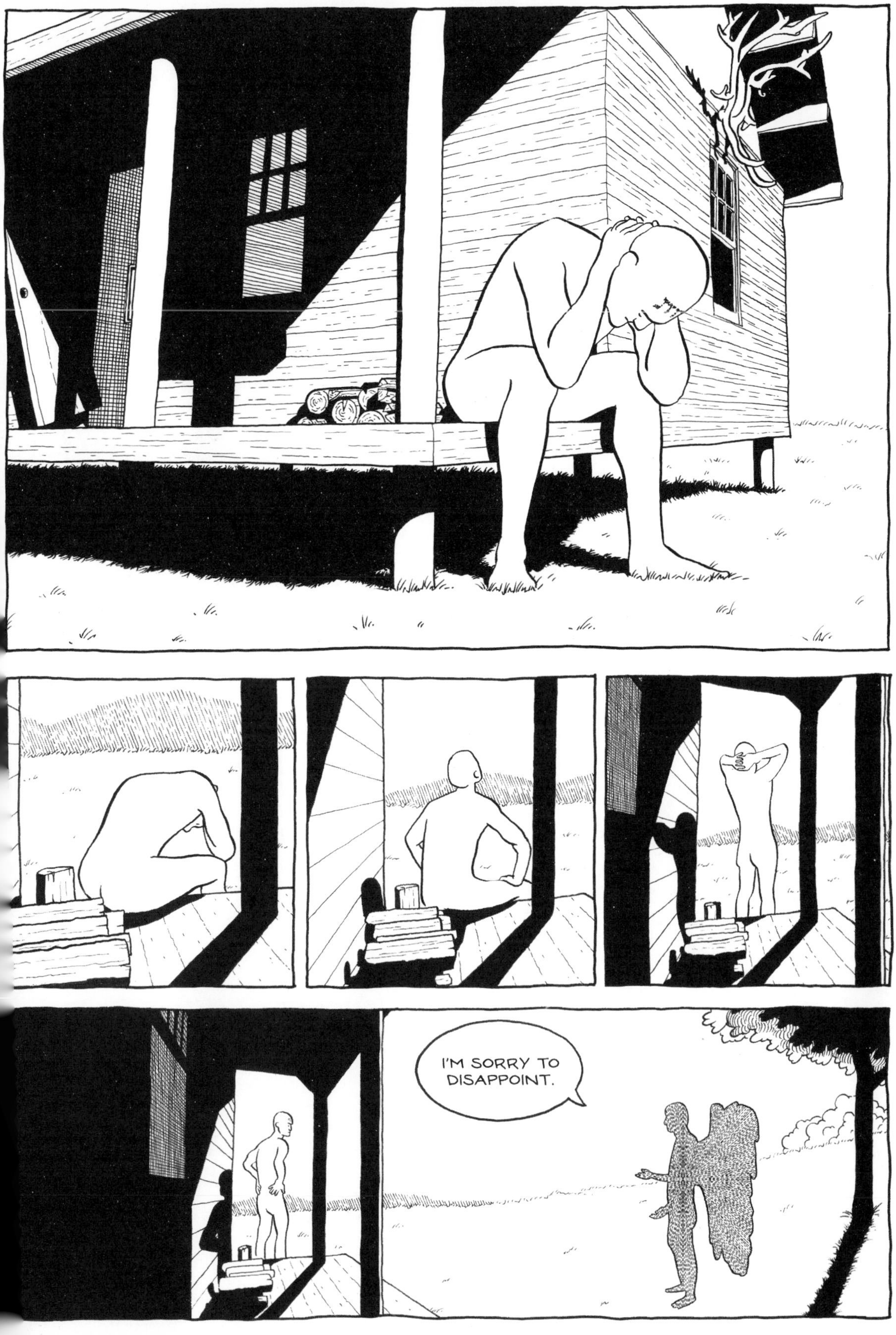
I'M SORRY TO DISAPPOINT.

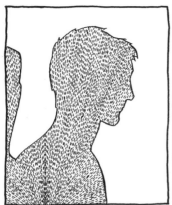

BUT YOU...
DIDN'T YOU...?

I HAD A HAND IN
SHEPHERDING YOU
FROM THE OTHER
SIDE, YES. BUT I AM
NOT YOUR FATHER.

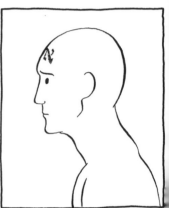

DID YOU NOT
REALISE...?

YOU KNOW HIM!
HE IS HERE, TOO -

JUST THE TWO OF
YOU, TOGETHER.

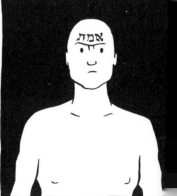

. . .
WHAT...
OH MAN, OH MAN!
HE'S GONE!
HE WAS...
MY DAD'S **GONE**!
HE GOT EATEN!
FUCKING CAT!
IT'S HIS FAULT!
HE SHANGHAIED US INTO DOING HIS DIRTY WORK.
DID YOU SEE THAT MONSTER HE FREED?
. . .
I'M GOING AFTER HIM. MAYBE MY FATHER'S STILL ALIVE.

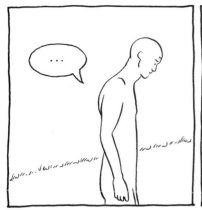

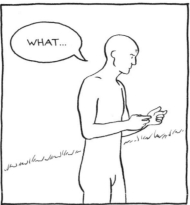

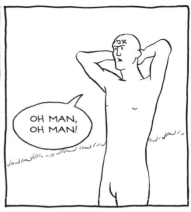

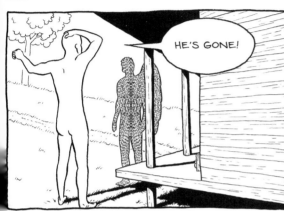

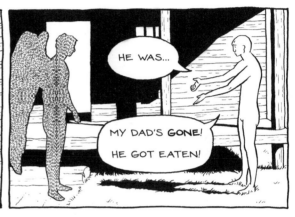

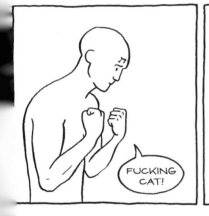

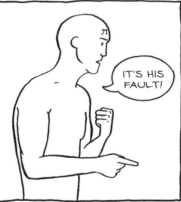

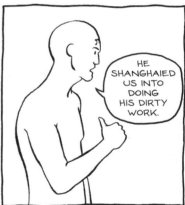

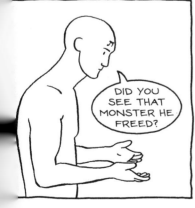

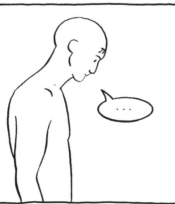

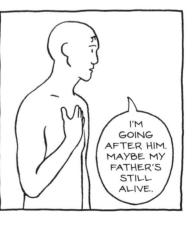

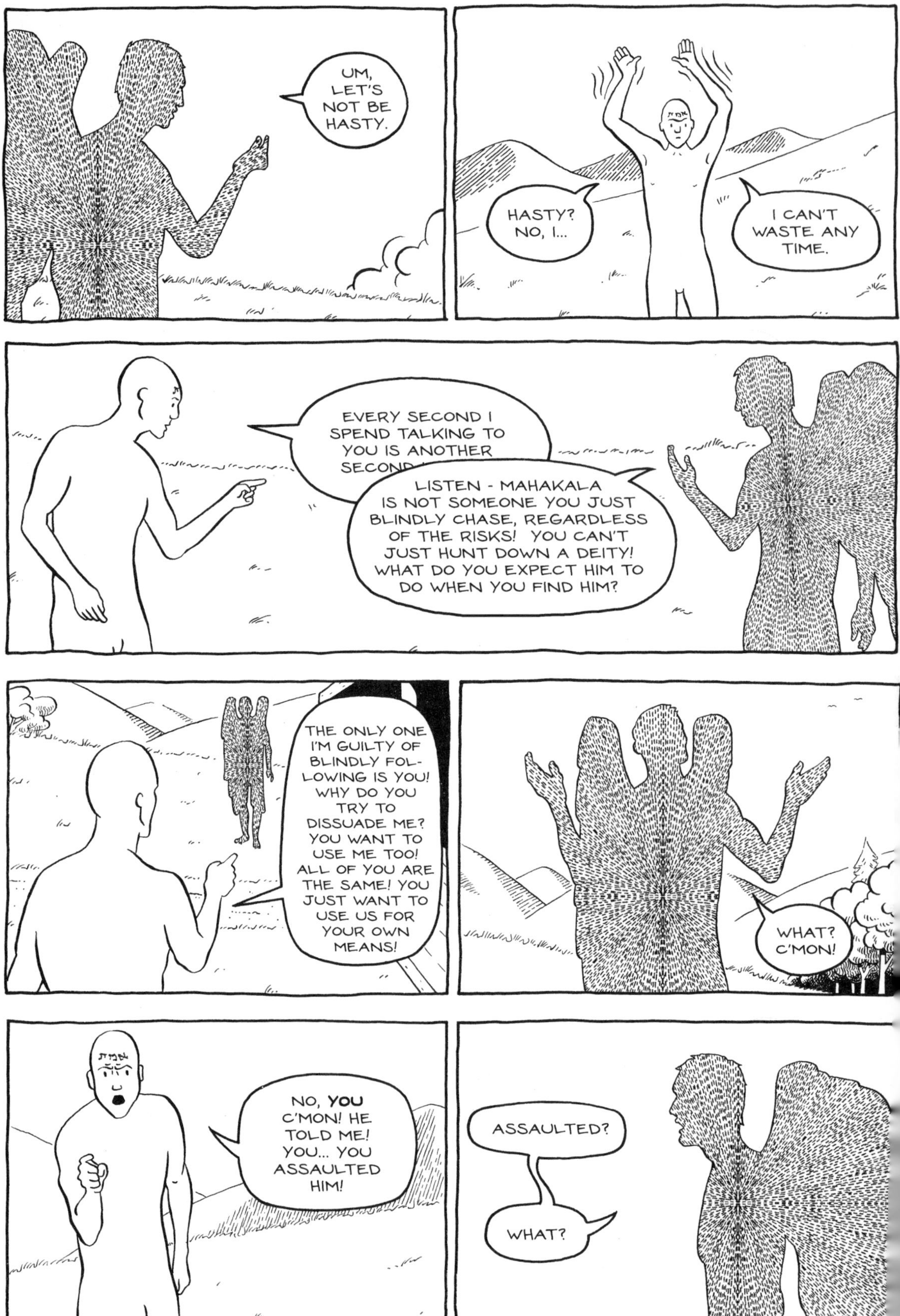
UM, LET'S NOT BE HASTY.
HASTY? NO, I...
I CAN'T WASTE ANY TIME.
EVERY SECOND I SPEND TALKING TO YOU IS ANOTHER SECOND
LISTEN - MAHAKALA IS NOT SOMEONE YOU JUST BLINDLY CHASE, REGARDLESS OF THE RISKS! YOU CAN'T JUST HUNT DOWN A DEITY! WHAT DO YOU EXPECT HIM TO DO WHEN YOU FIND HIM?
THE ONLY ONE I'M GUILTY OF BLINDLY FOL-LOWING IS YOU! WHY DO YOU TRY TO DISSUADE ME? YOU WANT TO USE ME TOO! ALL OF YOU ARE THE SAME! YOU JUST WANT TO USE US FOR YOUR OWN MEANS!
WHAT? C'MON!
NO, **YOU** C'MON! HE TOLD ME! YOU... YOU ASSAULTED HIM!
ASSAULTED?
WHAT?

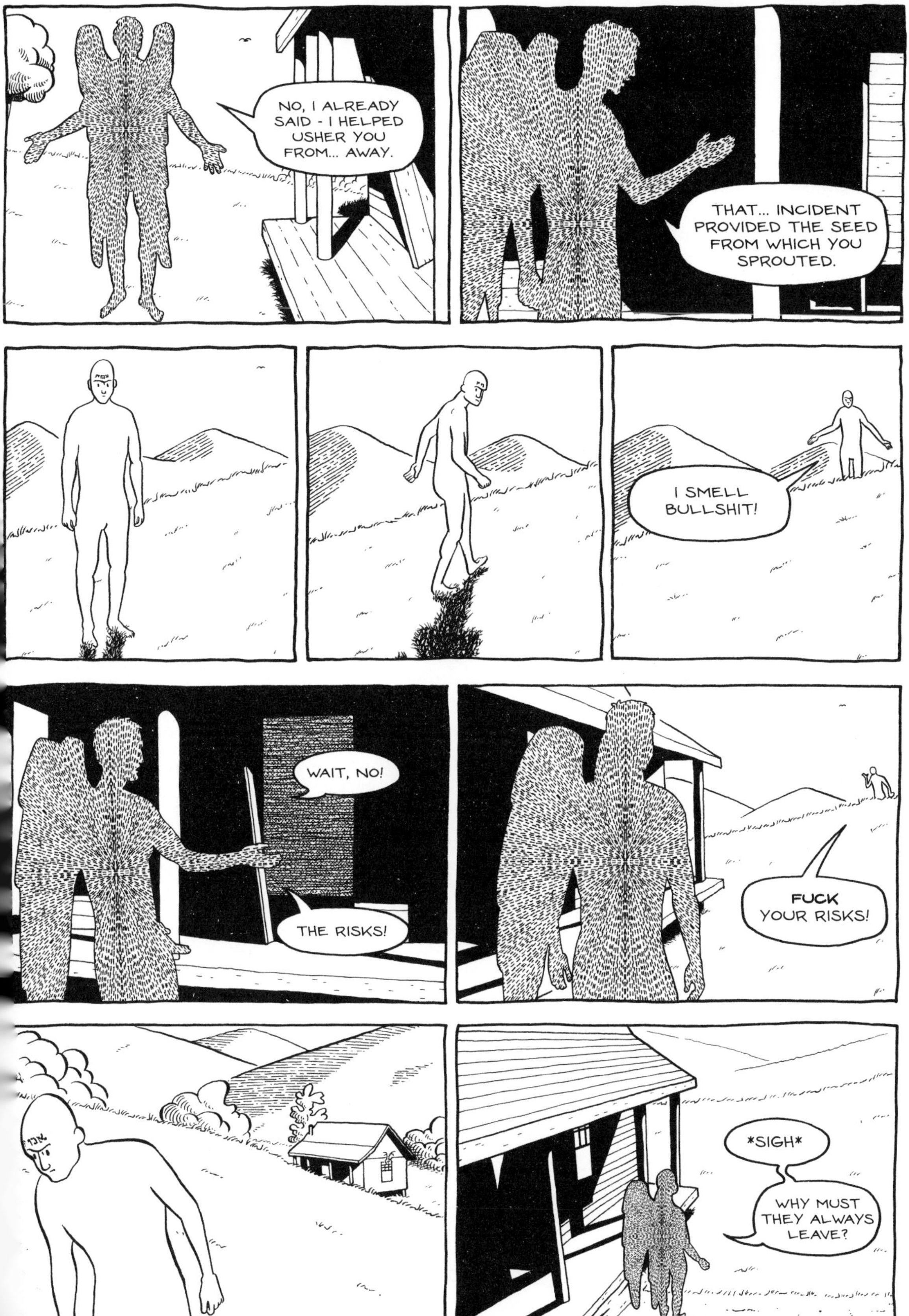
NO, I ALREADY SAID - I HELPED USHER YOU FROM... AWAY.
THAT... INCIDENT PROVIDED THE SEED FROM WHICH YOU SPROUTED.
I SMELL BULLSHIT!
WAIT, NO!
THE RISKS!
FUCK YOUR RISKS!
SIGH
WHY MUST THEY ALWAYS LEAVE?

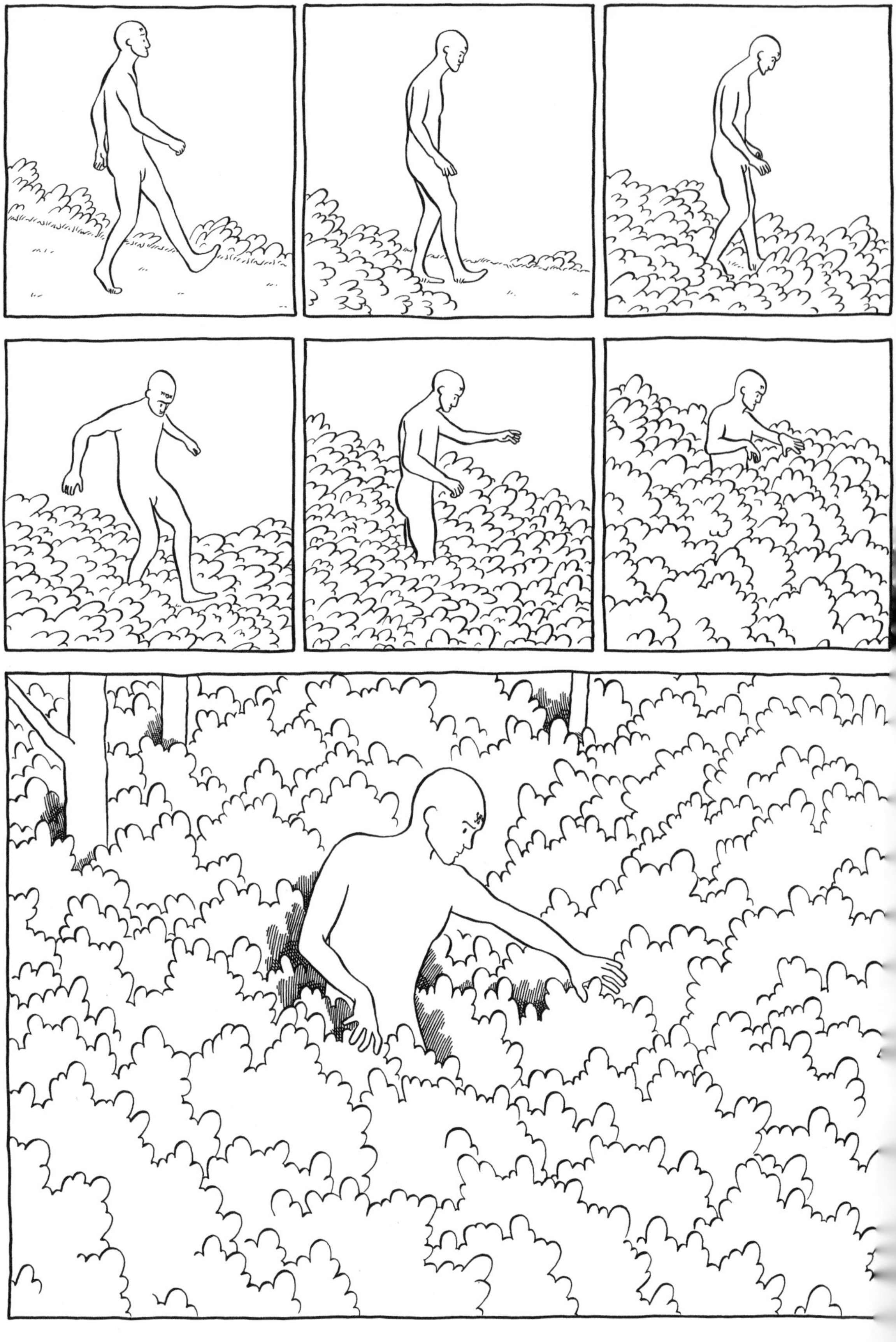

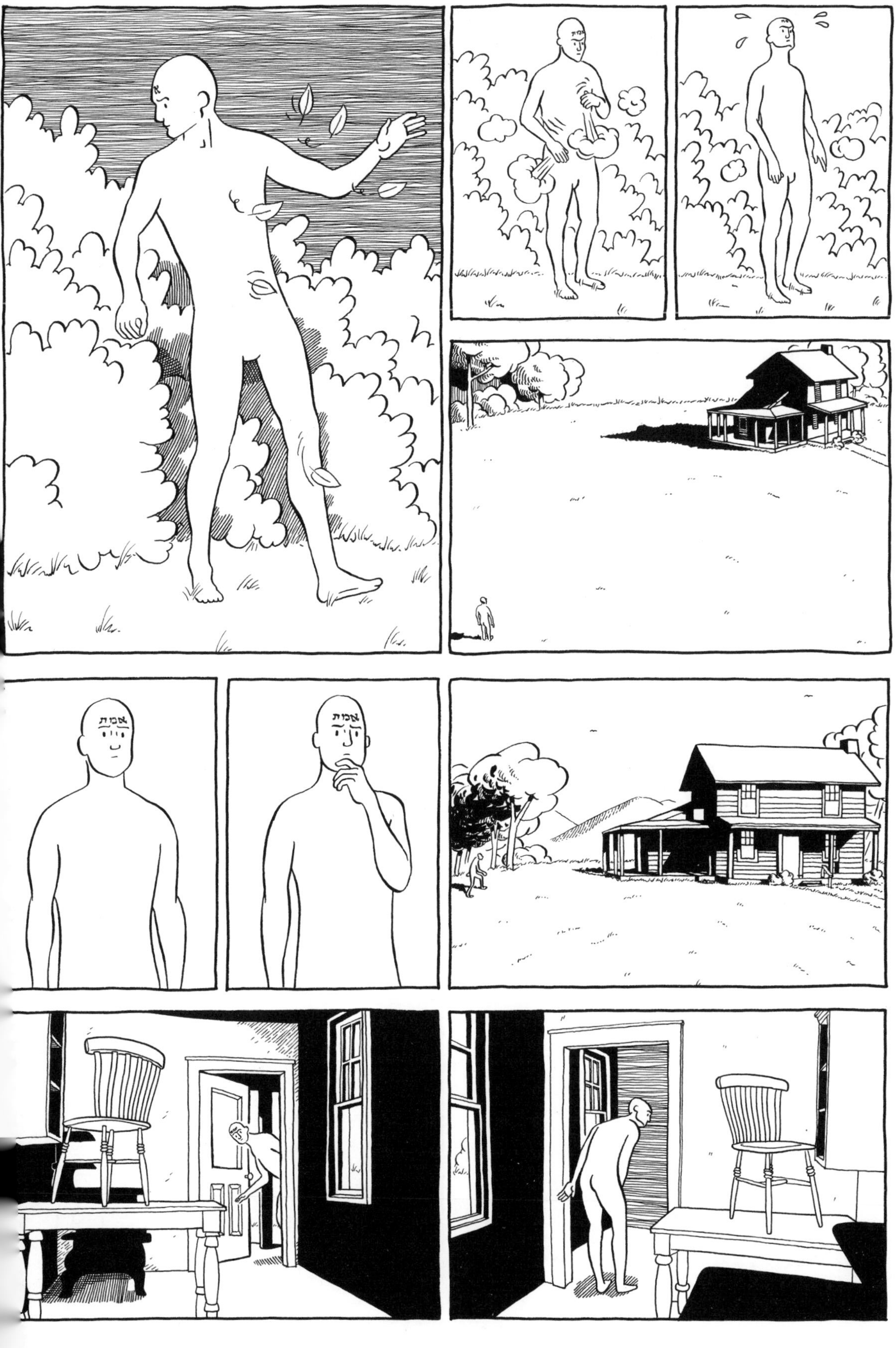
אמת

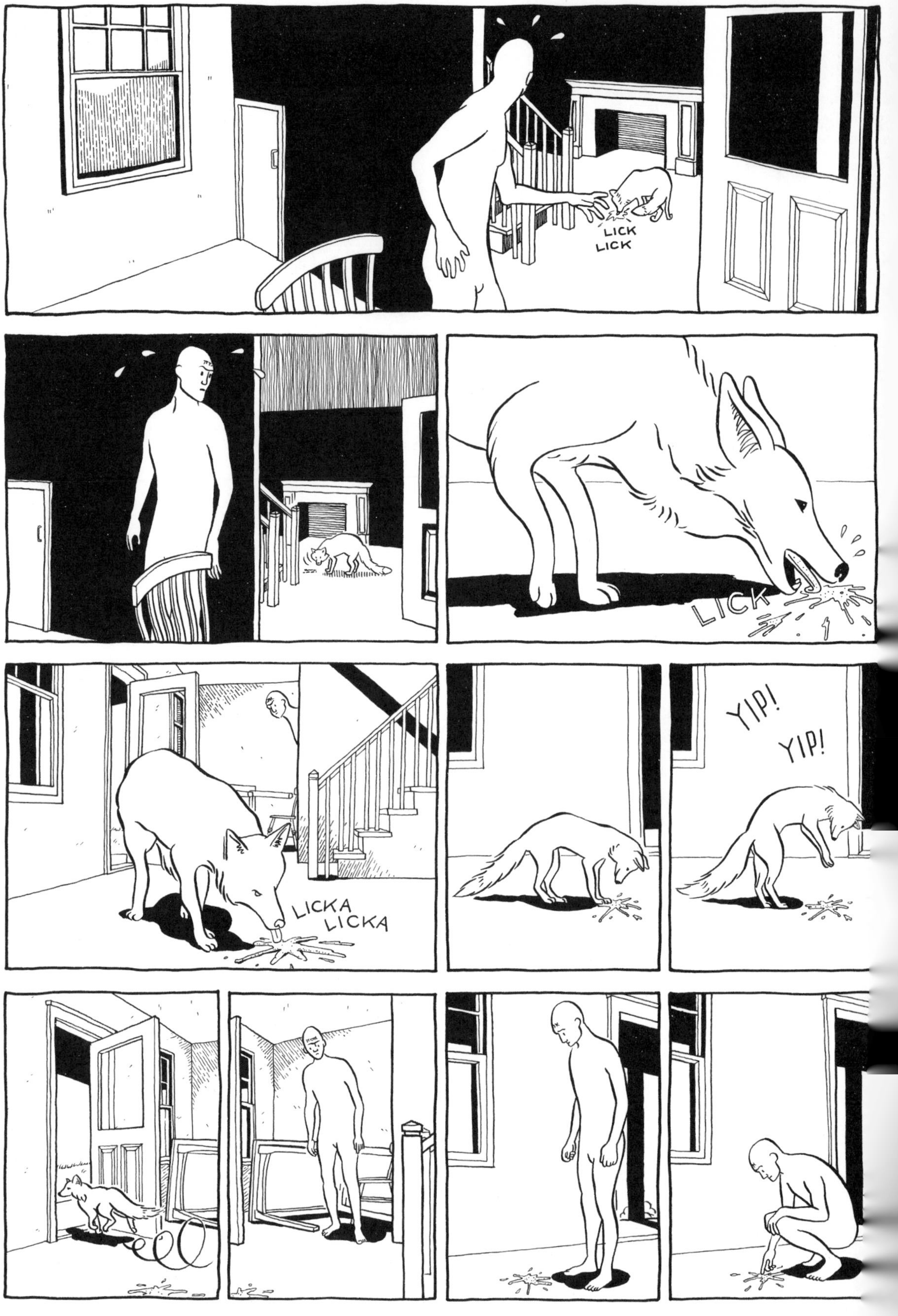
LICK
LICK
LICK
LICKA
LICKA
YIP!
YIP!

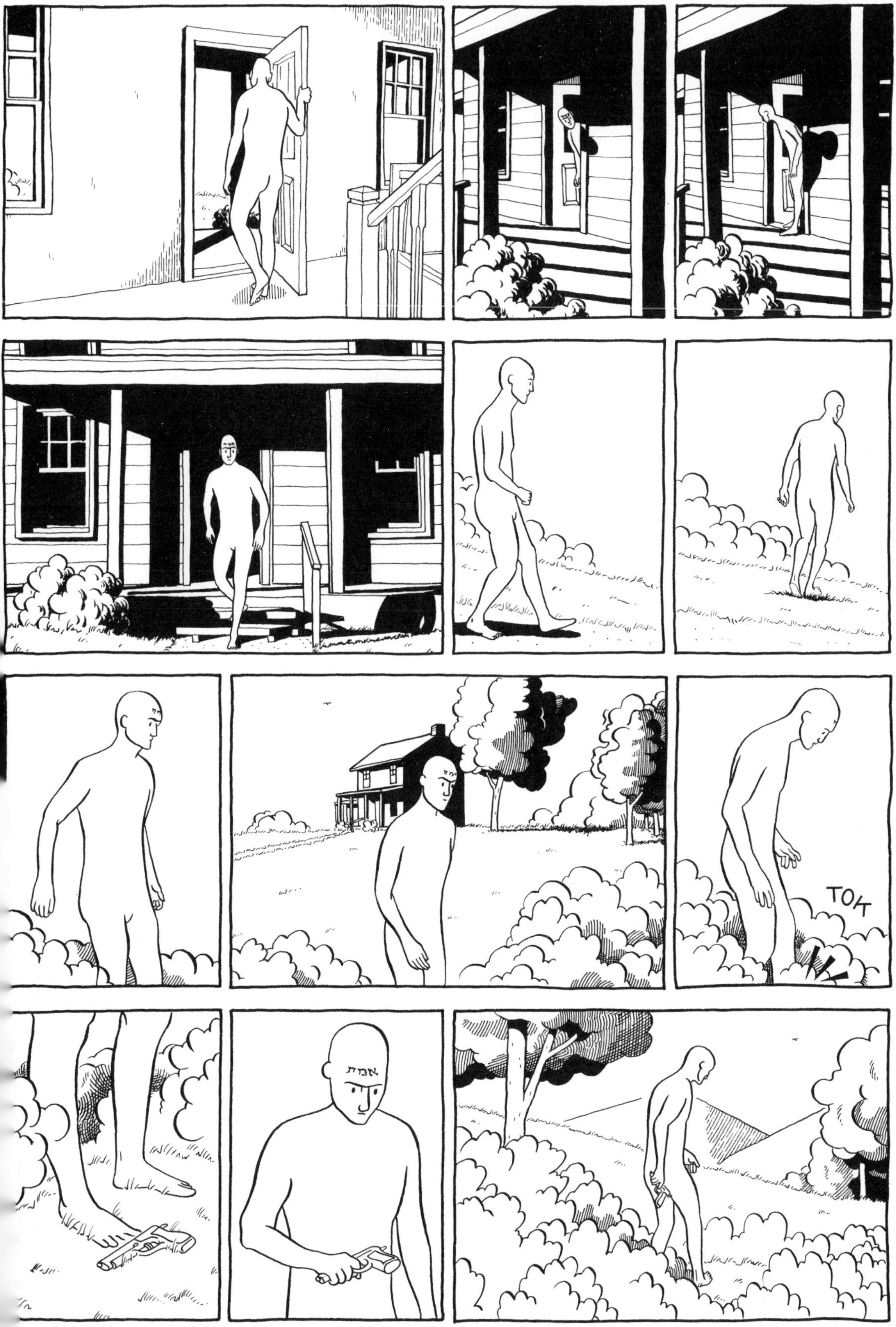
TOK

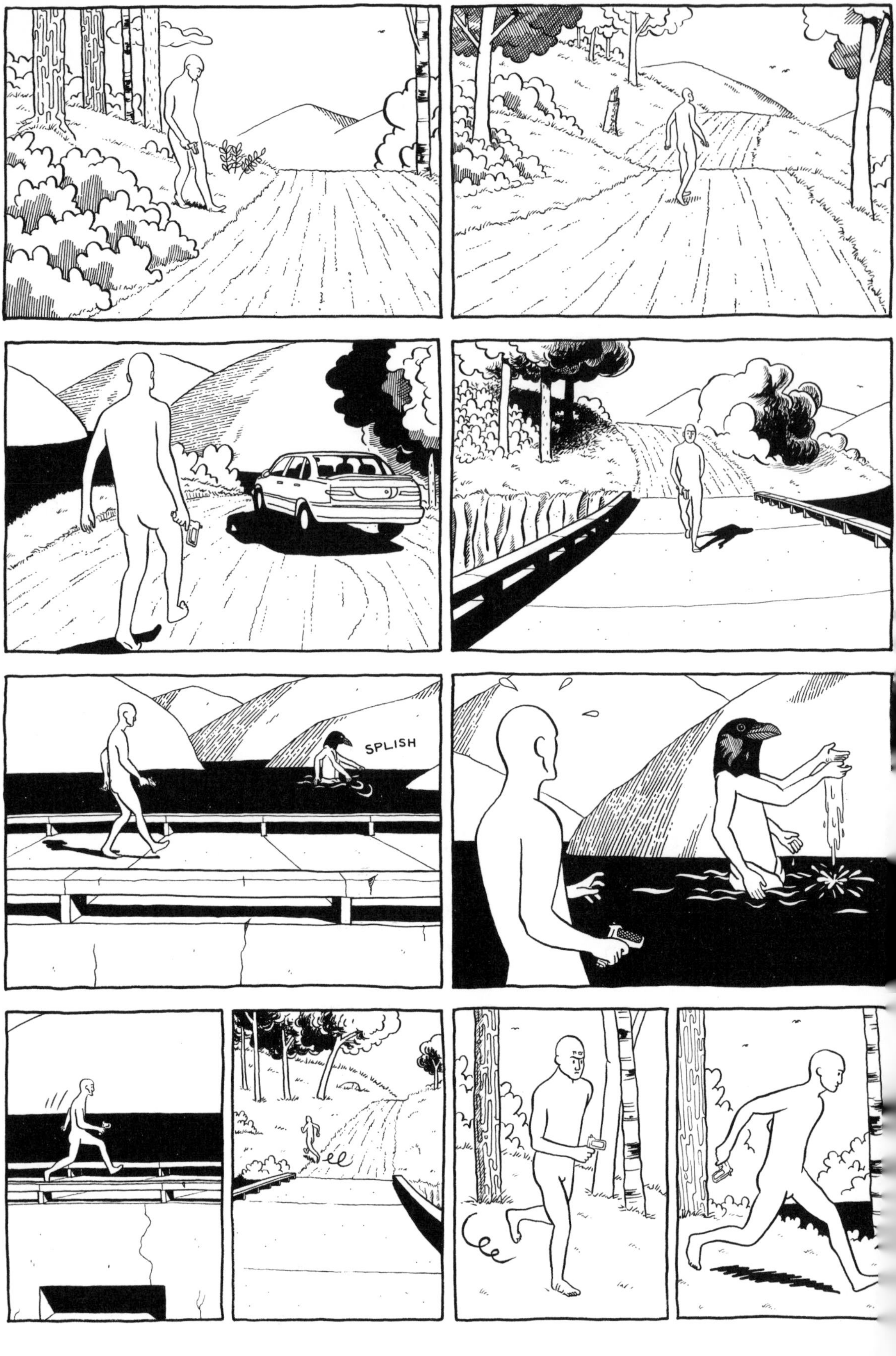
SPLISH

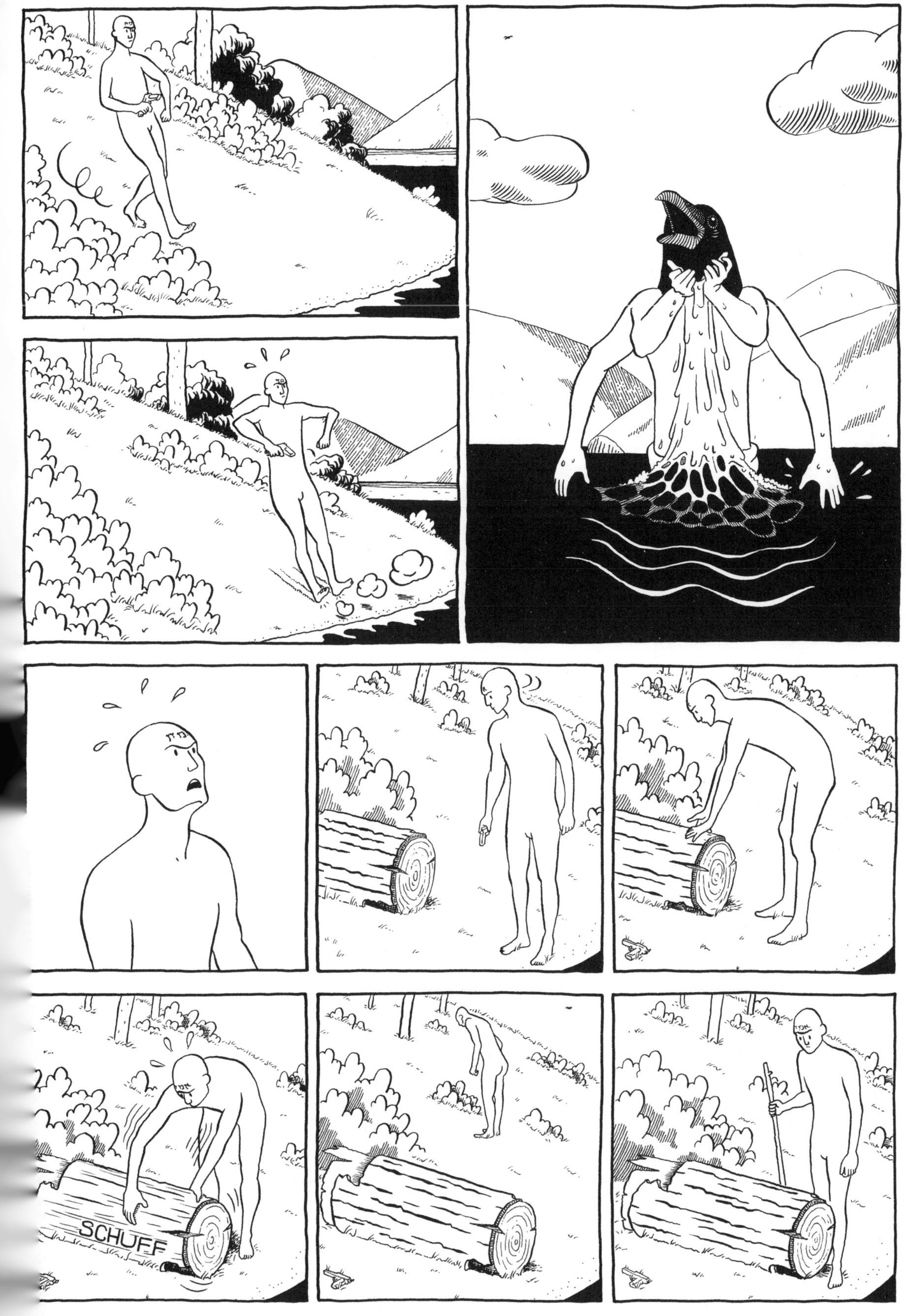
SCHUFF

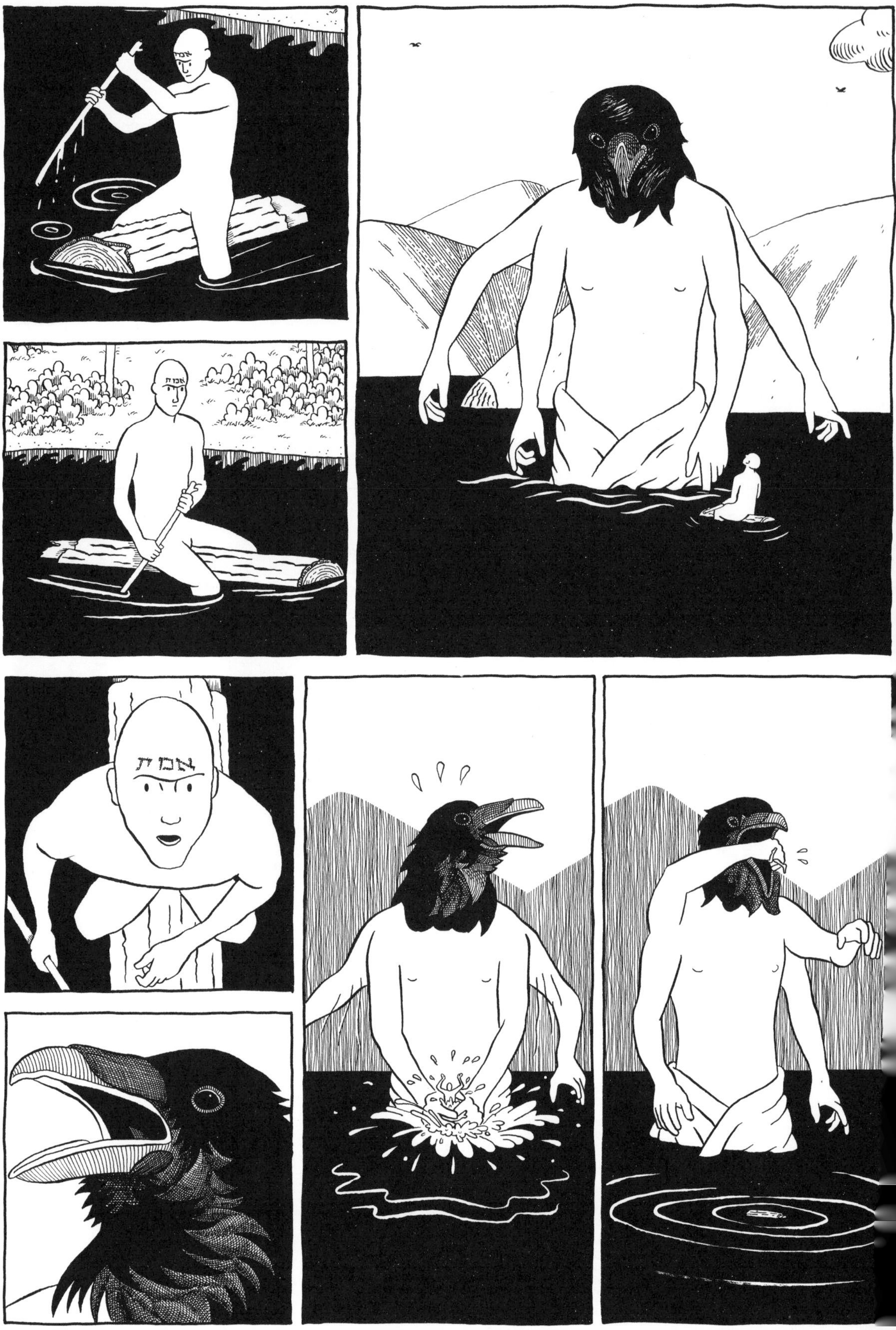
אמת

[redacted]

nine

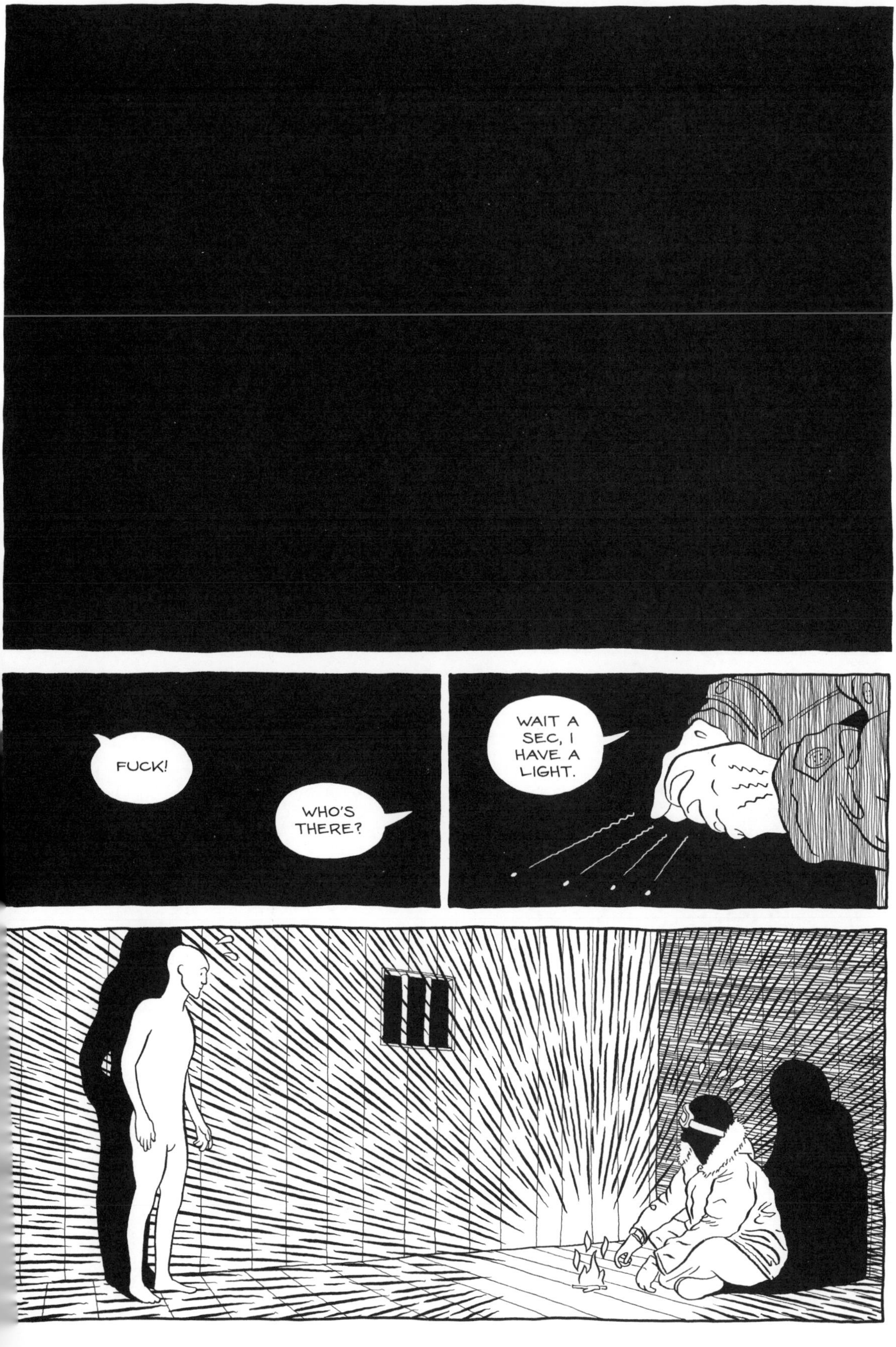
FUCK!
WHO'S THERE?
WAIT A SEC, I HAVE A LIGHT.

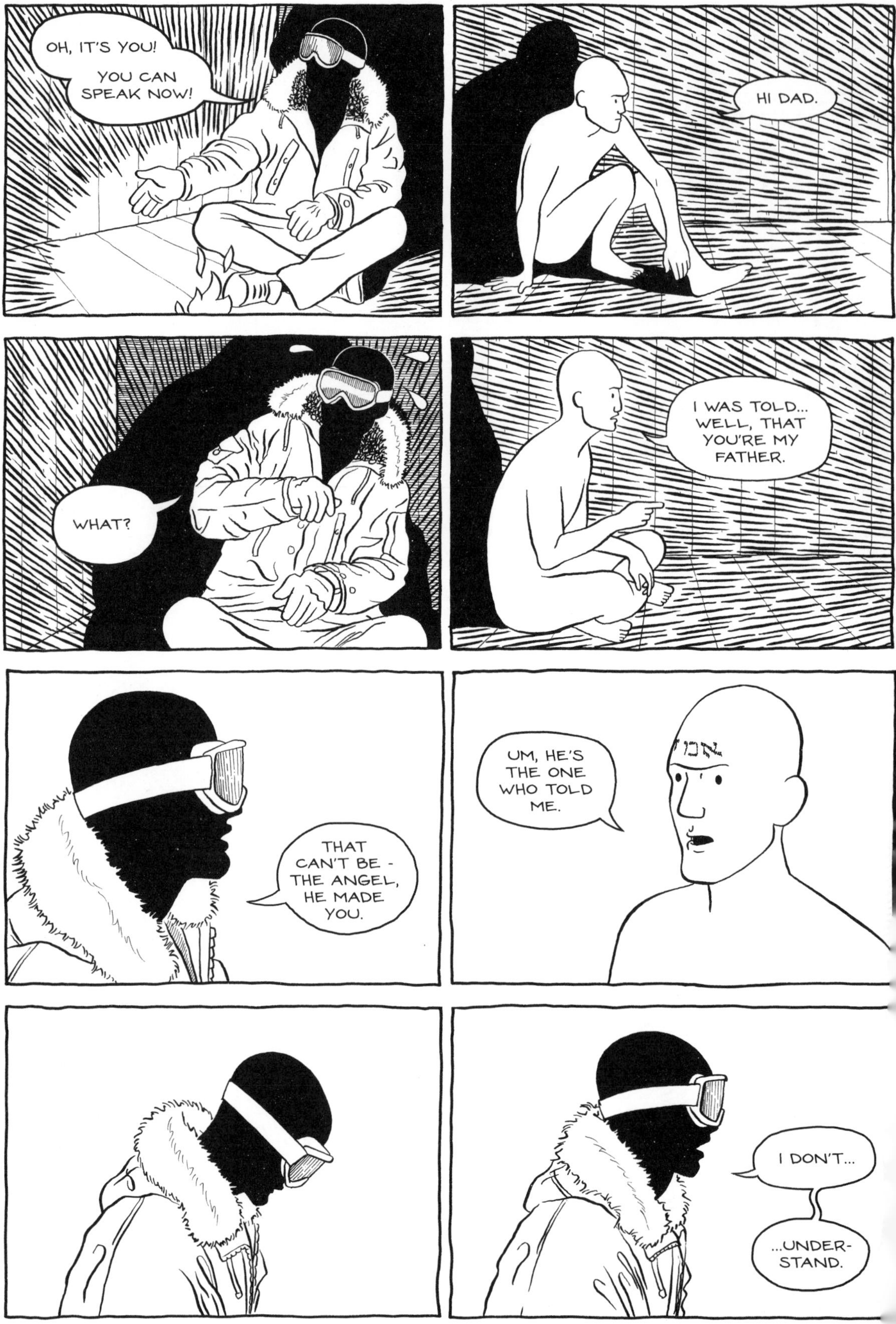

OH, IT'S YOU!
YOU CAN SPEAK NOW!
HI DAD.
WHAT?
I WAS TOLD... WELL, THAT YOU'RE MY FATHER.
THAT CAN'T BE - THE ANGEL, HE MADE YOU.
UM, HE'S THE ONE WHO TOLD ME.
I DON'T...
...UNDER-STAND.

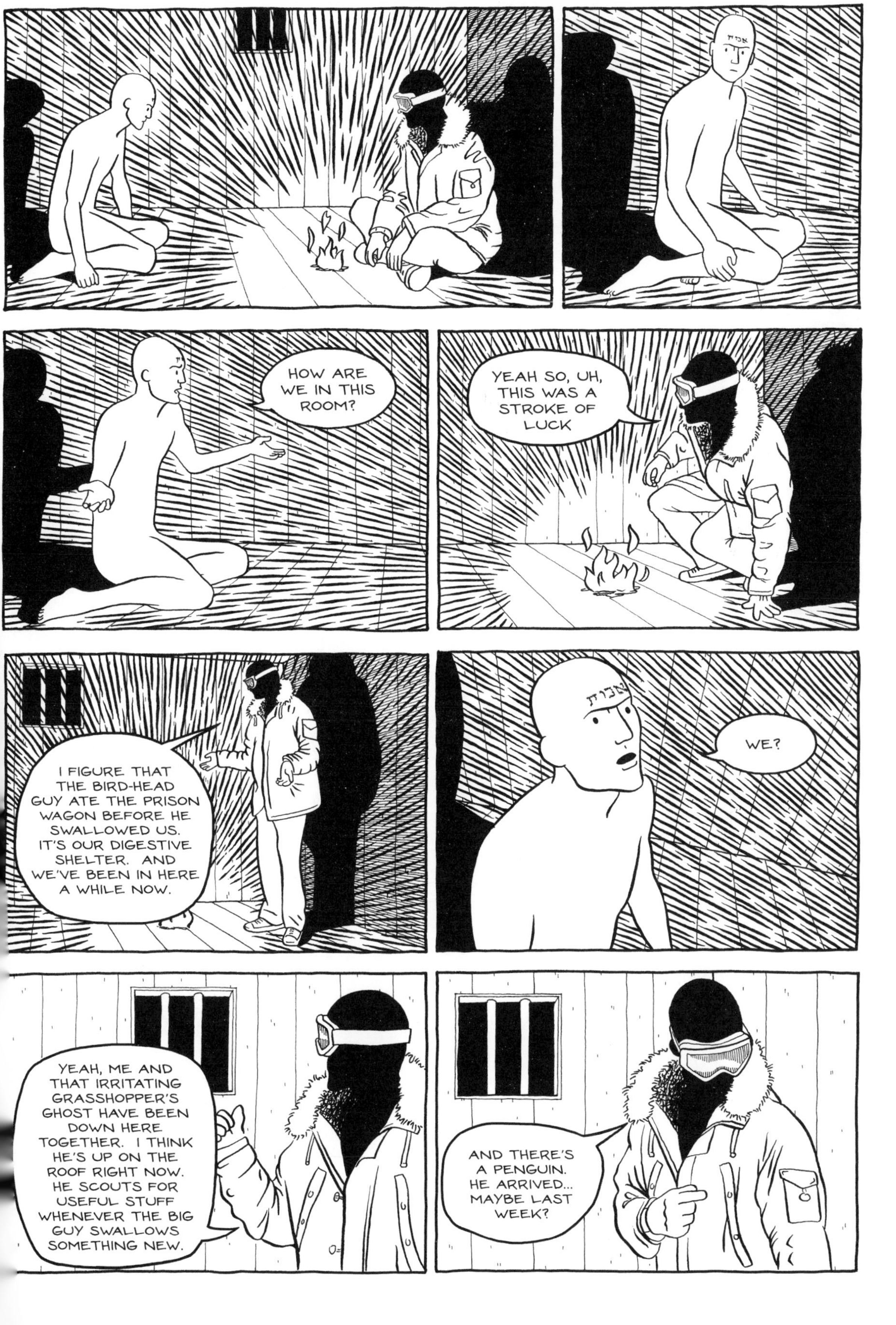
HOW ARE WE IN THIS ROOM?
YEAH SO, UH, THIS WAS A STROKE OF LUCK
I FIGURE THAT THE BIRD-HEAD GUY ATE THE PRISON WAGON BEFORE HE SWALLOWED US. IT'S OUR DIGESTIVE SHELTER. AND WE'VE BEEN IN HERE A WHILE NOW.
WE?
YEAH, ME AND THAT IRRITATING GRASSHOPPER'S GHOST HAVE BEEN DOWN HERE TOGETHER. I THINK HE'S UP ON THE ROOF RIGHT NOW. HE SCOUTS FOR USEFUL STUFF WHENEVER THE BIG GUY SWALLOWS SOMETHING NEW.
AND THERE'S A PENGUIN. HE ARRIVED... MAYBE LAST WEEK?

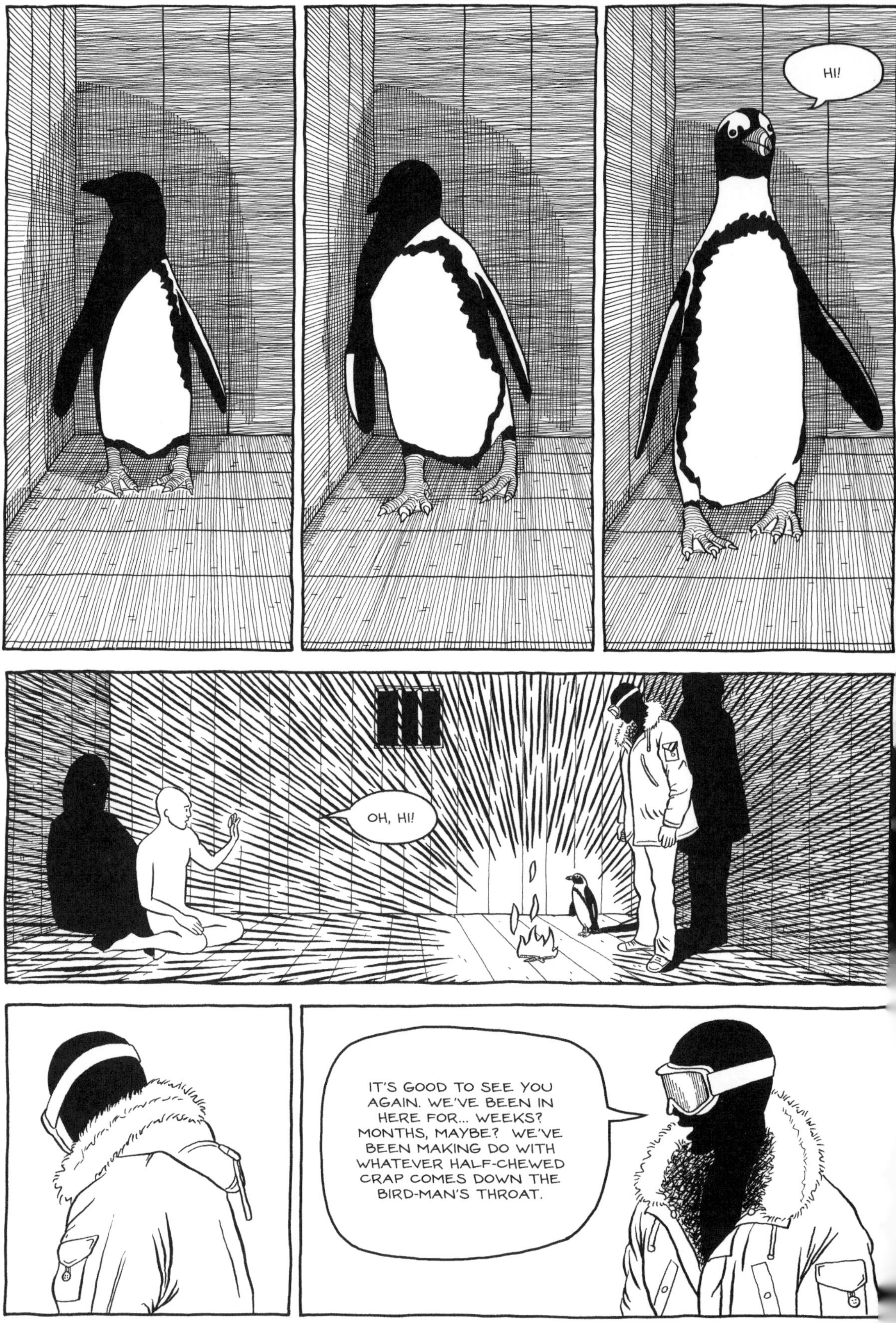
HI!
OH, HI!
IT'S GOOD TO SEE YOU AGAIN. WE'VE BEEN IN HERE FOR... WEEKS? MONTHS, MAYBE? WE'VE BEEN MAKING DO WITH WHATEVER HALF-CHEWED CRAP COMES DOWN THE BIRD-MAN'S THROAT.

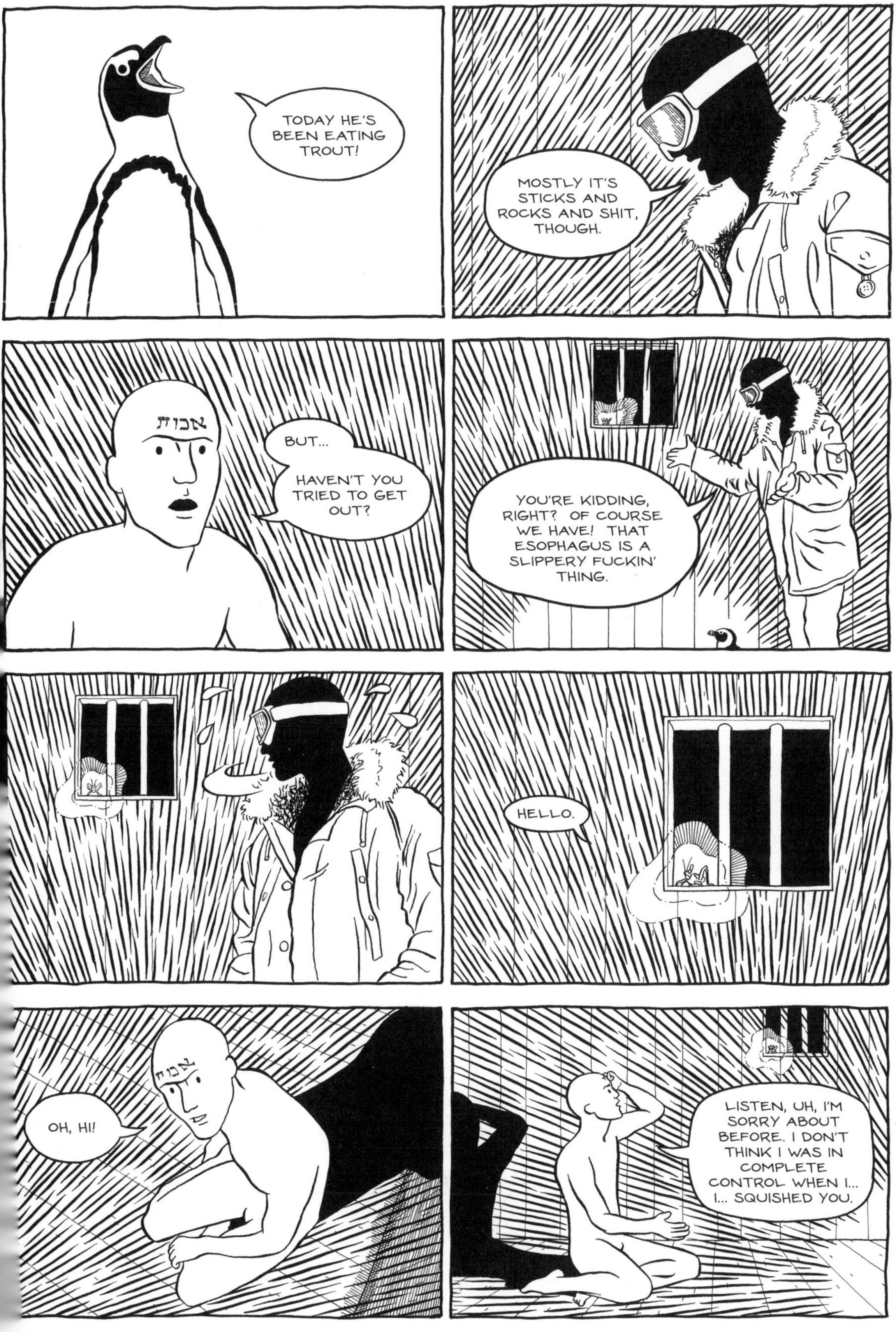
TODAY HE'S BEEN EATING TROUT!
MOSTLY IT'S STICKS AND ROCKS AND SHIT, THOUGH.
BUT...
HAVEN'T YOU TRIED TO GET OUT?
YOU'RE KIDDING, RIGHT? OF COURSE WE HAVE! THAT ESOPHAGUS IS A SLIPPERY FUCKIN' THING.
HELLO.
OH, HI!
LISTEN, UH, I'M SORRY ABOUT BEFORE. I DON'T THINK I WAS IN COMPLETE CONTROL WHEN I... I... SQUISHED YOU.

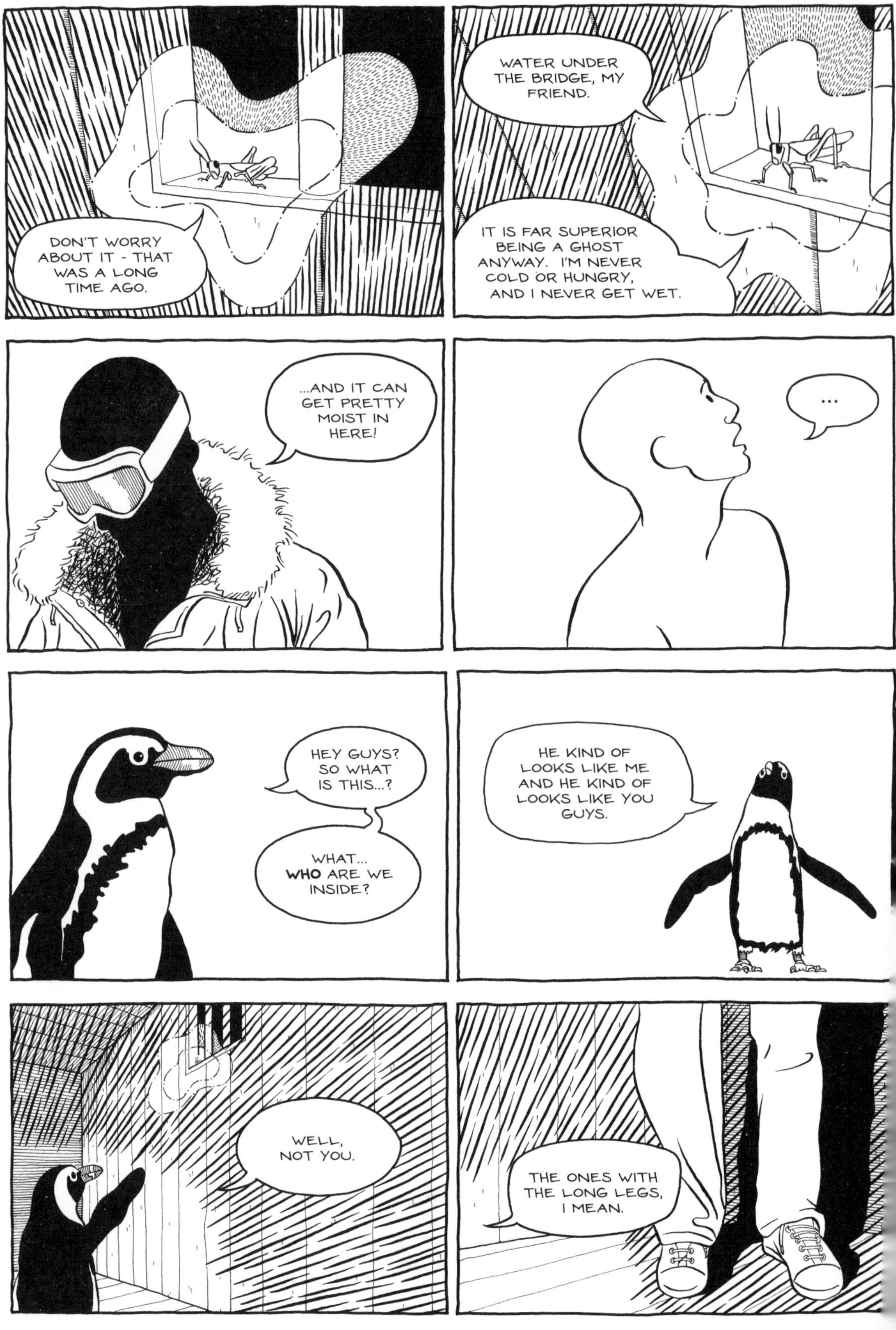
DON'T WORRY ABOUT IT - THAT WAS A LONG TIME AGO.
WATER UNDER THE BRIDGE, MY FRIEND.
IT IS FAR SUPERIOR BEING A GHOST ANYWAY. I'M NEVER COLD OR HUNGRY, AND I NEVER GET WET.
...AND IT CAN GET PRETTY MOIST IN HERE!
...
HEY GUYS? SO WHAT IS THIS...?
WHAT... **WHO** ARE WE INSIDE?
HE KIND OF LOOKS LIKE ME AND HE KIND OF LOOKS LIKE YOU GUYS.
WELL, NOT YOU.
THE ONES WITH THE LONG LEGS, I MEAN.

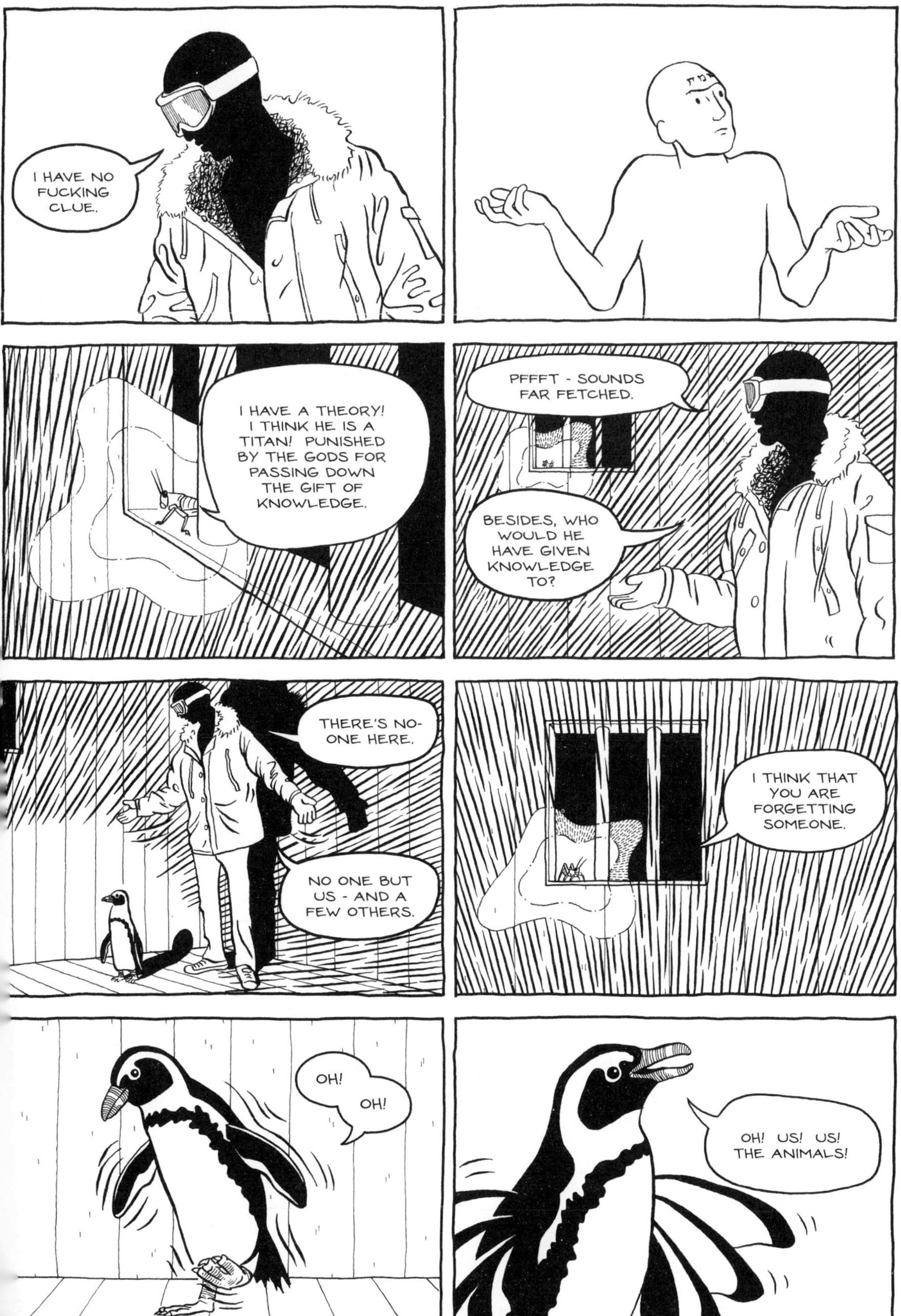
I HAVE NO FUCKING CLUE.
I HAVE A THEORY! I THINK HE IS A TITAN! PUNISHED BY THE GODS FOR PASSING DOWN THE GIFT OF KNOWLEDGE.
PFFFT - SOUNDS FAR FETCHED.
BESIDES, WHO WOULD HE HAVE GIVEN KNOWLEDGE TO?
THERE'S NO-ONE HERE.
NO ONE BUT US - AND A FEW OTHERS.
I THINK THAT YOU ARE FORGETTING SOMEONE.
OH!
OH!
OH! US! US! THE ANIMALS!

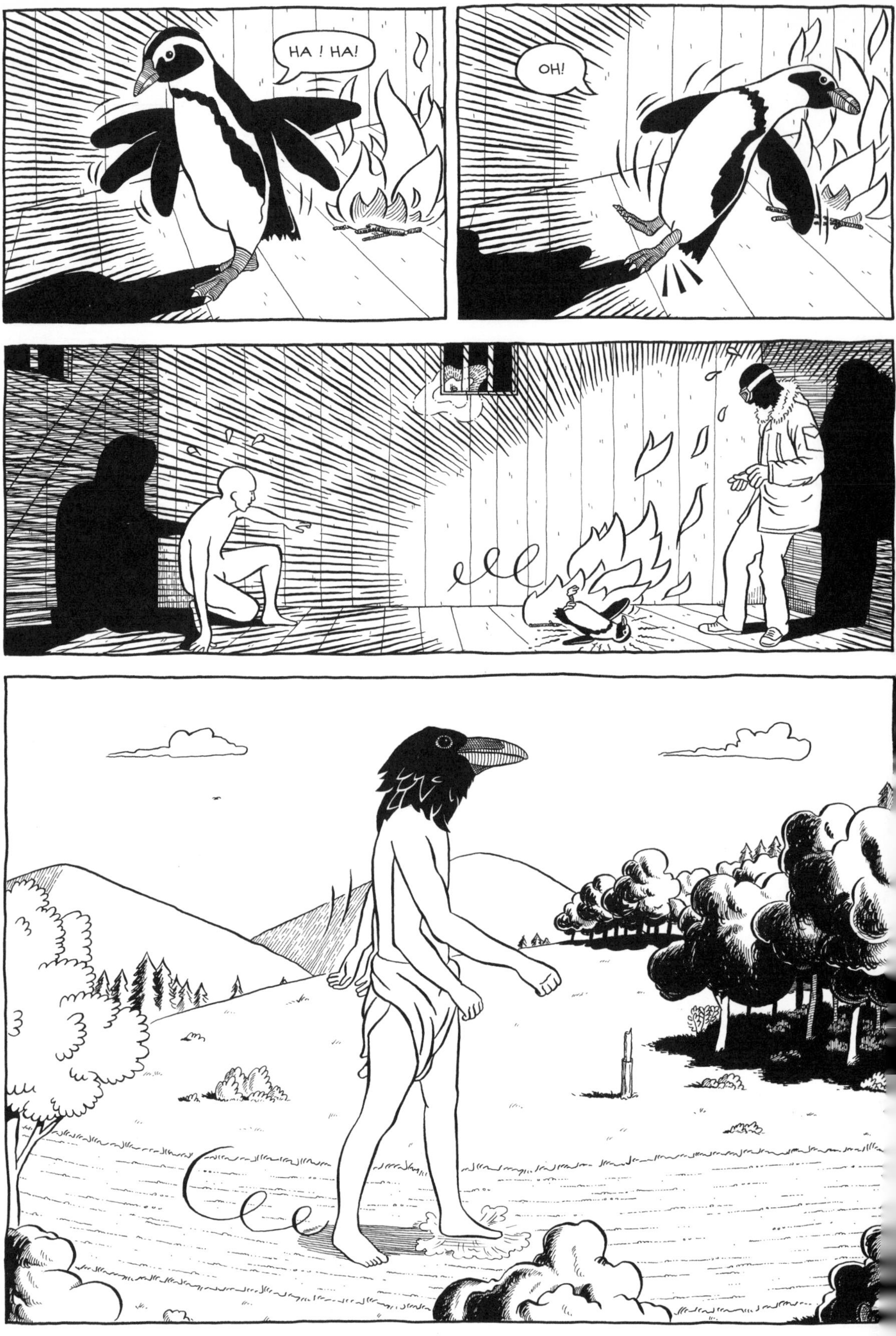
HA ! HA!
OH!

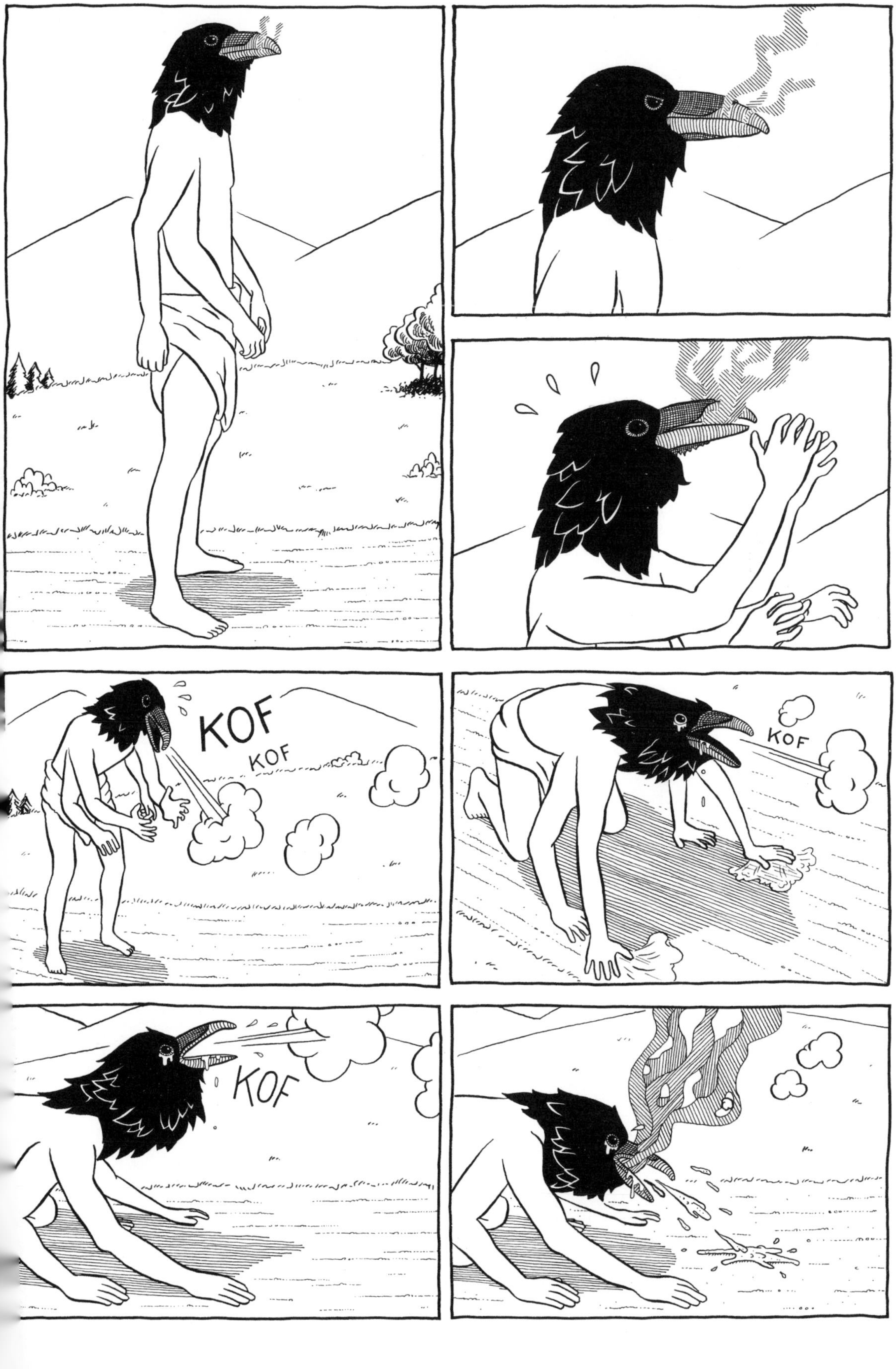
KOF
KOF
KOF
KOF

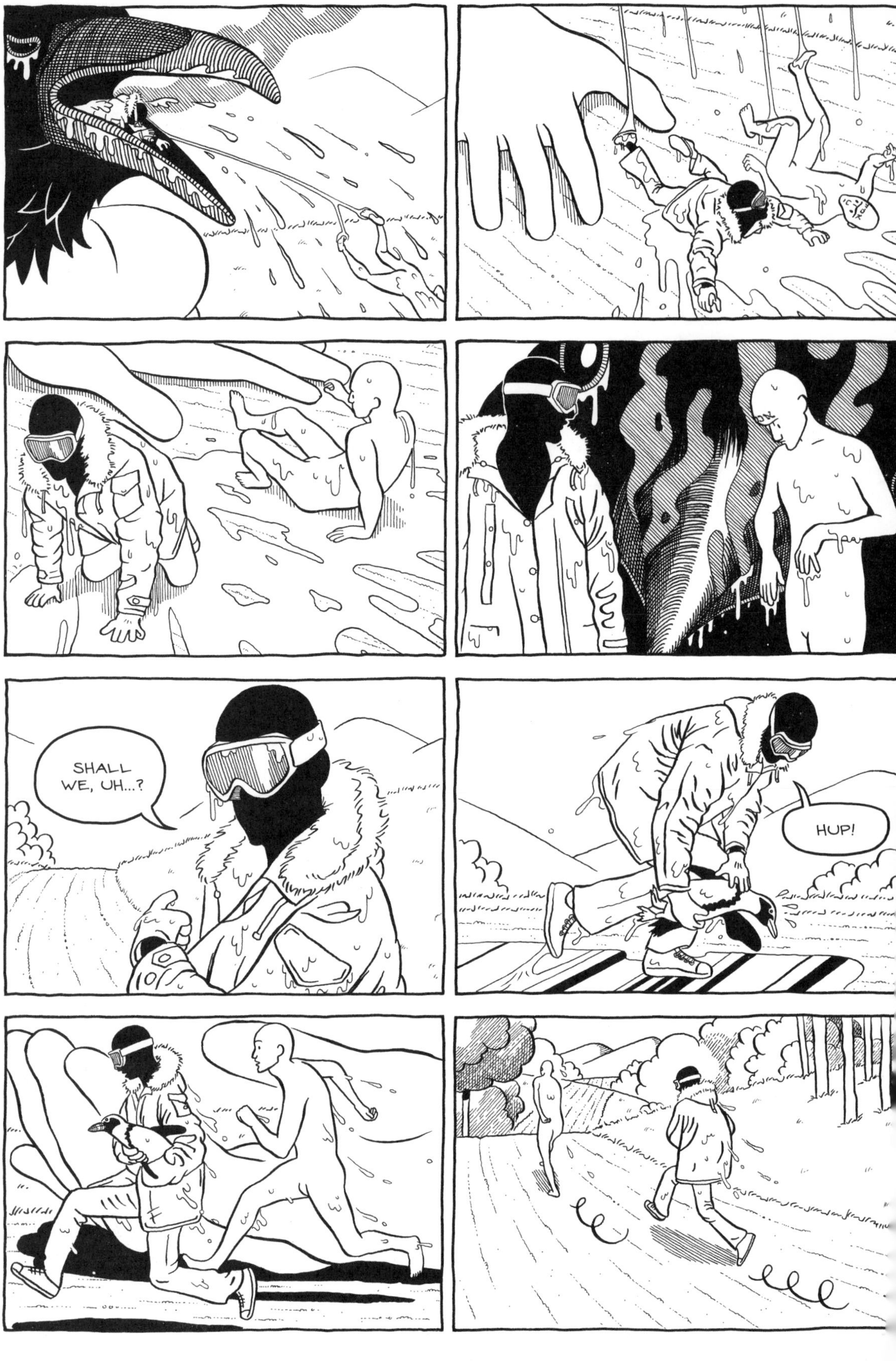
SHALL WE, UH...?
HUP!

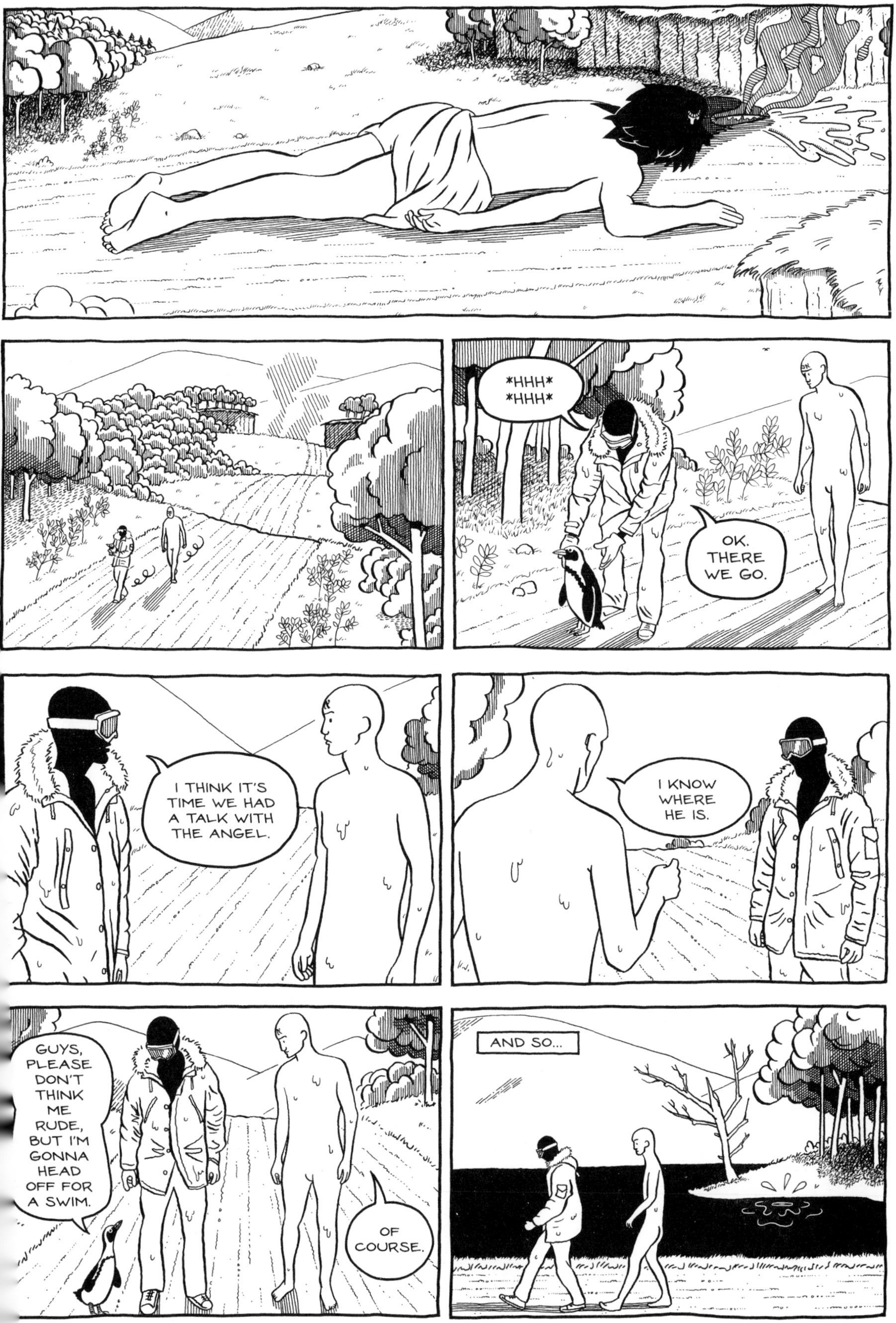
HHH
HHH
OK. THERE WE GO.
I THINK IT'S TIME WE HAD A TALK WITH THE ANGEL.
I KNOW WHERE HE IS.
GUYS, PLEASE DON'T THINK ME RUDE, BUT I'M GONNA HEAD OFF FOR A SWIM.
OF COURSE.
AND SO...

ten

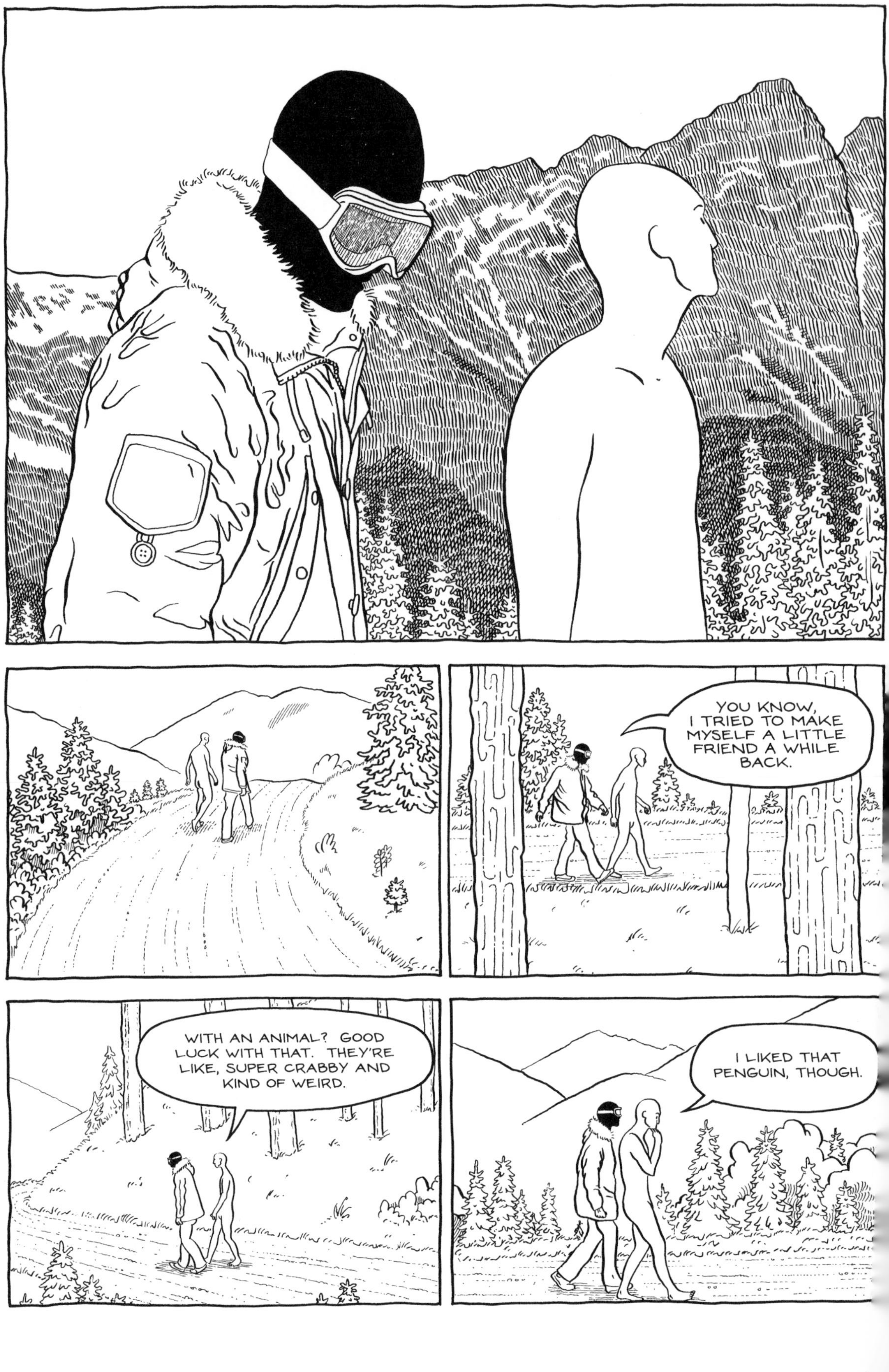
YOU KNOW, I TRIED TO MAKE MYSELF A LITTLE FRIEND A WHILE BACK.
WITH AN ANIMAL? GOOD LUCK WITH THAT. THEY'RE LIKE, SUPER CRABBY AND KIND OF WEIRD.
I LIKED THAT PENGUIN, THOUGH.

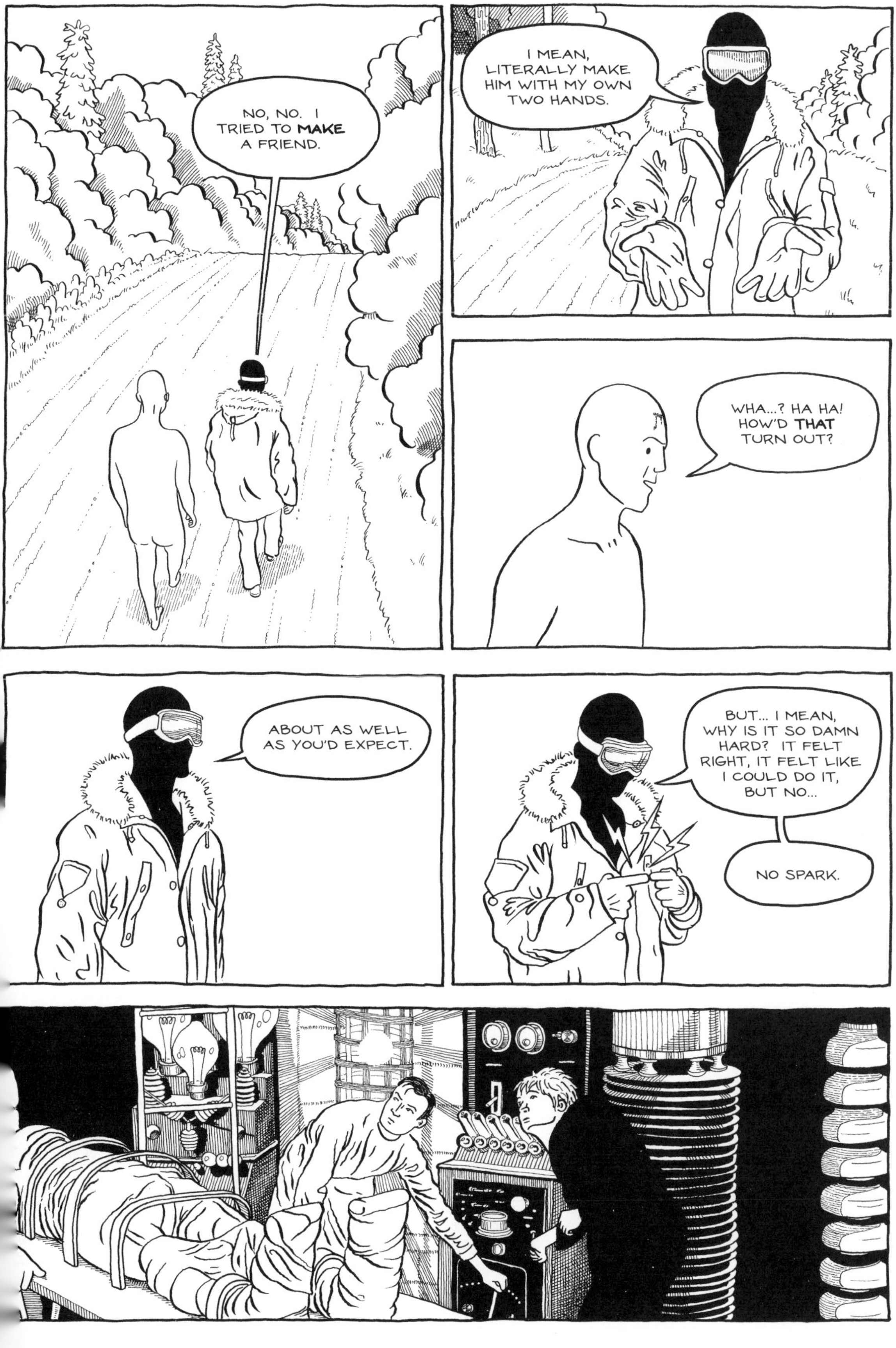
NO, NO. I TRIED TO **MAKE** A FRIEND.
I MEAN, LITERALLY MAKE HIM WITH MY OWN TWO HANDS.
WHA...? HA HA! HOW'D **THAT** TURN OUT?
ABOUT AS WELL AS YOU'D EXPECT.
BUT... I MEAN, WHY IS IT SO DAMN HARD? IT FELT RIGHT, IT FELT LIKE I COULD DO IT, BUT NO...
NO SPARK.

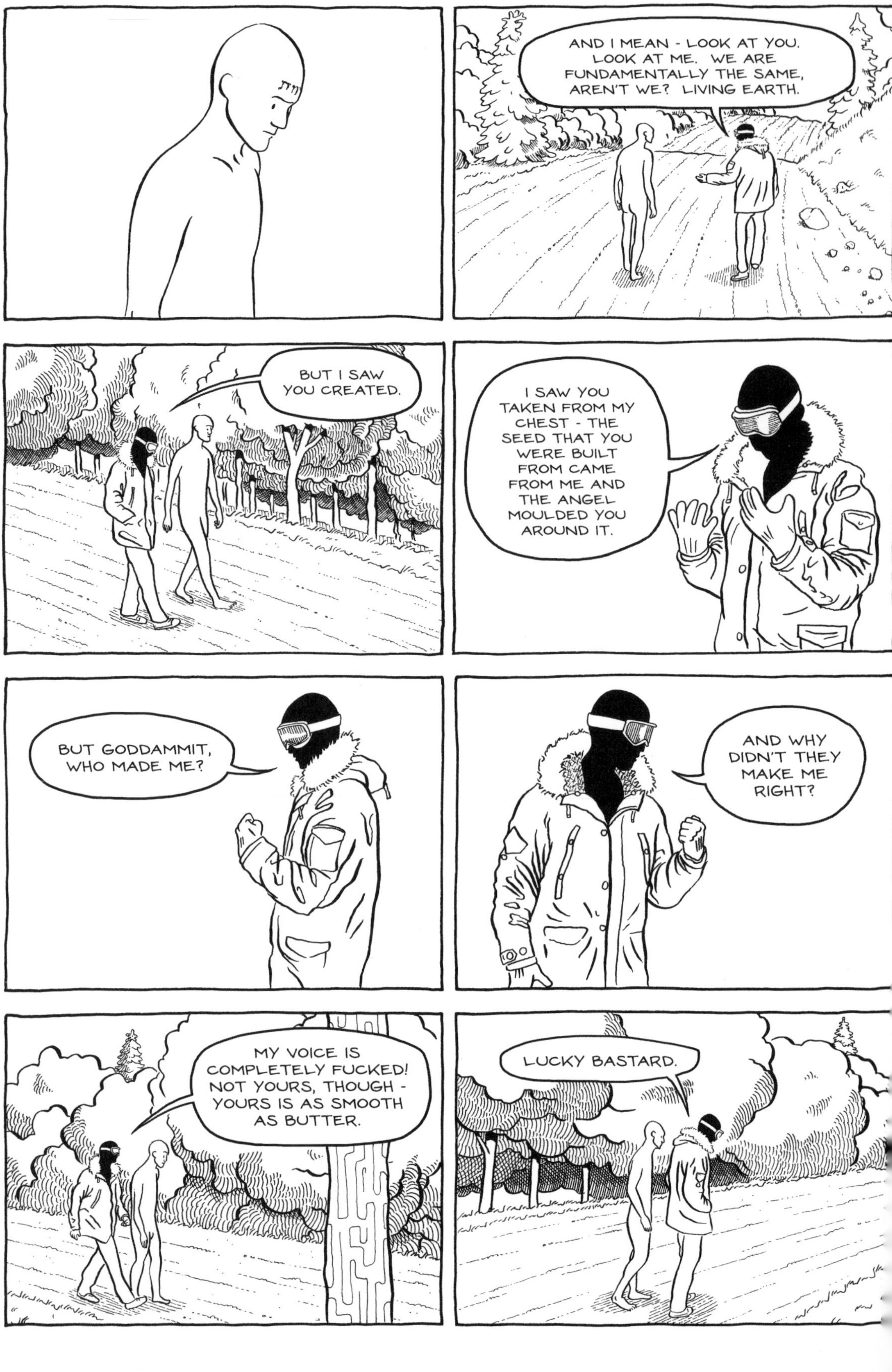
AND I MEAN - LOOK AT YOU. LOOK AT ME. WE ARE FUNDAMENTALLY THE SAME, AREN'T WE? LIVING EARTH.
BUT I SAW YOU CREATED.
I SAW YOU TAKEN FROM MY CHEST - THE SEED THAT YOU WERE BUILT FROM CAME FROM ME AND THE ANGEL MOULDED YOU AROUND IT.
BUT GODDAMMIT, WHO MADE ME?
AND WHY DIDN'T THEY MAKE ME RIGHT?
MY VOICE IS COMPLETELY FUCKED! NOT YOURS, THOUGH - YOURS IS AS SMOOTH AS BUTTER.
LUCKY BASTARD.

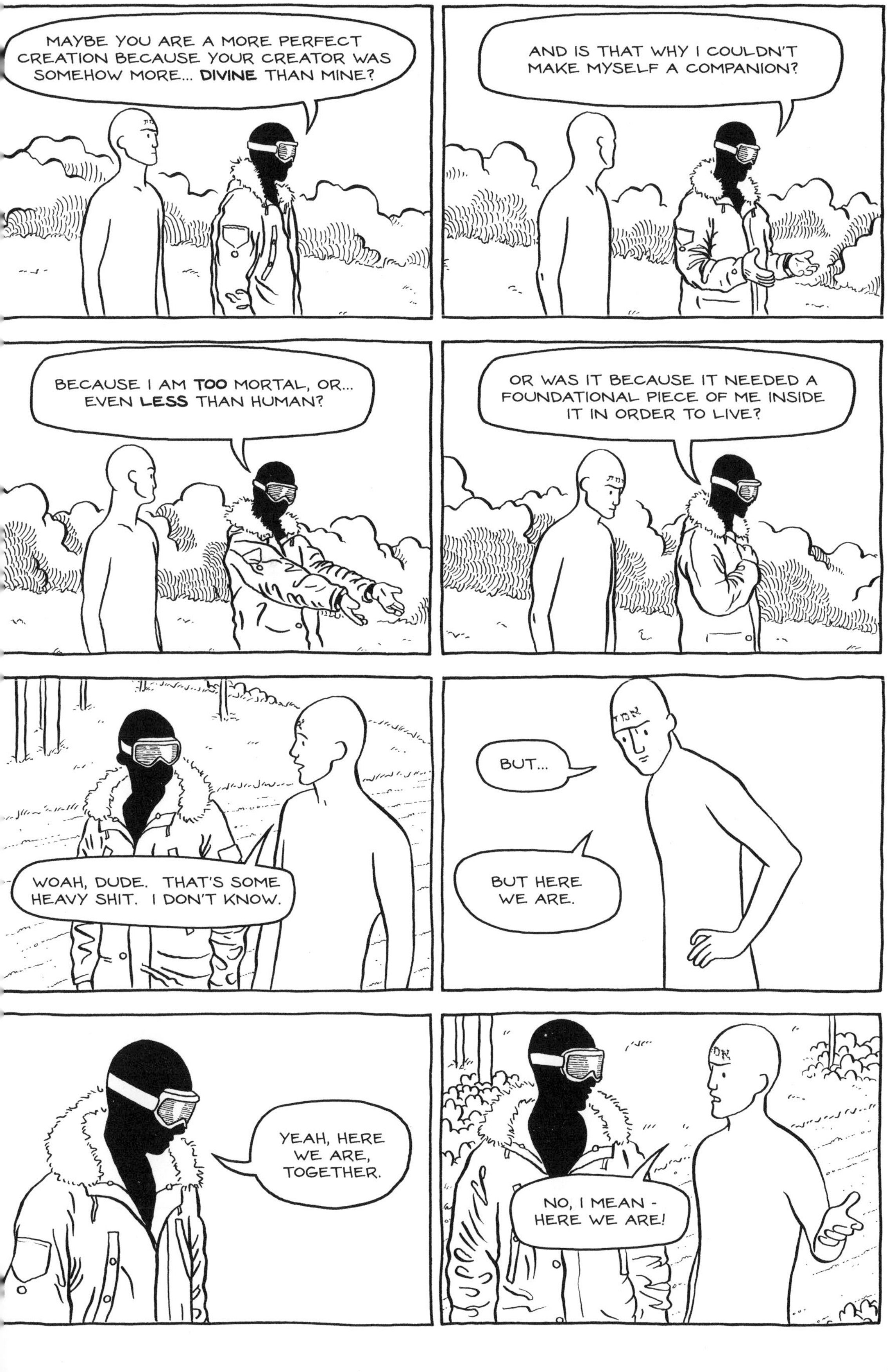
MAYBE YOU ARE A MORE PERFECT CREATION BECAUSE YOUR CREATOR WAS SOMEHOW MORE... **DIVINE** THAN MINE?
AND IS THAT WHY I COULDN'T MAKE MYSELF A COMPANION?
BECAUSE I AM **TOO** MORTAL, OR... EVEN **LESS** THAN HUMAN?
OR WAS IT BECAUSE IT NEEDED A FOUNDATIONAL PIECE OF ME INSIDE IT IN ORDER TO LIVE?
WOAH, DUDE. THAT'S SOME HEAVY SHIT. I DON'T KNOW.
BUT...
BUT HERE WE ARE.
YEAH, HERE WE ARE, TOGETHER.
NO, I MEAN - HERE WE ARE!

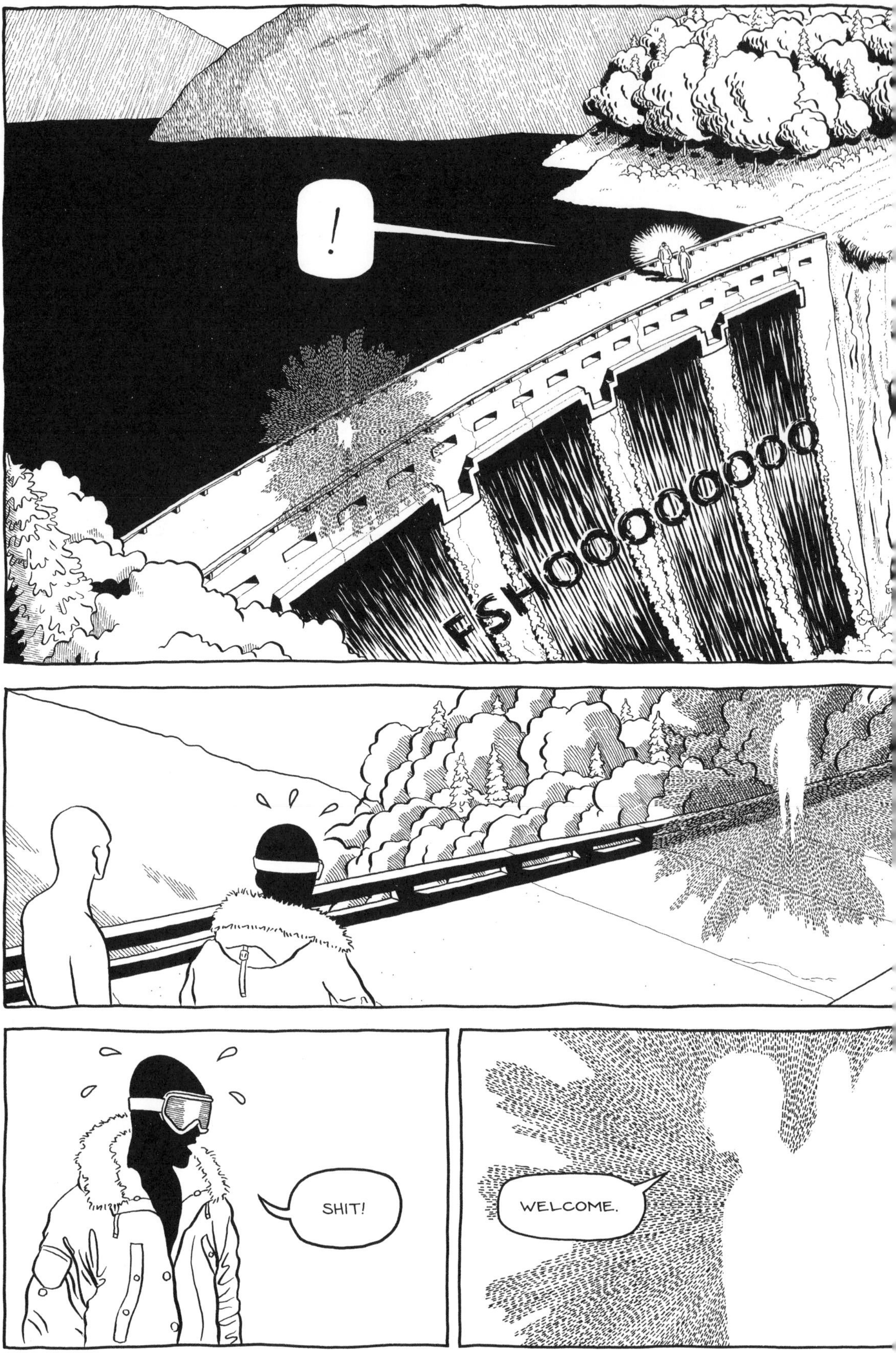
!
FSHOOOOOOOOOO
SHIT!
WELCOME.

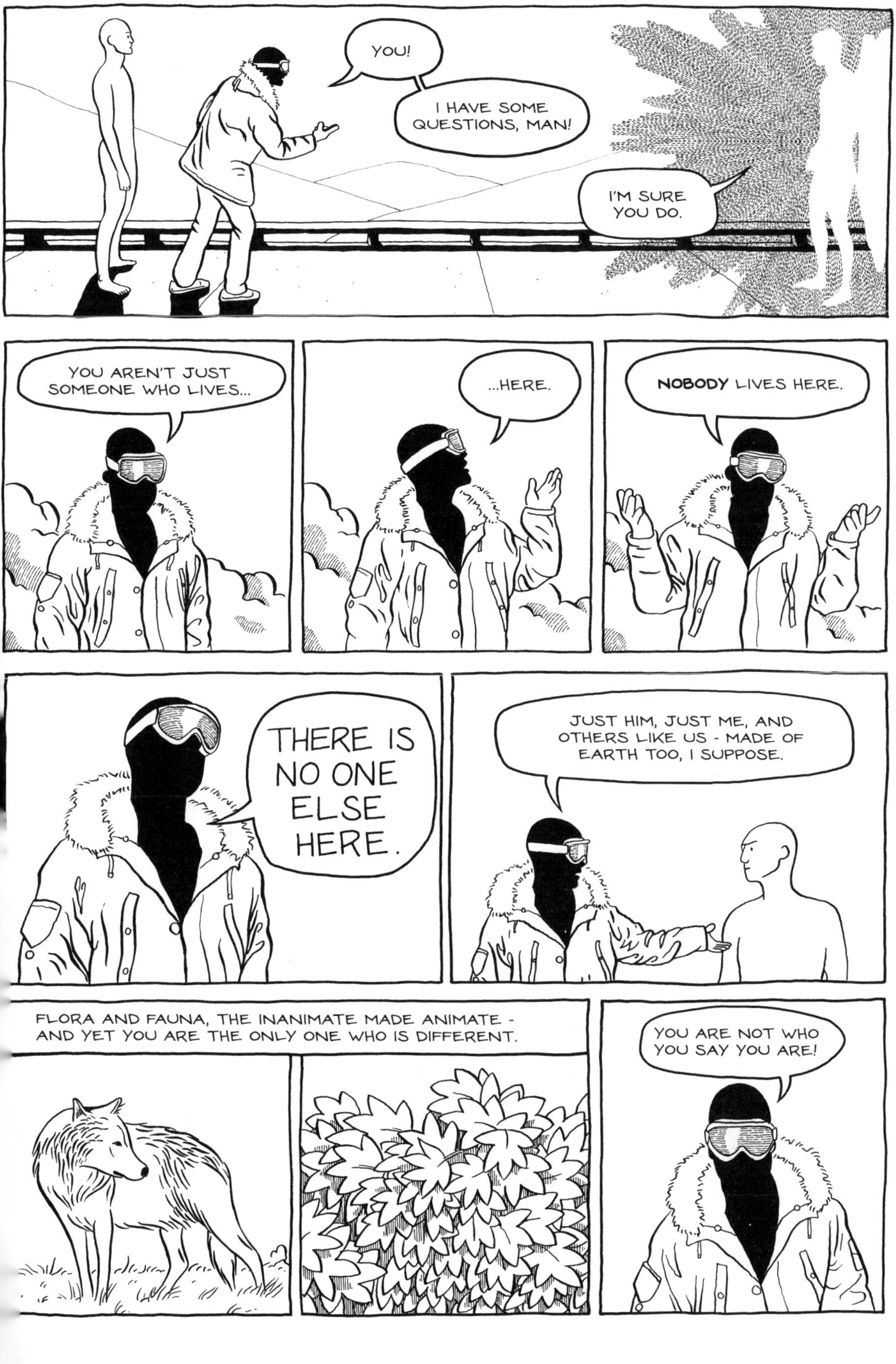
YOU!
I HAVE SOME QUESTIONS, MAN!
I'M SURE YOU DO.
YOU AREN'T JUST SOMEONE WHO LIVES...
...HERE.
NOBODY LIVES HERE.
THERE IS NO ONE ELSE HERE.
JUST HIM, JUST ME, AND OTHERS LIKE US - MADE OF EARTH TOO, I SUPPOSE.
FLORA AND FAUNA, THE INANIMATE MADE ANIMATE - AND YET YOU ARE THE ONLY ONE WHO IS DIFFERENT.
YOU ARE NOT WHO YOU SAY YOU ARE!

WOULD IT MAKE YOU MORE COMFORTABLE...
...IF I LOOKED LIKE THIS?
OR THIS?
WHAT?
YOU?
YOU!
IS THIS A FUCKING GAME TO YOU?
IS THIS SOME KIND OF... ...OF **HOAX**?

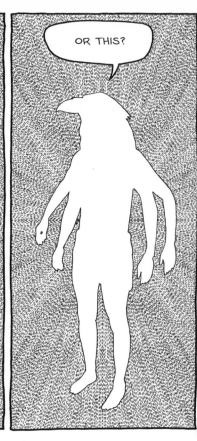

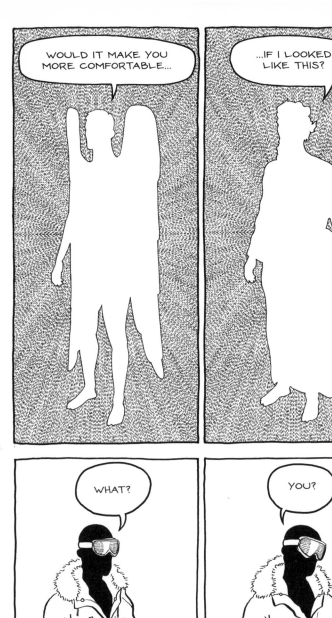

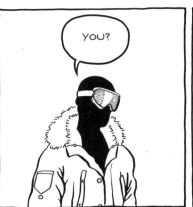

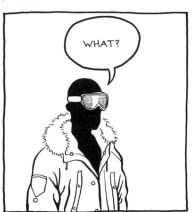

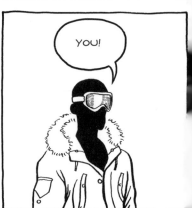

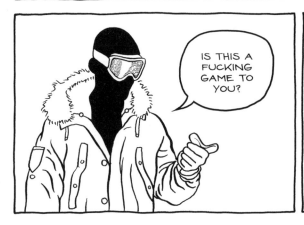

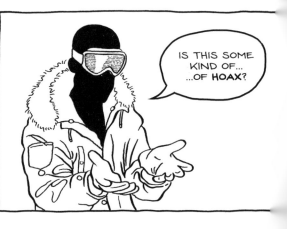

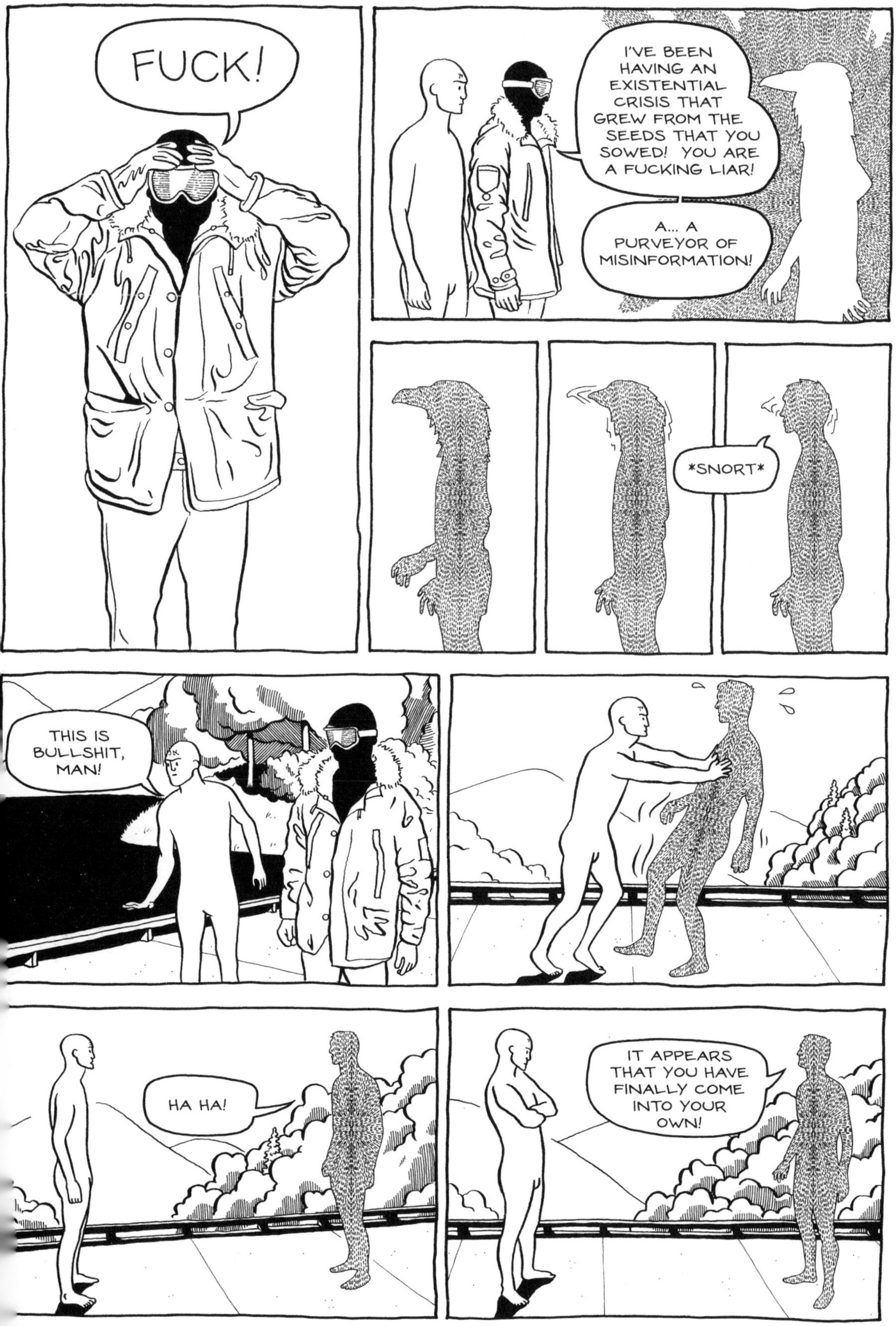
FUCK!
I'VE BEEN HAVING AN EXISTENTIAL CRISIS THAT GREW FROM THE SEEDS THAT YOU SOWED! YOU ARE A FUCKING LIAR!
A... A PURVEYOR OF MISINFORMATION!
SNORT
THIS IS BULLSHIT, MAN!
HA HA!
IT APPEARS THAT YOU HAVE FINALLY COME INTO YOUR OWN!

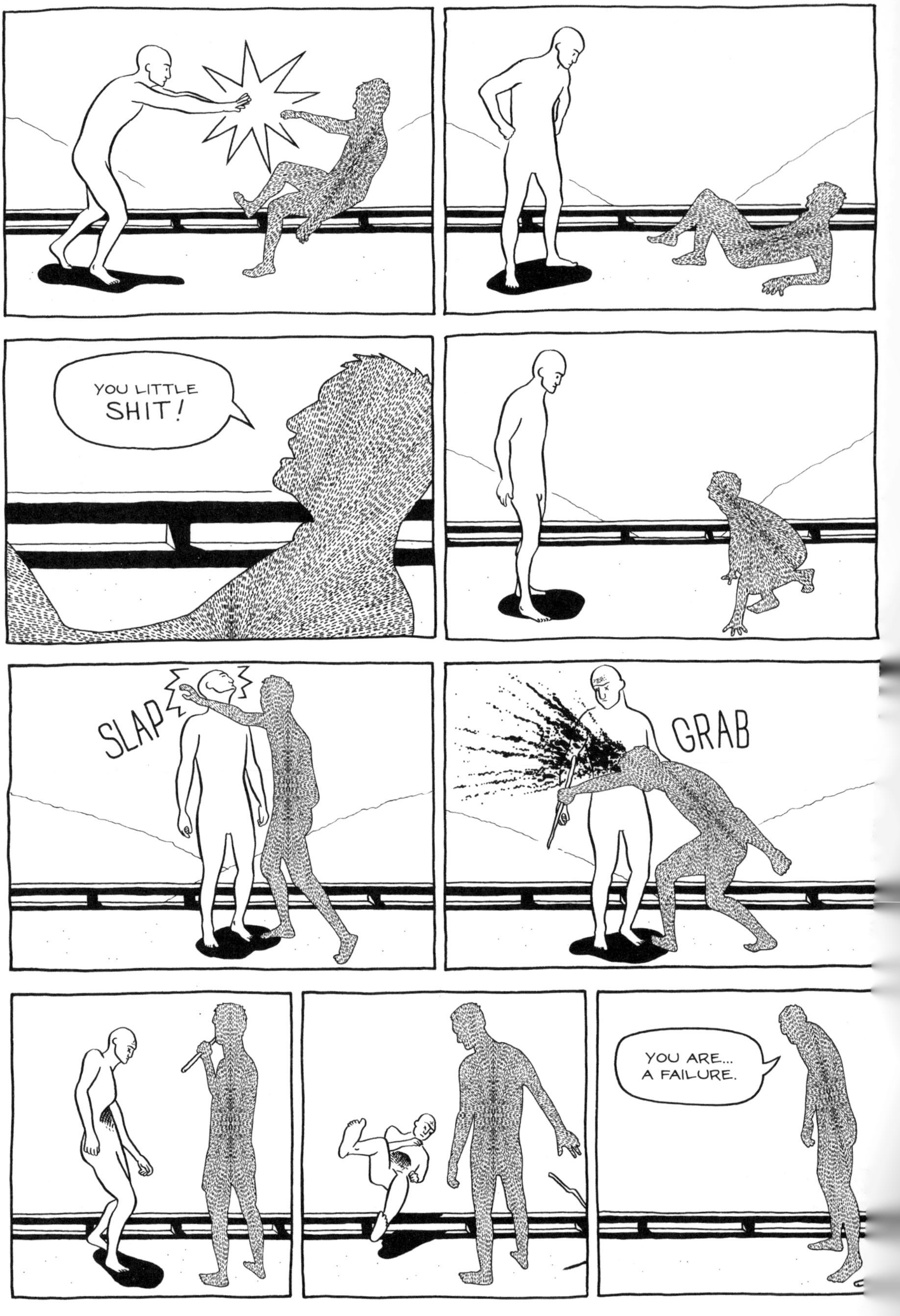
YOU LITTLE SHIT!
SLAP
GRAB
YOU ARE... A FAILURE.

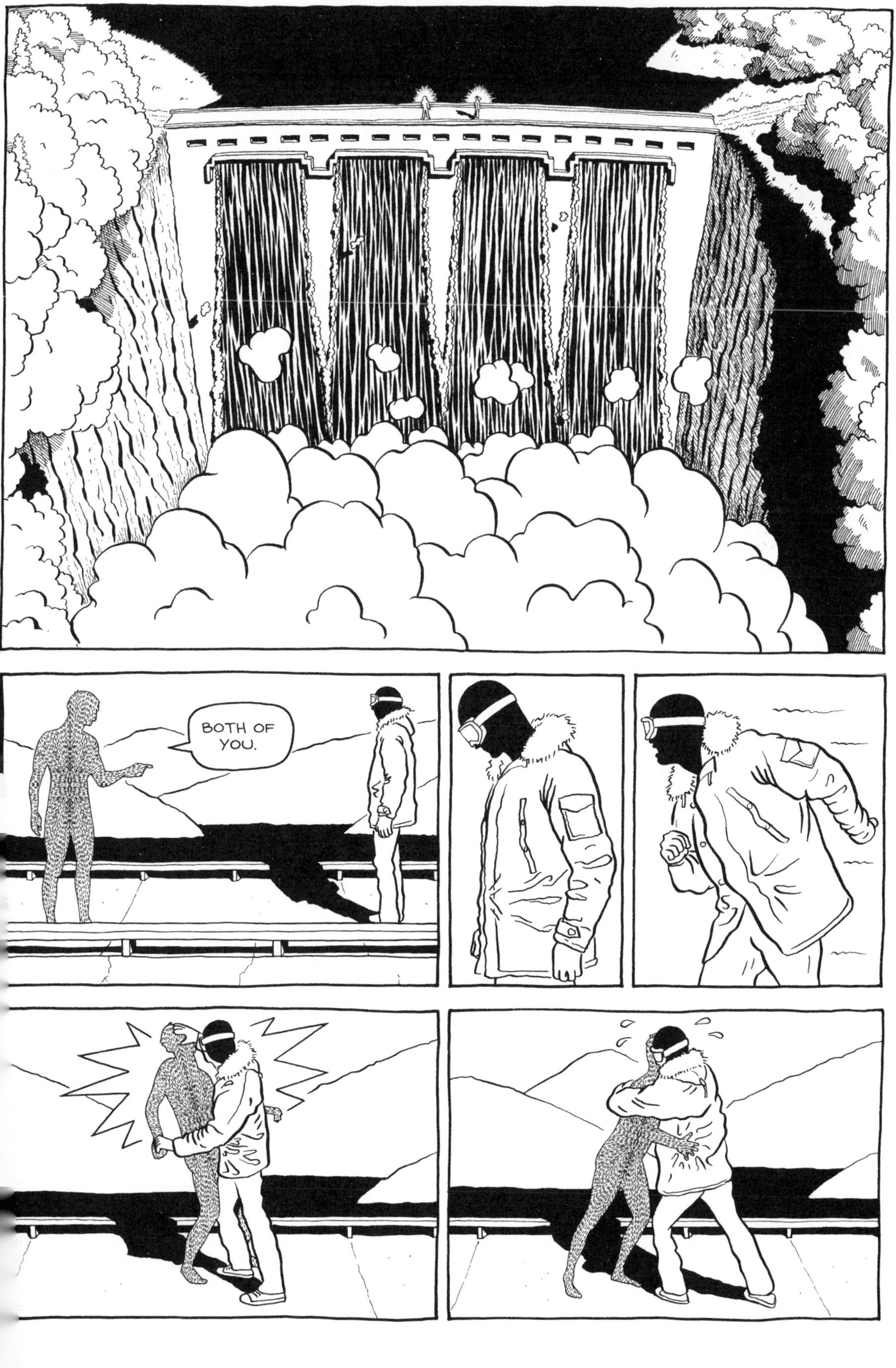
BOTH OF YOU.

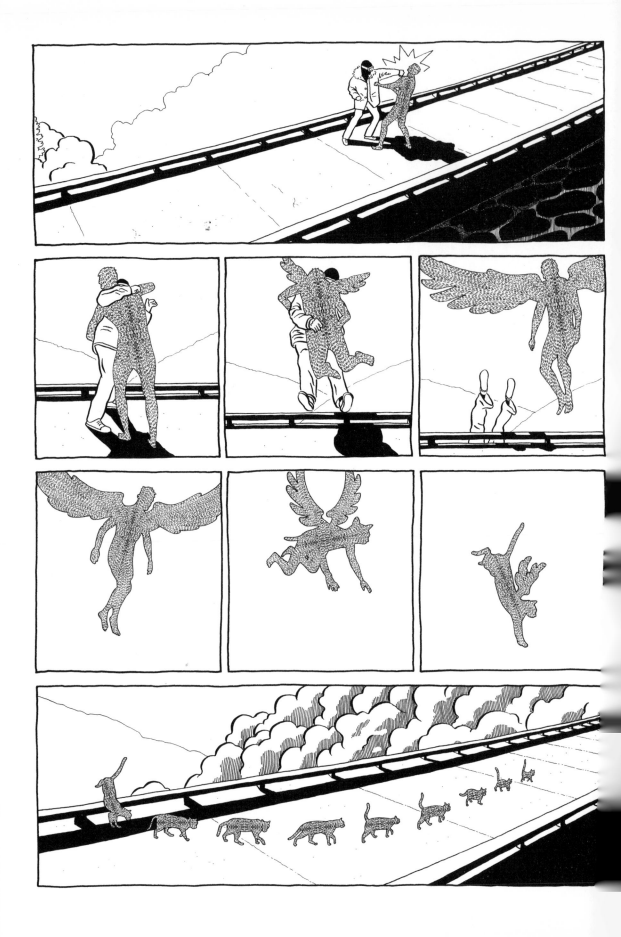

eleven

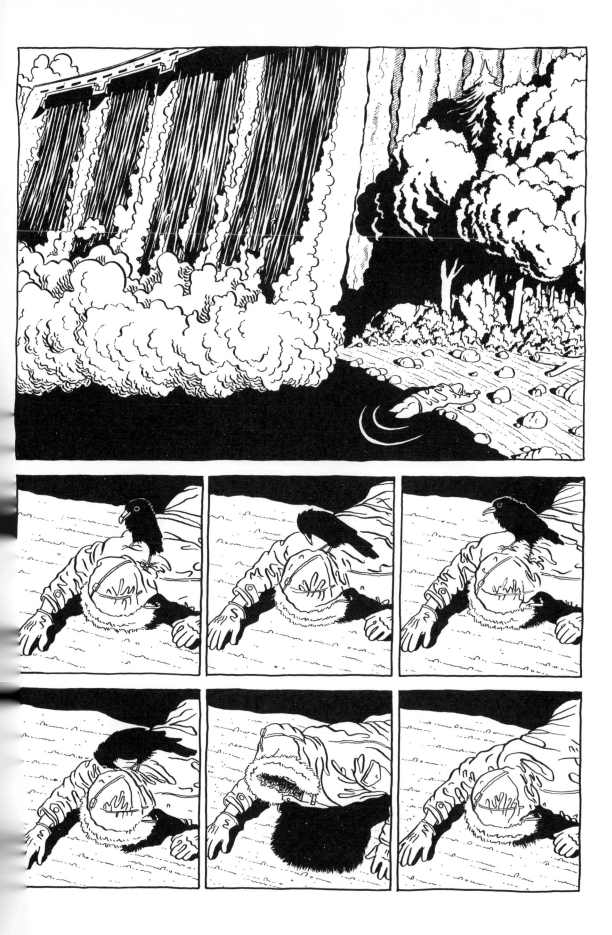

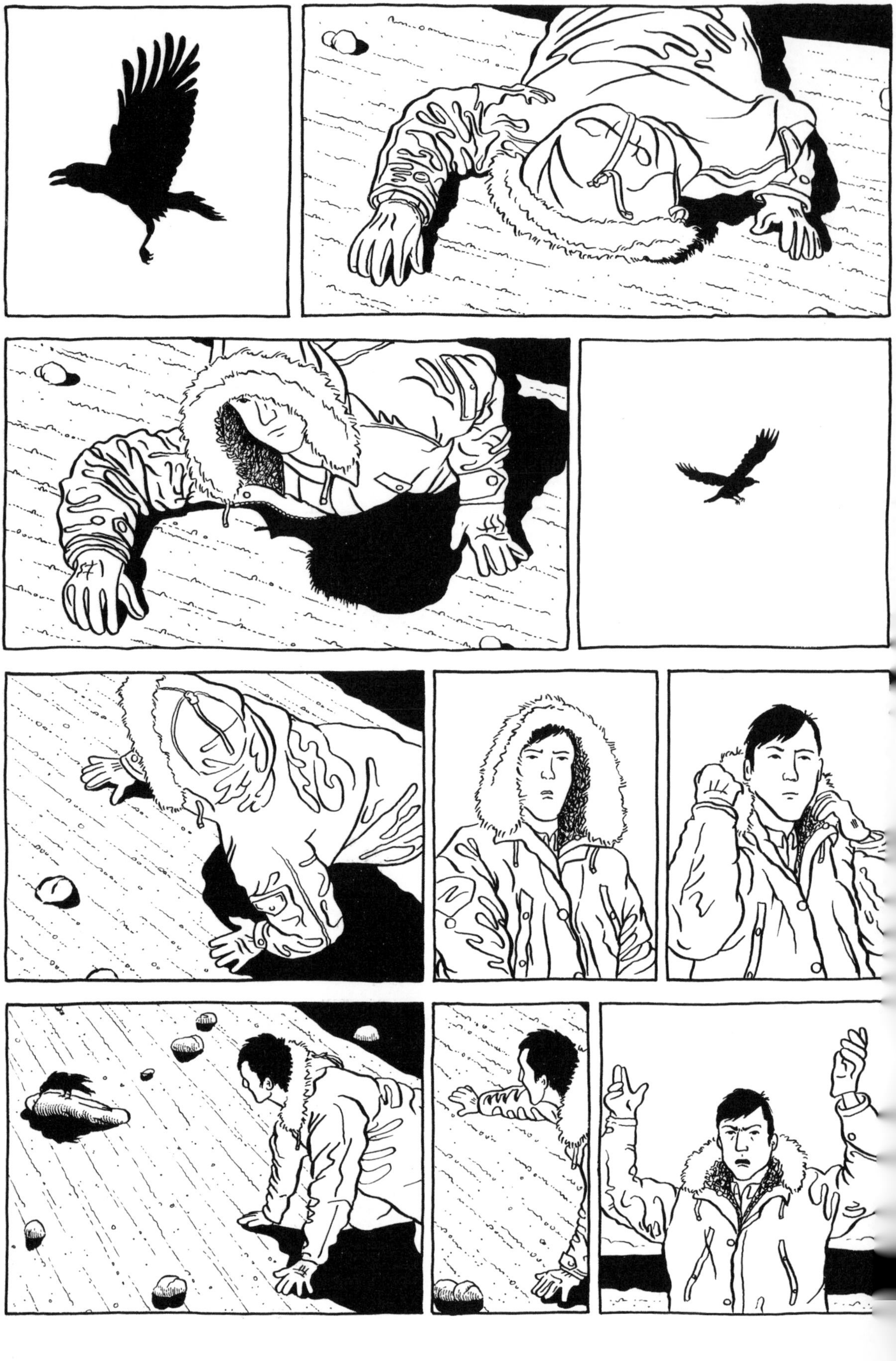

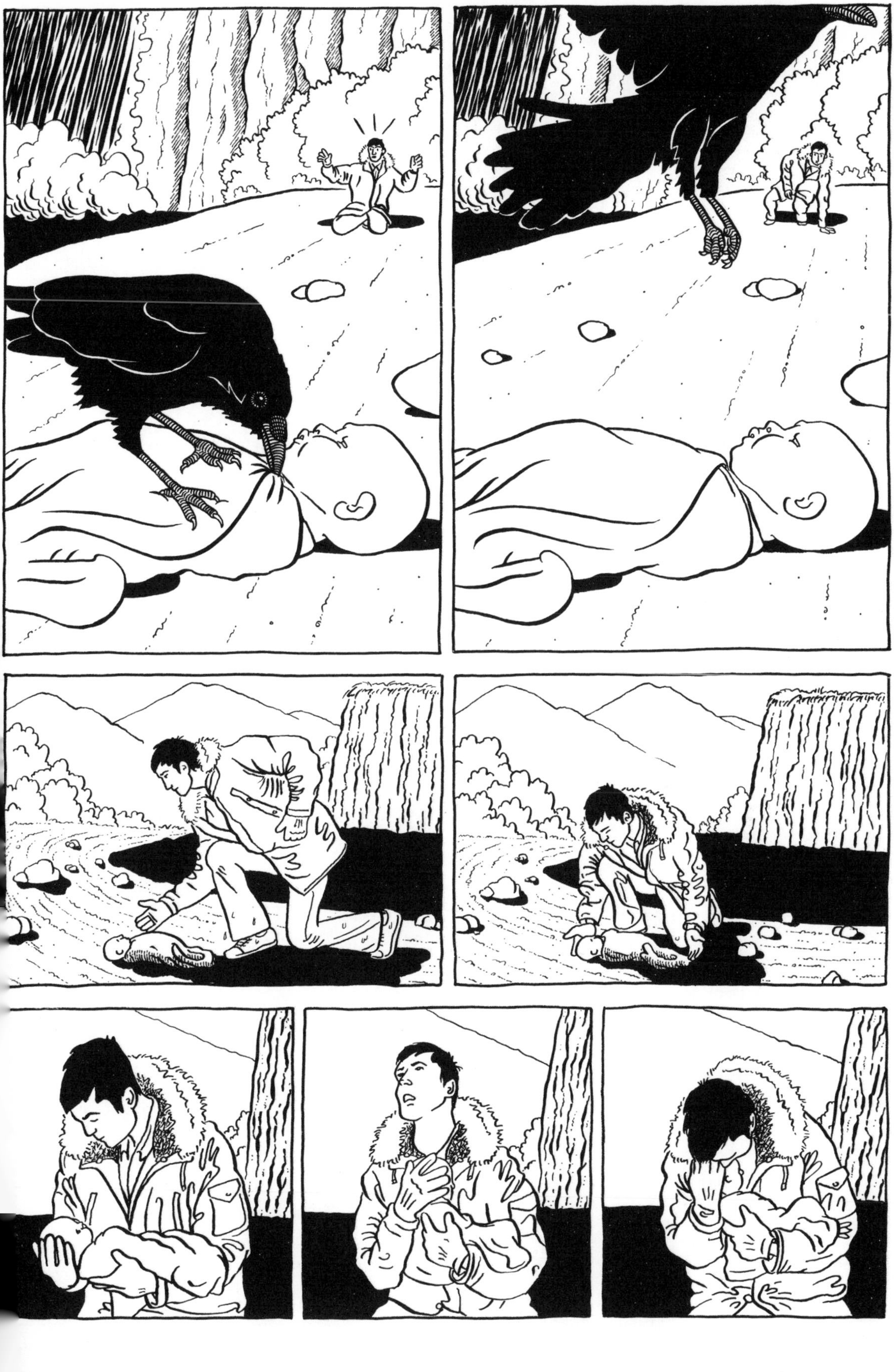

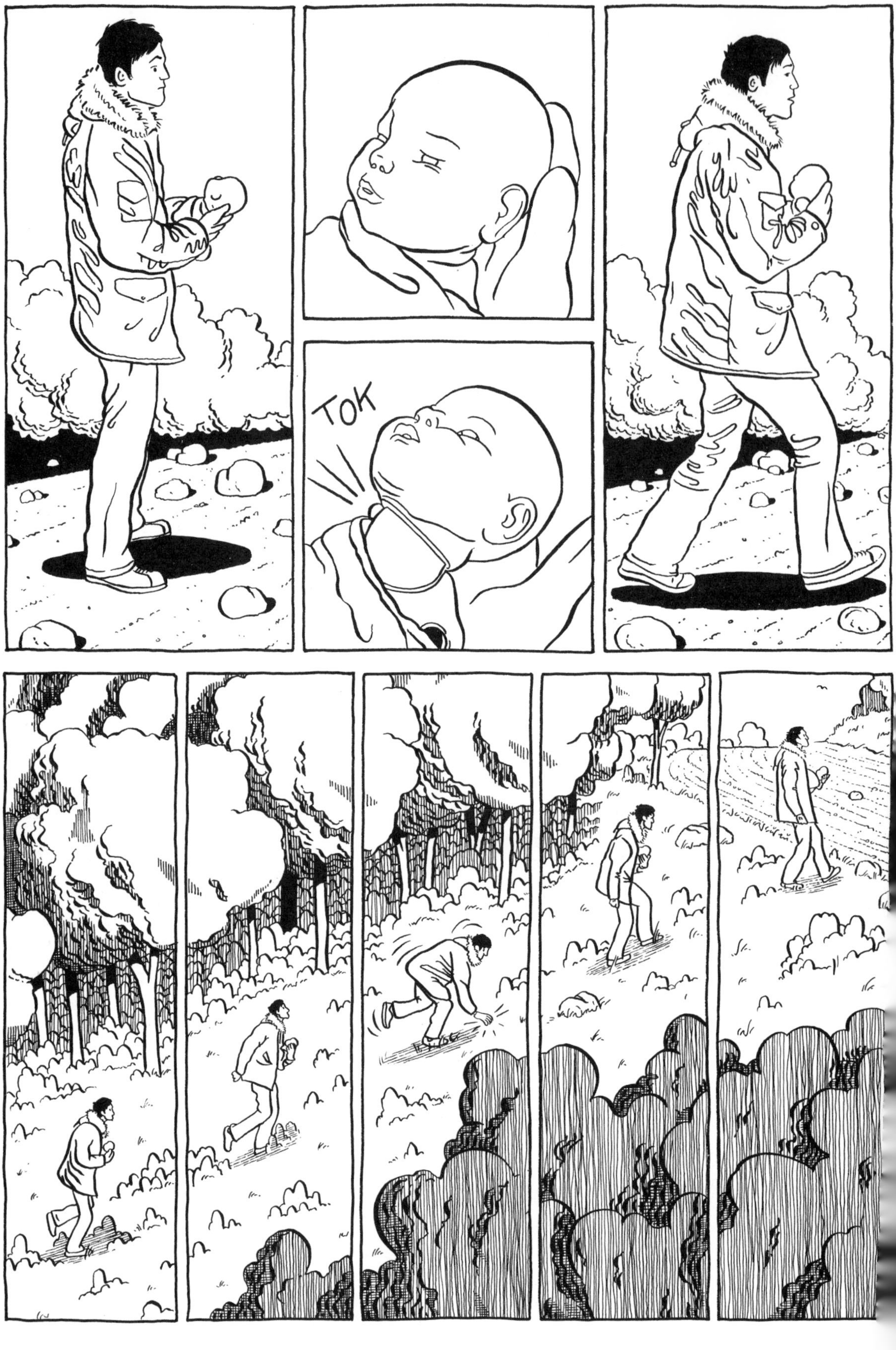
TOK

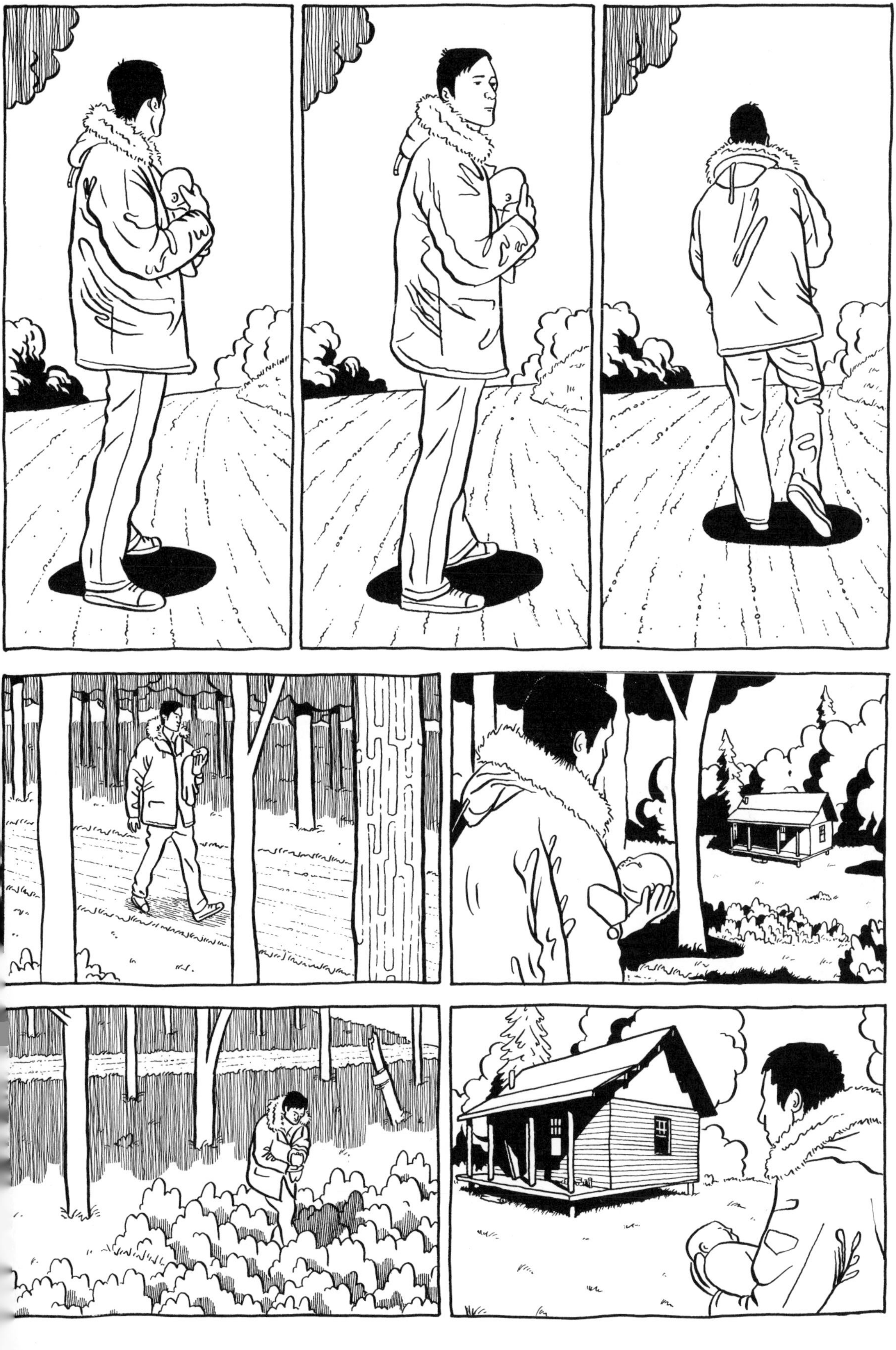

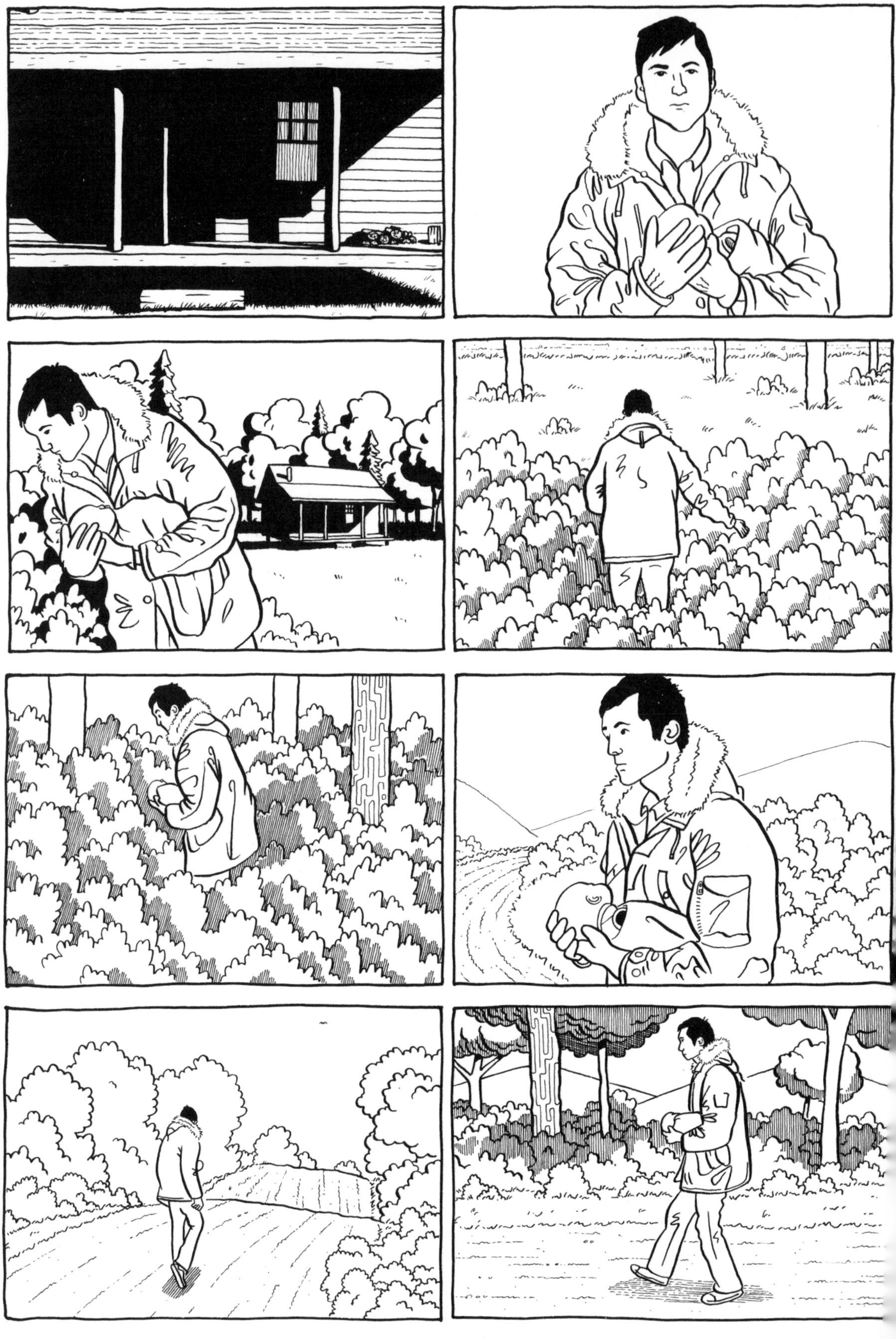

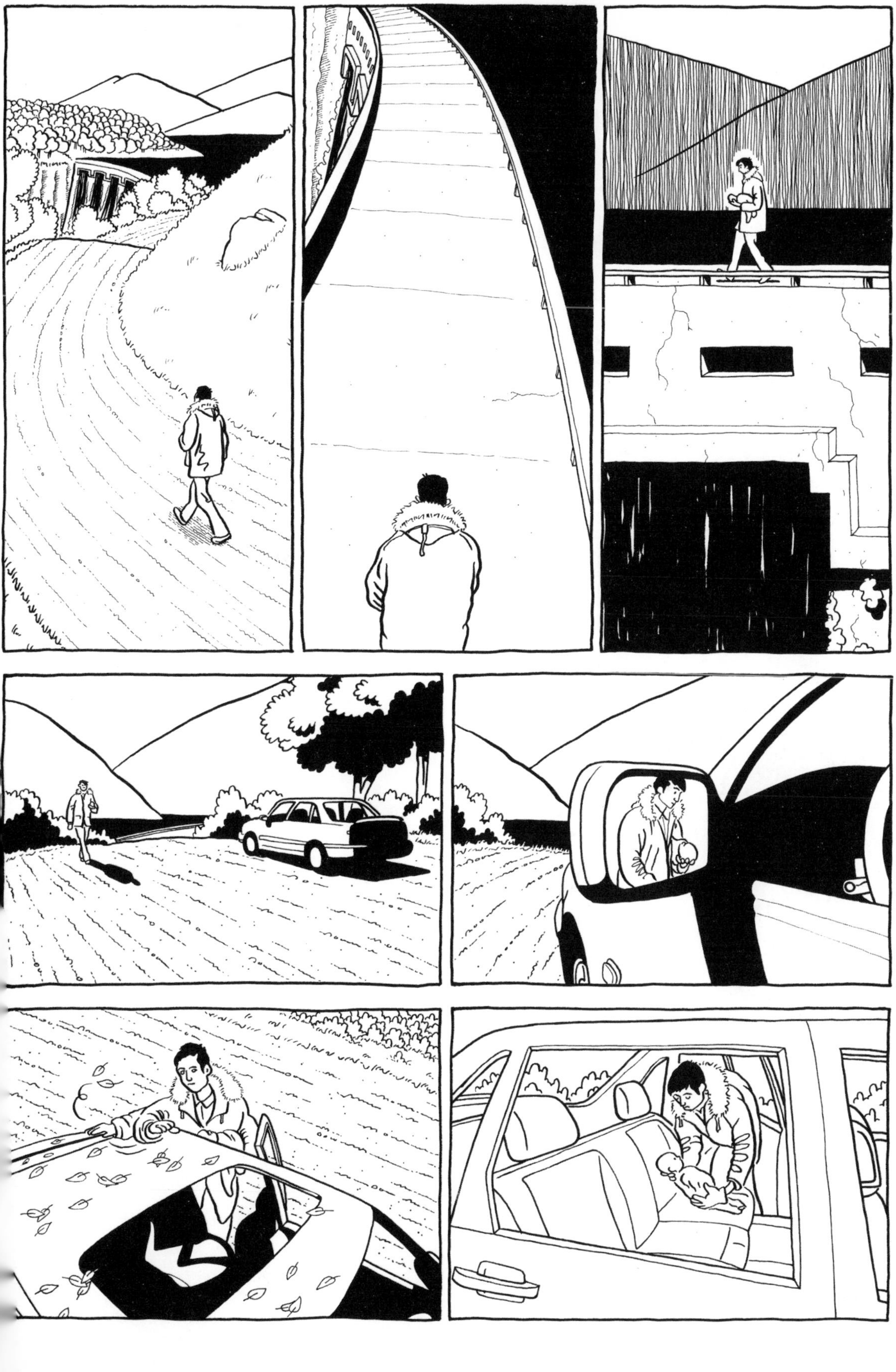

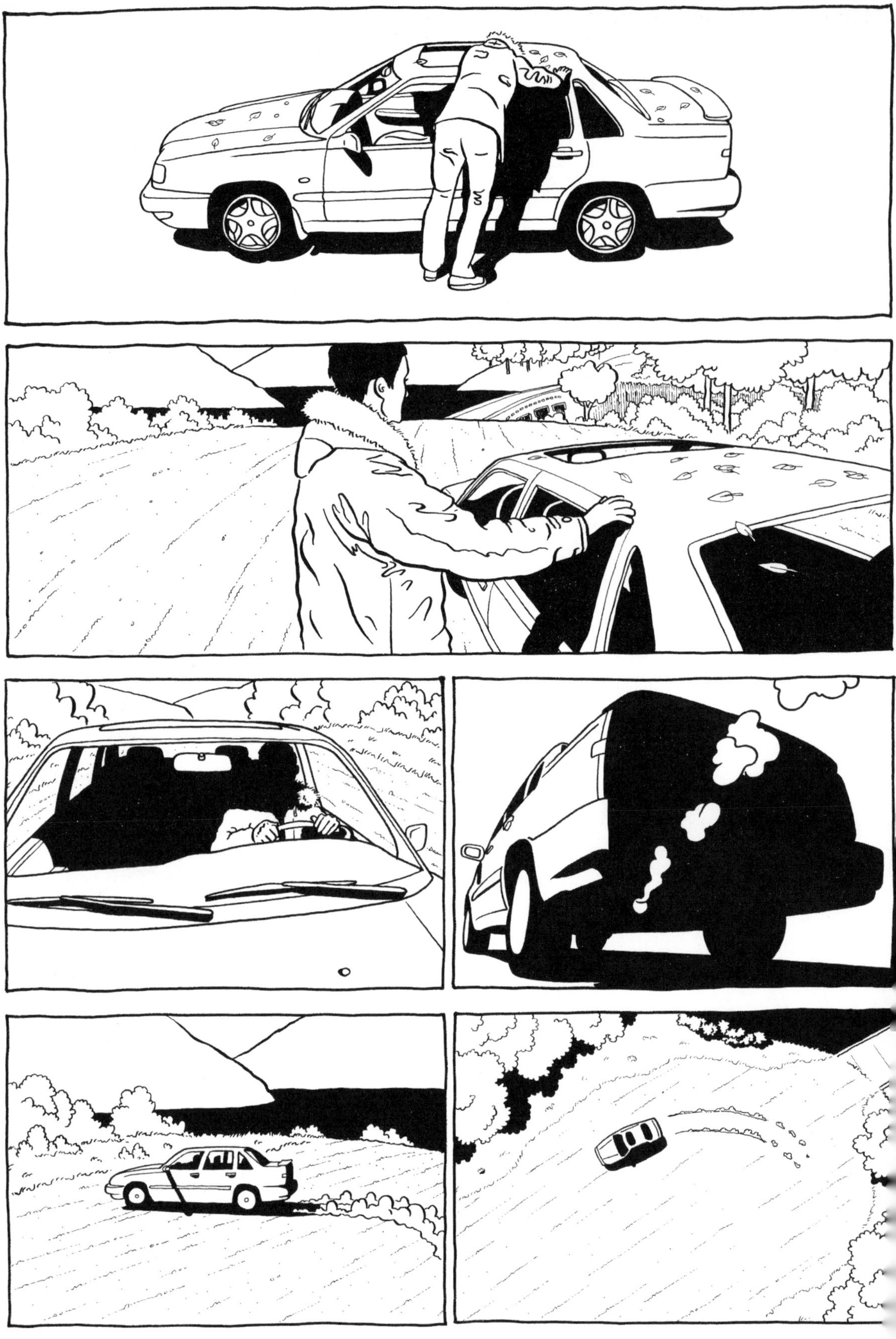

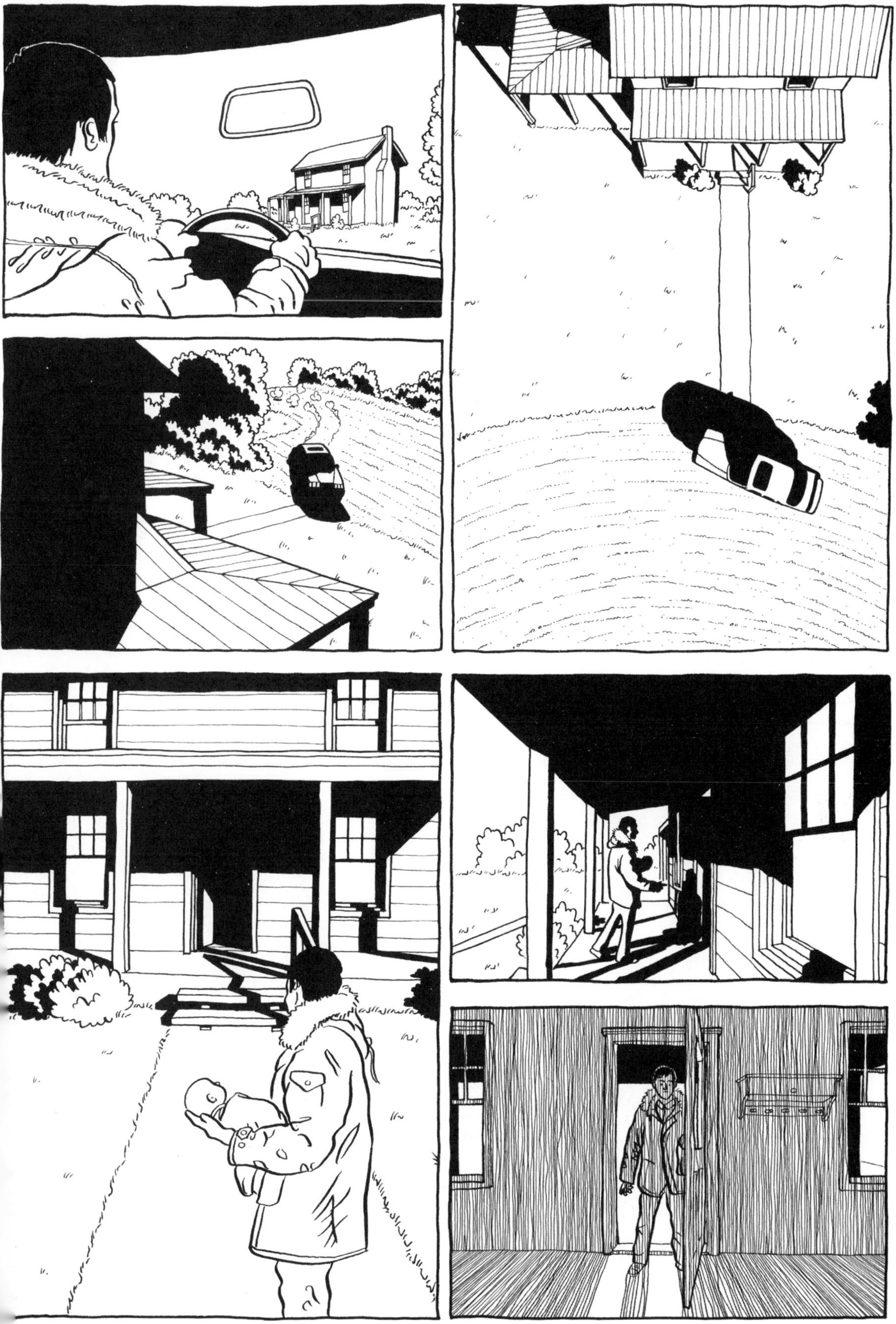

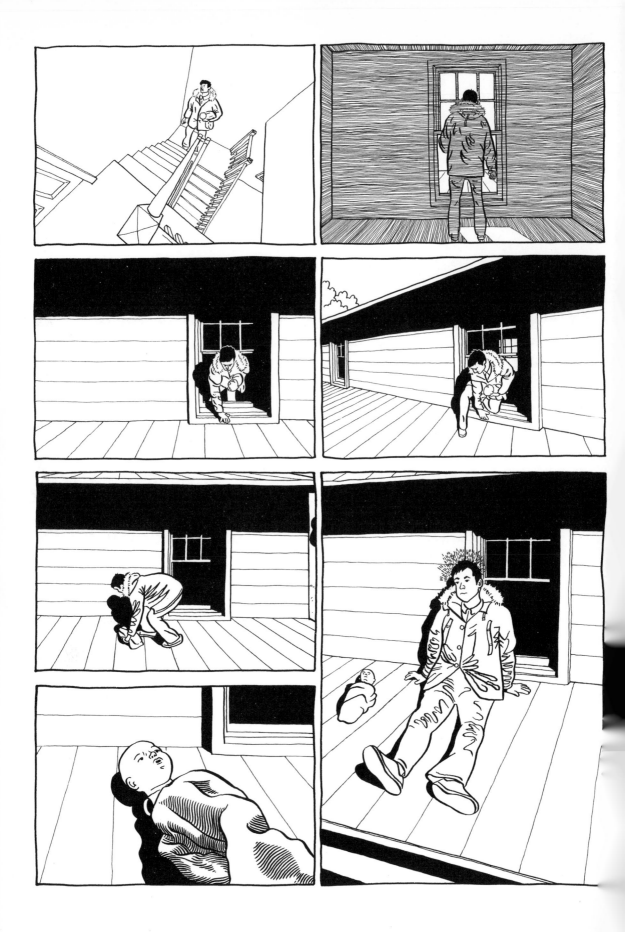

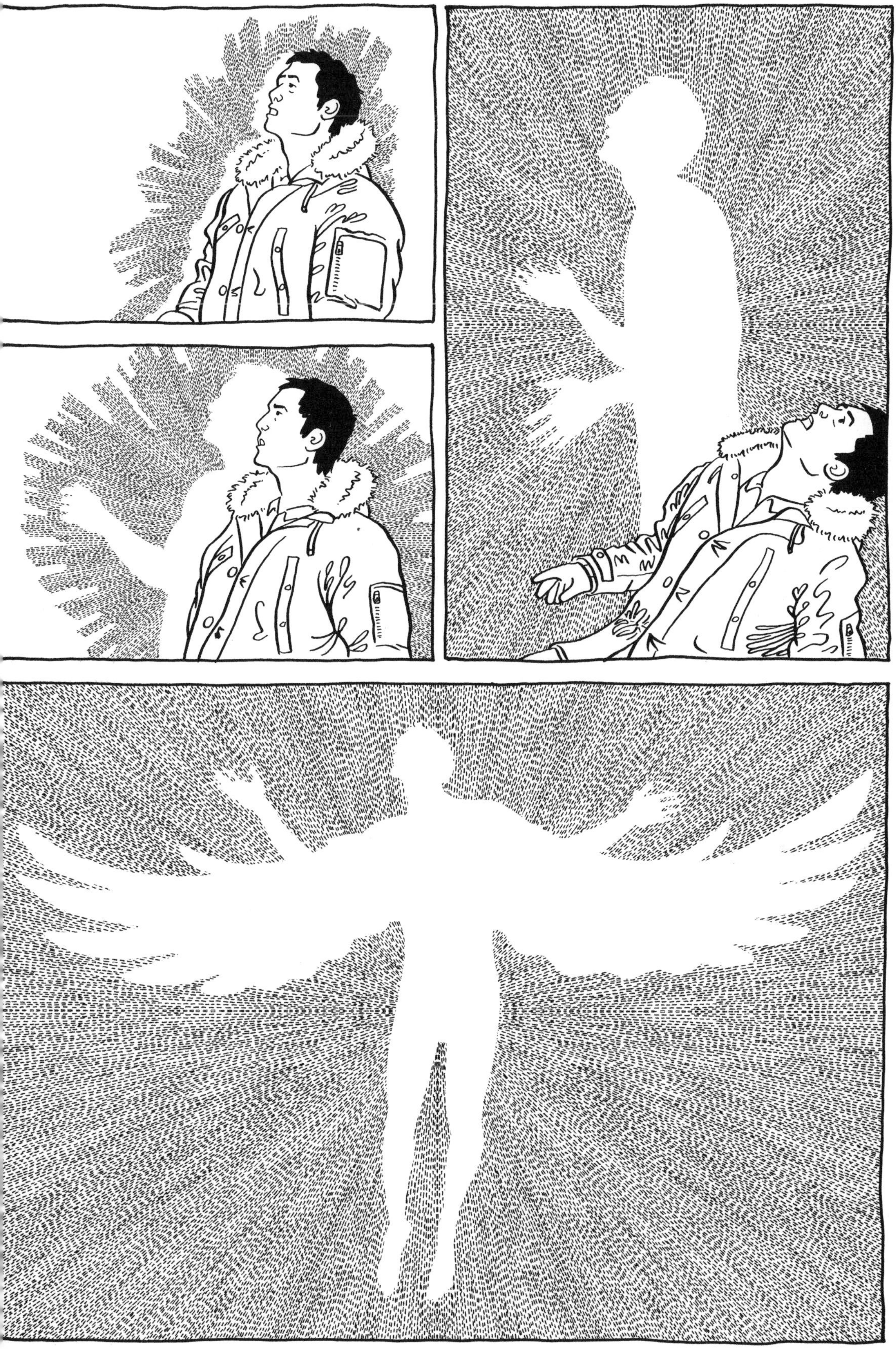

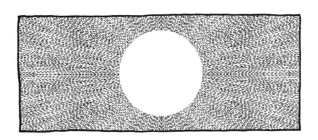

end

AARON COSTAIN IS AN ARCHITECT AND ILLUSTRATOR WHO LIVES IN TORONTO WITH HIS WIFE, DOG, AND CATS. HE WAS BORN IN VICTORIA, BRITISH COLUMBIA.

acknowledgements

THANKS TO MY FAMILY: MOM AND DAD, GRANDPA, NAOMI, AND ESPECIALLY RACHEL.

THANK YOU LEON AVELINO AND BARRY MATTHEWS, JOHN MARTZ, MATT FORSYTHE, ZACH WORTON, KATIE BEATON, JESSE JACOBS, ANNIE KOYAMA, TEAM SOCIETY LEAGUE, PETER BIRKEMOE, GRAHAM GAVINE, CARLO COLLODI, AND BILL REID.

THE FONT USED IN THIS BOOK WAS CREATED BY JOHN MARTZ.

CHAPTER THREE OF THIS BOOK WAS ORIGINALLY PUBLISHED IN ISSUE NINE OF CARTE BLANCHE, THE ONLINE MAGAZINE OF THE QUÉBEC WRITERS' FEDERATION.

ENTROPY WAS ORIGINALLY SERIALISED IN A DIFFERENT FORMAT BETWEEN 2006 AND 2016.